BOOKS BY KAY ARTHUR

Lord, Only You Can Change Me (January 1996)
Lord, I'm Torn Between Two Masters (April 1996)
Lord, Heal My Hurts
Lord, I Want to Know You
Lord, Is It Warfare? Teach Me to Stand
Lord, Where Are You When Bad Things Happen?
Lord, I Need Grace to Make It
Lord, Teach Me to Pray in 28 Days
God, Are You There? Do You Care? Do You Know About Me?
How to Study Your Bible Precept upon Precept
The International Inductive Study Series
Beloved: From God's Heart to Yours
His Imprint, My Expression
To Know Him by Name

LORD, IS IT WARFARE?

TEACH ME TO STAND

LORD, IS IT WARFARE?

TEACH ME TO STAND

KAY ARTHUR

MULTNOMAH BOOKS • SISTERS, OREGON

LORD, IS IT WARFARE? TEACH ME TO STAND

published by Multnomah Books
a part of the Questar publishing family

© 1991 by Kay Arthur

International Standard Book Number: 0-88070-882-4
(previously: 0-88070-593-0)

Cover design by Journey Communications

Printed in the United States of America

Most Scripture quotations are from:
New American Standard Bible (NASB) ©1960, 1977 by the Lockman Foundation

Also quoted:
The King James Version (KJV)

For information:
QUESTAR PUBLISHERS, INC. • POST OFFICE BOX 1720 • SISTERS, OREGON 97759

Library of Congress Cataloging-in-Publication Data:

Arthur, Kay. 1933-
   Lord, is it warfare?: teach me to stand / Kay Arthur.
         p.   cm.
   Includes bibliographical references.
   ISBN 0-88070-421-7
   1. Devil 2. Bible. N.T. Ephesians — Criticism, interpretation, etc. 3. Christian life — 1960
I. Title.
BT981.A77   1991
235'.4—dc20
                                                                              91-11779
                                                                                   CIP

98   99   00   01   02 — 10   9   8   7   6   5   4

CONTENTS

How to Use This Book 9

Chapter One   Lord, Is It Warfare? 11

Chapter Two   Lord, Why Did You Create the Devil? 31

Chapter Three Lord, Satan's Roaring — Need I Fear? 55

Chapter Four   Lord, I Don't Want to Buy Satan's Lie! 77

Chapter Five   Lord, the Enemy's Accusing Me! 95

Chapter Six   Lord, I Need a Kinsman Redeemer! 113

Chapter Seven Lord, Kinsman Redeemer, How Can Satan Be Defeated? . . 137

Chapter Eight Lord, How Do I Put on the Armor? Belt on Truth? 165

Chapter Nine   Lord, Teach Me about the Breastplate and Shoes 193

Chapter Ten   Lord, Satan's Attacking My Mind! My Shield! My Helmet! . 219

Chapter Eleven Lord, How Do I Take the Offense against Satan? 251

The Book of Ephesians 289

Group Discussion Questions 301

Notes 331

But the Lord is faithful, and He will strengthen and protect you from the evil one.

2 THESSALONIANS 3:3

HOW TO USE THIS BOOK

Let me tell you briefly about the book you're holding in your hands. You picked it up because its title interested you — it's a book on warfare, a subject we need to understand from a biblical perspective. And that's why I've written this book the way I have. It holds a unique place among books on the subject because it involves you.

My burden — and calling — is to help Christians (or interested or desperate inquirers) see for themselves what the Word of God has to teach on any given subject. That's why I write the *Lord* series. Many people are weak and unstable in their Christianity because they don't know truth for themselves; they only know what others have taught them.

This book involves you in a daily study of God's Word while it teaches you the subject of warfare. Each week's study of this particular book will take you an average of two to two-and-a-half hours if you do all of your assignments. The other *Lord* studies require less time, but because of the nature of this subject, you need to cover it thoroughly. It's an investment of time which will pay tremendous dividends. *Lord, Is It Warfare? Teach Me to Stand* is a tested study which has already had an impact on lives.

This book is ideal for personal devotions, home Bible studies, and Sunday School material. You don't need the following helps to do the study, but they are available, and many find that they enhance the study in a special way: supplementary teaching tapes on video and audio for adults and teens — one for each chapter in the book. These can be rented or purchased. There are also leaders' tapes to help you with the discussion and/or a leaders' manual. For more information on these supplementary items, please write: Precept Ministries, P. O. Box 182218, Chattanooga, Tennessee 37422, (423) 892-6814.

Much prayer and study has gone into this *Lord* book, and it's no accident you picked it up. May God train your hands for war!

Kay

LORD, IS IT WARFARE?

D A Y   O N E

O h, God, will I ever be free? I don't want to live like this for the rest of my life."

I knew my immoral thoughts weren't pleasing to God, but what could I do? I didn't want them running through my mind. They were unwelcome intruders, disturbing my peace, tormenting my soul.

I couldn't figure it out. Although I knew marriage was a covenant that wasn't to be broken, I would suddenly find myself wondering what it would be like to be married to someone else. Further, I knew God had told me to marry Jack! Why these unpredictable thoughts about other men? I was a child of God — I didn't want thoughts like these.

Sometimes I'd be driving along the freeway and remember an event from my immoral past. Then I'd try to figure out how and why I ever got into such compromising relationships. Depression would settle like a heavy fog.

Even when I was an unbeliever, I never intended to be immoral. Although I didn't have a personal relationship with Jesus Christ, I thought I was a Christian and knew that immorality was sin. Oh, I often fantasized, but that was in the privacy of my mind. My fantasy world was one I had enjoyed even as a child. I convinced myself that as long as I only thought these things, I was all right.

I never acted out my thoughts. They were just dreams — dreams to hold me until marriage. I had every intention of keeping my virginity until a ring was on my finger, and I did. I walked the aisle dressed in white. Physically I was a virgin, but not mentally.

Six years later I divorced my husband. Disillusioned and lonely, I shook my fist in the face of God and said, "To hell with You, God. I'm going to find someone to love me." Little did I realize that before the foundation of the world, God had said, "To heaven with you, Kay." His Son would take my hell so I could have His heaven.

In my search for love, I now gradually surrendered every moral conviction to my passion to be loved unconditionally, by someone other than my parents. I became what I thought I would never become — an immoral woman.

But then on July 16, 1963, at the age of twenty-nine, I became God's child. Wooed by His love and grace and consumed by a passion to be pleasing to Him, I finally came to the place where I told God I would remarry Tom. No, I didn't love him. But I knew that if God could change me so radically, He could do the same for Tom. And I wanted to be obedient.

I never had the opportunity to tell Tom I would come back. Tom committed suicide by hanging himself.

When God later brought Jack into my life, I was determined to be a godly wife. Why, then, was I wrestling with such ungodly thoughts? I knew that Jesus knew everything I was thinking. Thoughts like these belonged to my B.C. (before Christ) self, not to a Bible teacher with a growing ministry.

As I continued to study the Bible, I learned how to bring my thoughts under control. Every time a D.T. (dirty thought) would come to my mind, I would refuse it and think about something else. It may have knocked at the door of my mind a dozen times, but I persisted in slamming the door in its face each time. It was wearing, but it worked.

Yet, I couldn't control my dreams!

My immoral dreams would haunt me as I went about my day. Between the D.T.s and dreams, I wondered how Jack and I could ever add a man to the staff of our growing ministry. What if I became attracted to him?

Only God knew my agony. I had tried to tell another Bible teacher, but she wouldn't believe it. Not me! I couldn't be having problems like that! So I kept it all to myself. I'd go to bed, praying, pleading, reading my Bible or a good Christian biography, but the dreams still came.

Then one day, a day I'll never forget, God set me free! I discovered my problem! I was in warfare! When I finally recognized it as warfare, I knew what to do. What a relief!

How did God set me free? I'll share the details later in our study. At this point let me simply say that the attractions, the D.T.s, and the dreams were gone, destroyed by the sword of the Lord. Did they ever come back? Occasionally they tried. But I knew *who* sent them, and I'd have none of it!

I don't know what kind of a battle you're in, my friend, but I can tell you that if it's warfare, victory is assured. You simply need to know how to stand firm in the Lord.

If you're not in a battle, don't breathe a sigh of relief and think, *I don't need this study.* If you're a child of God, an attack *will* come. The question is, Will you know enough to recognize what's happening, and will you know how to win the war?

That is what this study on warfare is all about. Therefore, let's get started today. Why wait until tomorrow!

At the back of this book you'll find a copy of the entire book of Ephesians. A mother lode of truth on spiritual warfare runs through Paul's epistle to the Ephesians, a mother lode we are going to mine carefully in the weeks to come.

1. Today your assignment is to read carefully Ephesians 6:10–20. When you finish, write out below exactly whom your struggle is with.

2. Now, if you're brave enough, write down anything that has been tormenting you that you can't seem to shake or conquer. If you are hesitant to write it down because someone might see it, name it in your mind. Then talk to God about it. It's good to write out your prayers to God. So, I'll leave you some space to do so.

3. Finally, start memorizing Ephesians 6:10–11. As you will see later on, knowing these verses will help in warfare. Memorizing scripture is not as difficult as it may seem. Simply read the verses aloud three times in succession, three times a day, for three days. It's important to read aloud. One day you'll find you can say the verses from memory. It's also important to understand what you're memorizing, or otherwise you'll find yourself quoting verses simply by rote. So, take time to think about what you're reading.

Well, Beloved, we've begun our study! (I call you *Beloved* because that is what God calls you.) Please take to heart the fact that if you're going to benefit from this study, you must determine to do your daily assignments. Since there are many excellent books on spiritual warfare, we don't need another one unless it provides something unique. If you use this book as it is intended, you will get into the Word of God so that you personally learn truth and experience it.

You can use this book as it is designed by doing one day's study at a time, or you may find it more convenient to do a week's study in one day. However you choose to use it, begin each study with prayer. Ask God to open the eyes of your understanding and to lead you into truth. Stand firm against the enemy and all his strategies to keep you from this study. Victory is assured to those who know how victory is won and who war accordingly.

Just know, my friend, your study will not go unchallenged. Satan would love to keep you ignorant, misinformed, or fearful of the subject of spiritual warfare. However, in this case the old adage "ignorance is bliss" has to be the enemy's adage, not God's. Remember, Jesus said, "You shall know the truth, and the truth shall set you free" (John 8:32). Truth is always liberating!

D A Y   T W O

Have you ever felt like quitting because the hassle of Christianity was too much?

Do you ever doubt the truth of God's Word or the reality of Christianity? Have you ever been tormented by blasphemous thoughts against God?

Have you ever felt captivatingly drawn, almost magnetized, to the things of the world?

Is there anything you feel compelled to do or to believe, and yet you know it's not of God?

Are you bombarded with doubts about God's goodness — His love toward you?

Have you ever been plagued by feelings of worthlessness and/or inadequacy?

Even though you've confessed past sins, do you live under a cloud of condemnation?

Have you felt overwhelmed with depression?

Have you ever thought about suicide?

Have you ever been haunted by some derogatory remark, thought, memory, desire that you couldn't shake?

Or have you heard voices in your mind? Is your mind filled with incessant noise? Are you afraid to tell anyone?

Are you filled with anger, bitterness, or unforgiveness? Even though you realize you are wrong to harbor these feelings, do you feel powerless to deal with them?

Are you physically sick — yet the doctor cannot find the cause?

Have you ever been joyfully serving the Lord and been suddenly attacked unjustly?

Have you remembered that the Christian life is a warfare?

I believe many Christians live in defeat because they don't understand that when they become children of God they enter into war with the devil himself.

Not realizing that there is a war raging, they don't know victory is theirs for the taking. They simply need to find out what God's Word says and live in the light of it!

Ephesians 6:11 tells us to "put on the full armor of God, that you may be able to stand firm against the schemes of the devil." The English transliteration for the Greek word translated *schemes* in the New American Standard and New International versions, and *wiles* in the King James Version, is the word *methodia*.[1] According to Vine's *Expository Dictionary of Biblical Words*, *wiles* denotes "craft, deceit" (*meta*, "after," *hodos*, "a way"), "a cunning device, a wile."[2]

The same word is also used in Ephesians 4:14 where the literal translation of "they lie in wait [to deceive]" would be "[with a view to] the craft
[*methodia*] of deceit."[3]

If you take God at His Word, it is clear from Ephesians 6 that our enemy
is cunning and crafty — out to deceive you, me, and every other child of
God. You're not alone!

1. Go back and read the questions I asked you at the beginning of
today's study. Has the enemy deceived you in any of these areas? If so, next
to the question write out how.

Doesn't it make sense that Satan would want to keep you blind to the
fact that you are in a war? After all, you won't take up arms if you don't
believe there's a war.

2. Read through Ephesians 6:10–20 again, using the printed copy of
Ephesians provided for you. As you read, mark any key words or phrases
that are repeated. A key word is an important word that is used by the
author repeatedly in order to convey his message to his reader. For instance,
the phrase "the full armor of God" is repeated. You could color or underline
each occurrence of this phrase in blue, or you could draw a box around it
like this: the full armor of God . Color coding, along with diagrams, gives
you a wide variety of markings.

I'd suggest you buy some colored pencils and/or a Pentel pen with the
four-color heads so you can mark your Bible as you study. These do not
bleed through the pages of your Bible, but magic markers will. I'll tell you
more about marking key words later.

3. According to this passage, what is the child of God to do? List below
the specific instructions given in these verses.

At this point in our study you may not understand the full impact of the truths you are seeing. But by the end of our time together you'll not only understand these truths, you'll know how to apply them to your life!

Now that you are beginning to see that our study will be a process, be patient. You must lay a solid foundation of truth. You must understand God's Word so you can adhere to it, or you'll lose. So be patient with me as I lead you through truth. Our study time may be a little like Boot Camp in that it is not fun and games. But when you come face to face with the enemy, you'll be very glad you endured it because you'll know your weapons and how to use them. You'll also have learned to endure hardship as a good soldier of Jesus Christ!

As I tell my *Precept Upon Precept* Bible study students, "Hangeth thou in there." It is warfare, but victory is assured.

By the way, if you're thinking, *Hey, this is an awful lot of work*, you're right. Our *Lord* series books do not allow you simply to sit back and read. They wouldn't be as effective if that's all there was to it.

Now I'll tell you that your homework will be a little heavy this first week. Good way to encourage you, isn't it? Sorry. But the good news is that you'll need these truths immediately, and they will be yours. Persevere. Military training is never passive!

DAY   THREE

Apart from the Gospels, no book zeroes in on the Christian's warfare like Ephesians. Therefore, it's critical to thoroughly understand this book's historical, cultural, and religious context. You will then understand why Paul wrote Ephesians, addressing warfare and emphasizing the Christian's relationship to the principalities and powers behind it.

Ephesus was the fourth largest city in the Roman Empire in Paul's day. It was the home of the magnificent temple of the goddess Artemis, who was sometimes referred to as Diana. Artemis, a fertility deity whose image supposedly fell directly from heaven, was "grotesquely represented with turreted head and many breasts."[4] Of all the deities worshiped in Asia, none was more sought after than Artemis. Pilgrims came from all over the Mediterranean world to worship in her temple, which measured four times the size of the Parthenon in Athens.

Ephesus relied upon two important assets for its wealth and vitality. The first asset, her position as a center of trade, was lost by the time of the Apostle Paul.[5] The second asset, the worship of Artemis, then became her primary means of economic survival. The tourist and pilgrim trade associated with the temple and cult of Artemis made many Ephesians wealthy.[6]

Innkeepers and restaurant owners grew rich from the large influx of worshipers who traveled great distances to see the temple of Artemis, which was one of the seven wonders of the world. Silversmiths made their living by selling silver shrines and images of this goddess and her temple. Even the temple treasury served as a bank, loaning massive sums of money to many, including kings. And since Artemis was the patroness of sexual instinct, prostitutes sold their bodies without condemnation in the two-story brothel on the Marble Road.[7]

Yet for all the wealth it brought to Ephesus, the worship of Artemis left a void in the hearts of men.[8] Paul tells us in 1 Corinthians 10:19–21 that demons lurk behind idols. Therefore, the enemy was not about to let the disenchanted worshipers go. He would entice the Asians with magic, sorcery, and witchcraft. "Ephesus became the home of all sorts of magic and superstition. Even the phrase *Ephesia grammata* became common in antiquity for documents containing spells and magical formulae (cf. Athenaeus *Deipnosophistae* 12.548; Clement of Alexandria *Stromata* 5.242)."[9]

In addition to the temples of Artemis and lesser gods, Ephesus had the Library of Celsus, the third largest and most important library of that time. Had this library housed a Greek translation of the Old Testament, the Septuagint, and had the citizens of Ephesus read it, they could have known where such idolatrous and demonic worship would lead them. But no such copy was to be found in the Library of Celsus. It could only be found in the local synagogue.

While authors vied to get their books into this famous library[10] and, thus, gain access to the minds of men, God had another plan — a living epistle. He sent Paul. And the adversary roared!

1. Read Acts 19, and then list below the main events recorded in this chapter. As you do, keep in mind what you've just read about this prominent city.

2. How long did Paul stay in Ephesus?

3. Did you notice the conflict the gospel brings? Where? How? Does this bring you any comfort?

4. Look at Acts 19:37. What do you learn from this verse in respect to the way Paul handled the worshipers of Artemis?

5. Now, summarize what you learn from this passage about evil spirits or anything having to do with the enemy.

6. Finally, look up the following verses, and record what you learn. If you do not understand the terms used in these verses, you will find a page at the end of this chapter with their definitions.

a. Deuteronomy 18:9–14

b. Leviticus 19:26–28, 31

Now, if you have done any of these things, tell God that you realize you sinned and that you are sorry. Ask Him to cleanse and free you from any influence that has come into your life through these activities. Thank God for the blood of the Lord Jesus Christ which cleanses you from all sin. Tell Him you want to be filled with His blessed Holy Spirit and that you don't want any part in the things of darkness.

It would be good for you to write all this out in the form of a prayer to God.

Well, Beloved, you are on your way to gaining an understanding of why Paul wrote as he did to the church at Ephesus. Paul faced many of the things we will face as we live on the brink of the day of our Lord's second coming.

Remember, although our adversary, the devil, goes about "like a roaring lion, seeking someone to devour," you've nothing to fear if you know where and how to stand. And you will know, if you are faithful to finish this study.

DAY FOUR

After reading Acts 19, is it easier to understand the reference in Ephesians 6 to our warfare with spiritual forces of wickedness in the heavenly places? Ephesus was a hotbed of the occult. People lived in fear of what they could feel yet couldn't see. In their fear, they turned to all sorts of magic arts, charms, and sorcery.

Even Jewish exorcists were active. They knew there was a war that was not with flesh and blood, as evidenced in this statement from *Pseudepigrapha* (extrabiblical writings studied by the Jews): "'The earth is full of demons. Humanity is plagued by them. Almost all misfortunes are because of the demons: sickness, drought, death, and especially humanity's weakness about remaining faithful to the covenant. The region between heaven and earth seems to be almost cluttered by demons and angels; humanity is often seen as a pawn, helpless in the face of such cosmic force.'"[11]

How similar our western culture is becoming to the Ephesus and Asia of Paul's day! There's an increased fascination with the occult. The New Age movement offers to put people in touch with the god within. People from all walks of life, including children and teens, take on new identities as they enter the world of "Dungeons & Dragons." Witches and covens abound.

Films, TV, and recorded music evidence increasing control from the "dark side." Occult images fill even children's films, cartoons, and video games.

More than fifty "black metal" and "death metal" rock/rap groups preach satanic messages and even call for worship of the Prince of Darkness.

O Beloved, do not be spiritually naive. The war for the souls of people is escalating, and you and I have been commissioned by God to introduce them to Jesus Christ so He can "turn *them* from darkness to light, and *from* the power of Satan unto God" (Acts 26:18, KJV). Let's be about our Father's business even as Paul was!

Your assignment for today is to read through the first two chapters of Ephesians. Remember Ephesians is printed out at the end of this book. As you read, think about how the message applies to what we have discussed these past four days.

Mark the phrases *in Him, in Christ,* and *in Christ Jesus* in a distinctive way. Also mark the following words or phrases so you can easily spot them: *rule* and *rulers, power(s), authority* or *authorities, dominion, world, spirit, wickedness, darkness,* and *name.*

As you finish each week's study, take the truths you learned about your relationship to the Father, the Son, and the Holy Spirit, and turn them into an affirmational prayer of faith. As you pray, take a statement of truth from the Word of God, and make it your own by thanking God for it and applying it to your life. Paul prays this way for the Ephesians in 1:15–23.

Let me give you an example of what I'm suggesting, but don't let it limit you. Ephesians 1:3 says God has blessed you with every spiritual blessing in heavenly places in Christ Jesus. A prayer of affirmation might go something like this: "Father, I thank You that because I am Your child You have already blessed me with all the spiritual blessings I will ever need. (Then you would name those blessings which you gleaned from Ephesians 1 and 2.) Oh, Father, if I forget this, please remind me so I don't live like a spiritual pauper when I have everything I need in Christ Jesus."

Or your prayer of affirmation can be a commitment to believe a certain truth or to walk in obedience to something God has shown you is needed in your life.

Use a notebook or composition book to record these "Prayers of Affirmation." You should make this a weekly practice! Or you can do these daily if you desire. Make your prayers as brief or as long as you desire. They are for your benefit — and will help you greatly in warfare.

Ruth Paxson, in *The Wealth, Walk and Warfare of the Christian* says of Ephesians:

> One step over its threshold brings one into an atmosphere of unbounded spiritual affluence that creates within one's heart deepest peace and assurance. It is impossible to live habitually in Ephesians and be depressed.
>
> A vast deposit of riches has been made for the Christian in the bank of heaven. It is the oldest bank in existence. It dates way back to B.W. — before the world was. It does not belong to time and earth, but to eternity and heaven. Unlike the banks of earth, it is as unshakable and steadfast as the triune God who founded it. Its doors are never closed day or night to a child of God, and as for a run on it, nothing would please the heavenly Father more than to have a daily, hourly, moment-by-moment demand for its treasures.[12]

How different from the temple of Artemis! Let's study Ephesians and see the treasures stored there in our name.

Read through Ephesians 3 today, marking the same words you marked yesterday. When you finish, list below everything God tells you that belongs to those who are "in Him" in chapters 1 through 3. Look back at the phrases "in Him," "in Christ," and "in Christ Jesus" that you marked to help you make the list.

O Beloved, do you see that *in Him* you have everything you need? How wealthy are you? Meditate on what you have been given! When I say meditate, I mean to think it through, to chew it up and digest it — don't swallow it whole!

Now would be a good time to record a prayer of affirmation. Take one of these truths and lay hold of it in prayer.

DAY SIX

In the first three chapters of Ephesians, we learn of our wealth in Christ Jesus. In the last three chapters, we learn how to walk in the light of what we have. Your assignment today is to read chapters 4 and 5, marking the text as you have done previously.

Listen to the still, small voice of the Holy Spirit as He tells you how to walk. Every time you see *walk*, mark it in a distinctive way, and then list below what you learn about your walk. Glean your insights only from Ephesians!

Now then, let the Word of God examine your heart. What must you change? Confess? Continue in? Write it out.

DAY SEVEN

Christians in the West often remind me of ostriches because the minute they see something they'd rather not know, they bury their heads. Have you ever looked at an ostrich that has buried its head? It's quite comical. The ostrich can no longer see what he fears, but what he fears can see him! How could anyone miss those long skinny legs and that great big, feathery bottom?

The poor ostrich doesn't realize that burying his head will not remove him from danger. Do you think God made ostriches that way just to teach us a lesson?

Ignorance of the enemy and of warfare will not keep you out of the battle. Instead, it makes you extremely vulnerable. That's why God has been careful to let us know that there's an enemy who wants to wrestle us to the ground.

The word translated *struggle* or *wrestle* in Ephesians 6:12 speaks of "a 'hand-to-hand fight' — a fight characterized by trickery, cunningness, and strategy."[13] God doesn't tell us all this to scare us but to prepare us. We need to know why there's a struggle, why there's a conflict, and then we need to know how we're to live in the light of it.

So don't bury your head and leave your feathery bottom exposed! Remember, if you'll believe what He says and live as He tells you to live, you'll know the sweet taste of conquest!

Now read Ephesians 6 and mark the text as you have done these past few days.

When you finish, go back through the book of Ephesians and note where you have marked these words: *power, dominion, ruler, authority, world, darkness,* and *wickedness.* Then list everything Ephesians teaches you about these words and your relationship to them as a child of God.

Does the child of God need to bury his or her head? Answer that, and give your reason.

What do you need to remember this week? Satan would love nothing more than to keep you ignorant of truth, which sets you free. So determine that God's Word will have priority in your life. Look at what God did in Ephesus! He's the same yesterday, today, and forever. Record your affirmation of faith in your notebook.

And remember, you are beloved to Him — and to me.

DEFINITIONS OF TERMS
USED IN DEUTERONOMY 18:9–14
AND LEVITICUS 19:26–28, 31

1. *Casts spell:* the act of charming; "tying up" a person through magic; used in the sense of binding with a charm consisting of words of occult power.

2. *Divination:* the act of divining sorcery; soothsaying; pagan contrast to true prophecy or prophesying; man's attempt to know and control the world and future *apart* from the true God using means other than human; foretelling or foreseeing the future or discovering hidden knowledge through reading omens, dreams, using lots, astrology, or necromancy.

3. *Interpret omens:* a type of divination; seeking insight or knowledge through signs or events.

4. *Medium:* necromancer; one who foretells events or gains information by conversing with spirits of the dead; conjurer.

5. *Necromancer:* one who calls up the dead; medium.

6. *Spiritist:* familiar spirit; one who has esoteric knowledge through non-human means; diviner.

7. *Soothsaying:* witchcraft; observing clouds for augury; foretelling future events with supernatural power but not divine power; interpreting dreams; revealing secrets.

8. *Sorcerer:* magician; conjurer; enchanter; one who practices magic arts, sorcery, charms, with an intent to do harm or to delude or pervert the mind; one who claims to have supernatural power or knowledge through (evil) spirits.

9. *Witchcraft:* soothsaying; practice of witches; the use of formulas and incantations to practice sorcery; act of producing extraordinary effects by the invocation or aid of demons; the use of magic arts, spells, or charms.

LORD, WHY DID YOU CREATE THE DEVIL?

DAY ONE

How complete and accurate is your information on your enemy, the devil? In his autobiography, *Soldier,* General Matthew B. Ridgeway wrote, "There are two kinds of information that no commander can do without — information pertaining to the enemy which we call 'combat intelligence' and information on the terrain. Both are vital."

Accurate and up-to-date intelligence on the enemy is crucial in making tactical decisions in war. A thorough knowledge of the opponent's strength, his probable line of attack, and his tactics are vital in determining the course his land, sea, and air divisions will take. Major films such as *The Battle of Midway, A Bridge Too Far, Patton,* and *MacArthur* demonstrate in living color the importance of knowing your enemy. So does the black-and-white text of the Word of God! Therefore, our task this week is to gather intelligence information on our enemy, the devil.

All of us plummeted into death because Eve was deceived by the serpent — and Adam followed, eyes wide open! The crowning failure that toppled the diadem from King Saul's head came when he consulted the witch of Endor. David, along with his people, suffered greatly because Satan enticed him to number the children of Israel. King Ahab went to his death on the battlefield because he listened to a deceiving spirit which spoke through the mouth of a prophet. Daniel mourned, fasted, and agonized in prayer for three weeks, unaware of the heavenly conflict between God's angelic messengers and the unseen, but very real, prince of darkness who ruled over Persia. Satan was determined to keep Daniel in the dark, but God's angels prevailed.

It's imperative that we have accurate combat intelligence on our enemy! And that intelligence can be found in the Word of God.

The first chapter of Ephesians begins with an unparalleled eulogy of God who has blessed us with every spiritual blessing that we'll ever need. Praise is critical because God "inhabits the praises of His people," and the enemy hates praise that is offered to God. The chapter ends with the prayer that we might know three truths — truths critical in warfare because they give us a proper assessment of our position and power.

The first chapter also puts our focus where it should always be: on Christ, on who we are in Him, and on what we have in Him. Since you have already noted what we have "in Christ," we'll begin with Paul's prayer which outlines the three strategic truths. Look up Ephesians 1:15–23 and list these truths below. Each begins with a "what is" or "what are."

1.

2.

3.

In looking at these three facts, we discover the awesome and reassuring truth that our Lord Jesus Christ is seated with the Father in heavenly places far above all rule and authority and power and dominion and every name that is named, not only in this age, but also in the one to come. And, hallelujah, we come to understand that all things are in subjection to our Lord — including the enemy.

But if that's true, why all this conflict with the devil and his angels? Good question — one that will be answered before our study is over. However, at this point let's deal with what we know. We know we have an enemy who wants to throw us down and pin us to the ground. So let's see what we can learn about the devil himself, not to give him undue attention, nor to live in dread of him, but for the purpose of gaining accurate combat intelligence about him.

Since Satan is first mentioned in the third chapter of Genesis, let's begin there. However, before we study this passage, I want to make sure that you realize the Word of God is a progressive revelation of truth. By progressive revelation I mean God does not usually give us everything we need to know about a particular subject, person, or event in one book or chapter of the Bible. Instead, God's pattern is to reveal truth little by little, building on what has gone before. You might say that God builds truth precept by precept.

Insight or information on one subject may be spread out over the course of sixty-six books, written by about forty men under the inspiration of God and recorded over a span of 1,050 years. In order to have the whole counsel of the Word of God, you must know what is taught in the entire Bible about a particular subject. Therefore, as we cover the subject of spiritual warfare from the home base of Ephesians, we are going to incorporate all of Scripture into our study to ensure we have the complete picture. If you'll bear with me, my friend, you will learn much that will be very profitable to your Christian walk.

1. Read through Genesis 3 which is printed on the next page and mark every reference to the serpent. (Be certain you mark pronouns that refer to him.) You may want to use a symbol like this.   serpent

➤ GENESIS 3

¹ Now the serpent was more crafty than any beast of the field which the LORD God had made. And he said to the woman, "Indeed, has God said, 'You shall not eat from any tree of the garden'?"

² And the woman said to the serpent, "From the fruit of the trees of the garden we may eat;

³ but from the fruit of the tree which is in the middle of the garden, God has said, 'You shall not eat from it or touch it, lest you die.'"

⁴ And the serpent said to the woman, "You surely shall not die!

⁵ "For God knows that in the day you eat from it your eyes will be opened, and you will be like God, knowing good and evil."

⁶ When the woman saw that the tree was good for food, and that it was a delight to the eyes, and that the tree was desirable to make *one* wise, she took from its fruit and ate; and she gave also to her husband with her, and he ate.

⁷ Then the eyes of both of them were opened, and they knew that they were naked; and they sewed fig leaves together and made themselves loin coverings.

⁸ And they heard the sound of the LORD God walking in the garden in the cool of the day, and the man and his wife hid themselves from the presence of the LORD God among the trees of the garden.

⁹ Then the LORD God called to the man, and said to him, "Where are you?"

¹⁰ And he said, "I heard the sound of Thee in the garden, and I was afraid because I was naked; so I hid myself."

¹¹ And He said, "Who told you that you were naked? Have you eaten from the tree of which I commanded you not to eat?"

12 And the man said, "The woman whom Thou gavest *to be* with me, she gave me from the tree, and ate."

13 Then the LORD God said to the woman, "What is this you have done?" And the woman said, "The serpent deceived me, and I ate."

14 And the LORD God said to the serpent, "Because you have done this, cursed are you more than all cattle, and more than every beast of the field; on your belly shall you go, and dust shall you eat all the days of your life;

15 And I will put enmity between you and the woman, and between your seed and her seed; He shall bruise you on the head, and you shall bruise him on the heel."

16 To the woman He said, "I will greatly multiply your pain in childbirth, in pain you shall bring forth children; yet your desire shall be for your husband, and he shall rule over you."

17 Then to Adam He said, "Because you have listened to the voice of your wife, and have eaten from the tree about which I commanded you, saying, 'You shall not eat from it'; cursed is the ground because of you; in toil you shall eat of it all the days of your life.

18 "Both thorns and thistles it shall grow for you; and you shall eat the plants of the field;

19 By the sweat of your face you shall eat bread, till you return to the ground, because from it you were taken; for you are dust, and to dust you shall return."

20 Now the man called his wife's name Eve, because she was the mother of all *the* living.

21 And the LORD God made garments of skin for Adam and his wife, and clothed them.

²² Then the LORD God said, "Behold, the man has become like one of Us, knowing good and evil; and now, lest he stretch out his hand, and take also from the tree of life, and eat, and live forever" —

²³ therefore the LORD God sent him out from the garden of Eden, to cultivate the ground from which he was taken.

²⁴ So He drove the man out; and at the east of the garden of Eden He stationed the cherubim, and the flaming sword which turned every direction, to guard the way to the tree of life.

2. List everything you learn about the serpent, his tactics, his future, etc. (May I also suggest that from this point forward you keep a running list in your notebook of everything you are learning about the devil. I'll remind you from time to time.)

3. By now, you know that I believe the serpent is Satan, the devil. However, how do you know that what I believe is right? How did I come to that conclusion? Since we have the whole counsel of God, let's leave the first book and go to the last to see what it says about who the serpent is.

Look at Revelation 12:9.

a. Write out the verse.

b. What parallels do you see between this verse and what you learned in Genesis 3?

4. If these were the only two passages about the enemy that you had access to, what could you learn from them that you could apply to your own life?

Well, Beloved, we have begun our second week of study. I know God will use these insights to strengthen you and further His kingdom — that's why I'm excited about this study! Press on.

D A Y   T W O

Where did this serpent, Satan, come from? Has he always existed, or was he created? If he was created, is there another creator other than God? Did God create him as an evil being? These are all legitimate questions. I believe that if it's important for us to have the answers, we'll find them in His Word. However, if God leaves something unexplained, then we must apply Isaiah 50:10: "Who is among you that fears the LORD, that obeys the voice of His servant, that walks in darkness and has no light? Let him trust in the name of the LORD and rely on his God."

Traditionally there are two passages of Scripture which some theologians believe give us a glimpse into how Satan became the enemy of God. I want us to examine these two passages, cross-reference them, and see what "intelligence" we can gather about our enemy.

1. The first passage is Ezekiel 28:11–19. Some theologians believe that the "king of Tyre" is a reference to Satan. The passage is typed out for you, so read through it quickly. Then reread it and mark or color in a distinctive way every pronoun (him, you, your) which refers to the "king of Tyre." Also mark every reference to God. When I mark *God* and references to Him, I use a triangle like this one ⟨God⟩ and color the inside of it yellow.

➤ EZEKIEL 28:11–19

11 Again the word of the LORD came to me saying,

12 "Son of man, take up a lamentation over the king of Tyre, and say to him, 'Thus says the Lord GOD, "You had the seal of perfection, full of wisdom and perfect in beauty.

13 "You were in Eden, the garden of God; every precious stone was your covering: The ruby, the topaz, and the diamond; the beryl, the onyx, and the jasper; the lapis lazuli, the turquoise, and the emerald; and the gold, the workmanship of your settings and sockets, was in you. On the day that you were created they were prepared.

14 "You were the anointed cherub who covers, and I placed you *there*. You were on the holy mountain of God; you walked in the midst of the stones of fire.

15 "You were blameless in your ways from the day you were created, until unrighteousness was found in you.

16 "By the abundance of your trade you were internally filled with violence, and you sinned; therefore I have cast you as profane from the mountain of God. And I have destroyed you, O covering cherub, from the midst of the stones of fire.

17 "Your heart was lifted up because of your beauty; you corrupted your

wisdom by reason of your splendor. I cast you to the ground; I put you before kings, that they may see you.

18 "By the multitude of your iniquities, in the unrighteousness of your trade, you profaned your sanctuaries. Therefore I have brought fire from the midst of you; it has consumed you, and I have turned you to ashes on the earth in the eyes of all who see you.

19 "All who know you among the peoples are appalled at you; you have become terrified, and you will be no more.""''"

2. Now then, list everything you learn from this passage about the "king of Tyre." Tomorrow we'll discuss what you have observed.

DAY   THREE

Some believe Ezekiel 28 is a prophetic passage which refers to Satan. Others believe it is simply a lamentation against an earthly king. One commentator says that in Ezekiel 28:2, 9 the king of Tyre is told two different times that he is "only human." I could not agree more. However, in Ezekiel 28:11–19, the scene seems to change. Therefore, before we assume that Ezekiel 28:11–19 does not refer to Satan, let's examine this passage.

Ezekiel 28:2 begins with the Lord saying, "Son of man [this is the way God refers to Ezekiel throughout this book], say to the leader of Tyre, 'Thus says the Lord GOD, "Because your heart is lifted up and you have said, 'I am a god, I sit in the seat of gods, in the heart of the seas'; yet you are a man and not God, although you make your heart like the heart of God.""'

Ezekiel 28:2 makes it clear that the *leader* of Tyre is a man. However, in 28:11–19, there is a definite transition as the Lord tells Ezekiel to take up a lamentation against the *king* of Tyre, not the *leader* of Tyre.

The English transliteration of the Hebrew word for *leader* in 28:2, is *nāgîd,* which means a ruler, leader, prince, captain. According to the *Theological Wordbook of the Old Testament,* it is used about fifty times as applied to leaders in several fields: governmental, military, and religious. The word usually is singular and refers to the man at the top, the king, the high priest, etc., but there are also places where the word refers to leaders and captains in the army. The word is used with reference to the Messiah in Daniel 9:25, i.e., "Messiah the Prince."

In Ezekiel 28:12 a different Hebrew word, *melek,* is used for the *king* of Tyre. Since every word of God is pure, "God-breathed," and, therefore, chosen by God, it seems that a distinction is being made between two different authorities. *Melek* occurs over 2,500 times in the Old Testament and has a wide range of meaning. It may refer to an emperor of an empire or to a chieftain of a tiny city-state. It is the most commonly used word for chief magistrate.

Ezekiel 28:11–19 is a dirge, a lament as in a funeral. In the Greek the root of the word *lament* means "to strike a note or a chant, a wail, or mourn." Although this king began well, he ended up cast out of the mountain of God onto the ground where he became a spectacle before kings. (The Hebrew for the word *kings* in verse 17 is the plural form of *melek.*)

It is most interesting that this king is called a cherub, not a man. Also don't miss that the passage says he was a cherub who was in Eden, the garden of God.

Remember what you read in Genesis 3? After Adam and Eve sinned and were cast out of the garden of Eden, God stationed cherubim (plural of *cherub*) to guard the way to the tree of life so that man could not return to it. Remember too that there is no biblical record of any human except Adam and Eve ever being in the garden of Eden, or as Ezekiel calls it, the "garden of God."

It's interesting too, isn't it, that this cherub spoken of in Ezekiel 28 was created by God, rather than born of man, and that he was placed in the garden by God.

Could this cherub be a man? Ezekiel says that this cherub was blameless from the day he was created. Psalm 51:5 tells us that man is born in sin. Adam and Eve were the only humans created by a direct act of God. Every other person on the face of the earth can trace their genealogy back to Adam and Eve. In fact, Eve's name means "the mother of all the living" (Genesis 3:20). Now, contrast these facts with the fact that the *melek*, the anointed cherub in Ezekiel 28:11–19, was blameless from his creation until unrighteousness was found in him. This king of Tyre doesn't sound like a man to me. Does he to you?

There is one more passage we need to study tomorrow. Today you have a lot to digest. Review what we talked about in the light of your list of observations regarding the "king of Tyre."

You might also want to write down any questions you have at this point and then see if I cover them tomorrow.

As we close, I want you to know that I'm thrilled you're willing to study to show yourself approved unto God, a workman who won't be ashamed because you have put forth the effort and time it takes to handle the Word of God accurately.

What you're learning is intelligence information, and it's foundational to warfare! It isn't superfluous.

What have you learned that you can turn into a prayer?

Have you ever had anyone challenge you with questions like these: "Well, if God made everything, then how did the devil get here? Did God make him? What kind of a God would do that?"

How did you answer? Were you right?

Many scholars believe Isaiah 14:3–15 gives us further insight into how Satan became the adversary of God and man. As in other Old Testament prophetic passages, sometimes there can be a dual reference to the present and to the future, the former serving as a foreshadowing of someone or something yet to come. Such references occur often in prophetic passages regarding our Lord's first and second comings and the day of the Lord.

Isaiah 14:3–15 is printed out for you. Read it over and over, asking yourself the "5 W's and an H — who, what, when, where, why, and how" (especially note the "when").

Ask God to open the eyes of your understanding as you read. Remember, it is our responsibility to study His Word, but truth is revealed (1 Corinthians 2:9–16)

► ISAIAH 14:3–15

3 And it will be in the day when the LORD gives you rest from your pain and turmoil and harsh service in which you have been enslaved,

4 that you will take up this taunt against the king of Babylon, and say, "How the oppressor has ceased, *and how* fury has ceased!

5 "The LORD has broken the staff of the wicked, the scepter of rulers

6 Which used to strike the peoples in fury with unceasing strokes, which subdued the nations in anger with unrestrained persecution.

7 "The whole earth is at rest *and* is quiet; they break forth into shouts of joy.

8 "Even the cypress trees rejoice over you, *and* the cedars of Lebanon, *saying,* 'Since you were laid low, no *tree* cutter comes up against us.'

9 "Sheol from beneath is excited over you to meet you when you come; it arouses for you the spirits of the dead, all the leaders of the earth; it raises all the kings of the nations from their thrones.

10 "They will all respond and say to you, 'Even you have been made weak as we, you have become like us.

11 'Your pomp *and* the music of your harps have been brought down to Sheol; maggots are spread out *as your bed* beneath you, and worms are your covering.'

12 "How you have fallen from heaven, O star of the morning, son of the dawn! You have been cut down to the earth, you who have weakened the nations!

13 "But you said in your heart, 'I will ascend to heaven; I will raise my throne above the stars of God, and I will sit on the mount of assembly in the recesses of the north.

14 'I will ascend above the heights of the clouds; I will make myself like the Most High.'

15 "Nevertheless you will be thrust down to Sheol, to the recesses of the pit.

This Isaiah 14 passage does not seem to refer to any earthly king. Why? Because this king, whoever he is, fell from heaven. He was cut down to earth because of his ambition to ascend into heaven. He wanted to make himself like the Most High, to raise his throne above the stars of God and to sit on the mount of assembly in the recesses of the north.

Doesn't this account sound like the same song, second verse of Ezekiel 28:11–19? It does to me! When this passage from Isaiah is cross-referenced with other scriptures, we begin to get a clearer understanding of the whole scenario of the origin of sin. Let's look at one cross-reference.

Begin with 1 Timothy 3:6: "And not a new convert, lest he become conceited and fall into the condemnation incurred by the devil."

1. Can you see any way in which this verse would help support the belief that Isaiah 14:12–14 is referring to the devil? Explain your answer.

In the *Linguistic Key to the Greek New Testament,* Rienecker and Rogers state that "condemnation incurred by the devil" (1 Timothy 3:6) could be translated "condemnation reserved for the devil."[1] If this is so, 1 Timothy 3:6 tells us that pride brought Satan into condemnation. No other scripture highlights that fact like Isaiah 14. Interesting, isn't it? It also lets you know what God thinks about pride.

2. What do you learn from 1 Timothy 3:6 that you can apply to your own life...or that you should remember when appointing leaders in the church?

Can you see, Beloved, how the enemy would try to lure us into the same sin as his — pride? Does what you've seen give you any insight into why God is opposed to the proud (1 Peter 5:5)? (Don't forget to add all you've learned about the enemy to your list in your notebook.)

Did God create anything that was evil? What does the Word say?

    1. Look up the following verses and then record what you learn about God's creative acts.

        a. John 1:1–3

        b. Nehemiah 9:5–6 (Note the word *host* — this includes angelic beings.)

        c. Colossians 1:15–16

    Colossians 1:15–16 leaves no doubt that even invisible thrones, dominions, rulers, and authorities were created by our Lord Jesus Christ, the incarnate Word of God. But would a righteous and holy God create evil beings? I don't believe so.

    Genesis 1 repeatedly tells us that God saw what He created and that it was good. How then did Satan become the adversary? If Genesis is true, then where did demons come from?

Let's review what we learned in Ezekiel and Isaiah and move on from there. If the anointed cherub is Satan, the passage tells us that he was perfect until he sinned. This beautiful creation of God, like other angelic beings, possessed a free will — and he exercised it.

Corrupted by his splendor, he wanted to raise his throne above the stars and sit on the mount of the assembly. He wanted to be like the Most High. Consequently, he became the classic illustration of 1 Timothy 3:6: "Pride goes before a fall."

O Beloved, can you see that Satan would like to snare you and me in the same trap? Be careful, my friend, be careful! Examine your heart. Ask God to show you any snare of pride that the enemy might have set for you.

Write your own prayer.

DAY SIX

Well, we've seen where we believe Satan came from, but what about demons? Again we face the question, "If God created all things, where did rulers and spiritual forces of wickedness and darkness come from?" Our answer is found in the word *stars!*

The word *star* appears twice in Isaiah 14:12–14. Remember, the "king" of Isaiah 14 was called the "star [*helel* — shining one] of the morning," and it was the "son of the dawn" who wanted to raise his throne above the stars of God.

A star wanted to have a throne above the stars? Are we talking about literal stars? Let's do a little searching in the Word and find out.

➤ J O B 3 8 : 4 – 7

⁴ "Where were you when I laid the foundation of the earth! Tell *Me*, if you have understanding.

⁵ Who set its measurements, since you know? Or who stretched the line on it?

⁶ "On what were its bases sunk? Or who laid its cornerstone,

⁷ When the morning stars sang together, and all the sons of God shouted for joy?"

When writing poetically, authors commonly state the same truth in two ways. Therefore, in Job 38:7 it is possible that the author is speaking of the same group in two different ways when he speaks of the "sons of God" and of "the morning stars."

1. There are two other places besides Job 38:7 where "sons of God" (*bēnê 'elōhîm*) is used in the Book of Job. Read these verses and record what you learn about the "sons of God."

a. Job 1:6

b. Job 2:1

2. What do you learn from these verses about Satan? Do they parallel in any way what you saw in Ezekiel 28 and Isaiah 14?

3. Look up the following verses and note what you learn about stars.

a. Revelation 1:20

b. Revelation 9:1–2

c. Revelation 12:3–4 compared with 12:7–9

Now, let's discuss these verses. I believe the morning stars that sang at creation were angelic beings, *bēnê ʾelōhîm* (sons of God). I also believe that Satan was one of them. However, when he became enamored with himself, he wasn't content to be a star among stars. He wanted to raise his throne above God and above the stars of God. He wanted to usurp God's authority.

Revelation confirms that stars can refer to angels. In Revelation 1:20 when God explains the mystery of the seven stars in His right hand, He tells us "the seven stars are the angels of the seven churches."

Then again in Revelation 9:1 we see that a star which had fallen to the earth from heaven is given the key to a bottomless pit. The verb *fallen* is in the perfect tense in the Greek, which means a past completed action with a present and continuing result. In other words, this star (angel) fell from heaven sometime in the past and remains in that fallen state. I believe this angel is one who chose to side with Satan when Satan revolted against God.

There is no redemption for Satan or angels. Those angels who defected with Satan sealed their fate for eternity at that moment. How blessed we are to have a Redeemer!

When the star of Revelation 9 opens the bottomless pit, he releases locusts of a horrendous description. These locusts possess great power and torment people for a period of five months. In Revelation 9:11 we learn that the locusts have a "king over them, the angel of the abyss; his name in Hebrew is Abaddon, and in the Greek he has the name Apollyon." *Abaddon* means "destruction," and *Apollyon* is translated as "destroyer." Could this king be Satan, who comes to kill and destroy?

The dragon mentioned in Revelation 12:4 is described in 12:9 as the devil and Satan, the serpent of old — a serpent who swept away a third of the stars of heaven with his tail. Could it be that in this passage God pulls back the curtain even more so that we can understand what happened to a third of the angels?

4. Let's look at one more set of verses. Then I'll put it all together as I see it, and you can see if you agree. Note what the following verses teach in respect to God's throne, God's power, and the angels.

   a. Psalm 103:19–22

   b. Hebrews 1:7–9, 13–14 (As you read these verses, you need to realize that the author's purpose in this chapter, as indicated in verse 4, is to show that Jesus is better than the angels.)
   (1) Record what you learn about angels.

   (2) Note in verses 7 and 8 the contrast between angels and Jesus.

   (3) Now note the relationship of Jesus to angels in Hebrews 1:9.

   (4) What place did Satan want?

So where do evil spirits, demons, and fallen angels come from? Although there's not much information in the Bible specifically on the fall of angels, let me give you my understanding of God's Word on this subject. As I fit all of the pieces of scripture together, remember all you've learned so far.

When God created the heavens and the earth, I believe the angelic host was already in existence because according to Job 38:7 they sang together for joy. However, one of the highest cherubim, puffed up because of his beauty and splendor, determined he would be like the Most High. He wanted to raise his throne above the stars, or angels, of God and sit in God's place on the mount of the assembly in the recesses of the north. (As a point of interest we learn from Job that God's throne is in the north.) This pride resulted in his fall.

When Satan fell, he took some angelic beings with him. I believe the account of Revelation 12:4 confirms this belief. Remember it says that the dragon's tail swept away a third of the stars of heaven and threw them to the earth. I believe the third of the stars mentioned here was a third of the angelic beings. These became what we call "fallen angels," evil spirits, or demons.

When this revolt took place, God cast Satan out of heaven. Prior to his fall he apparently had access to Eden, the garden of God, because as we saw, the Word of God opens with the creation and fall of man — man created innocent but seduced and deceived in the garden by the serpent of old, Satan. With this seduction, Satan became the ruler of the world who rules over the sons of disobedience (John 14:30; Ephesians 2:1–3).

The fate of the devil and his angels was sealed the day they sinned. There's no redemption for angels. Thus, God prepared a lake of fire for the devil and his angels (Matthew 25:41). However, Satan and his angels will not be the only ones to inhabit that eternal lake of fire.

When Satan walked into the garden of Eden, he wanted to gain control over the human race. He succeeded. He deceived Eve, and through Eve he reached Adam. Adam listened to the voice of his wife rather than to God. He ate of the forbidden fruit, and at that moment sin entered the world, and death by sin. Humanity was lost…lost to God, lost to eternal life…eternally doomed. Yet on that same day God graciously promised One who would bruise the head of the serpent. He would send His Son as our Kinsman Redeemer, break the power of sin and death, and free us from Satan's domain of darkness.

Satan may have walked into the garden, but he slithered out. His fate was sealed. God said to the serpent, "Because you have done this, cursed are you more than all cattle, and more than every beast of the field; on your belly shall you go, and dust shall you eat all the days of your life; and I will put enmity between you and the woman, and between your seed and her seed; he shall bruise you on the head, and you shall bruise him on the heel" (Genesis 3:14–15).

From that day forward there has been enmity between Satan and the seed of the woman, the Lord Jesus Christ. That's why we must learn all we can about spiritual warfare.

Revelation 12:7 tells us about a war in heaven which is yet to be fought. Michael and his angels will wage war with the dragon and his angels, and Michael will win! Those who belong to God will triumph ultimately!

O precious one, so many wonderful truths lie before us — truths which will set you free, truths that will enable you to be strong in the Lord and in the strength of His might. Press on, valiant warrior to know the truth and to live in the freedom of it!

DAY SEVEN

Both Christians and Satanists alike refer to Satan as Lucifer. This particular name for the prince of darkness came from the King James translation of Isaiah 14:12, "How art thou fallen from heaven, O Lucifer, son of the morning."

According to the *Strong's Exhaustive Concordance of the Bible,* the Hebrew word *hêylêl* or *hêlēl,* translated *Lucifer,* means "in the sense of brightness, the morning star." Its derivation is *hâlal,* which means "to be clear" — either clear in sound or in color, thus, to shine. The *Theological Wordbook of the Old Testament* says the word means to "praise, boast," which, of course, is what the cherubim and seraphim do continuously before the throne as they worship God.

It's interesting, isn't it, that this shining bright one who was created to praise God and bring Him glory would instead become God's archenemy and rival and be called "the prince of darkness"? And all because he was caught up with his own beauty and splendor!

As we bring this week's study to a close, let's look at the five "I wills" of Isaiah 14:3–15. We who were created for God's glory alone can learn a lesson from what we see here so that we aren't caught in the same snare of pride.

Listen to pride's discordant words:

"I will ascend to heaven."

"I will raise my throne above the stars of God."

"I will sit on the mount of assembly in the recesses of the north."

"I will ascend above the heights of the clouds."

"I will be like the Most High."

O Beloved, what motivates you? What are your ambitions? Are they self-promoting? Are you hungry for power? Do you have a "need" to be in control? Are you ambitious — scrambling, maneuvering to sit in the seat of leaders? Are you constantly pushing yourself for recognition and achievement? Have you forgotten the following admonition?

Have this attitude in yourselves which was also in Christ Jesus, who, although He existed in the form of God, did not regard equality with God a thing to be grasped, but emptied Himself, taking the form of a bond-servant, *and* being made in the likeness of men. And being found in appearance as a man, He humbled Himself by becoming obedient to the point of death, even death on a cross. Therefore also God highly exalted Him, and bestowed on Him the name which is above every name, that at the name of Jesus EVERY KNEE SHOULD BOW, of those who are in heaven, and on earth, and under the earth, and that every tongue should confess that Jesus Christ is Lord, to the glory of the Father. (Philippians 2:5–11)

Is your vocabulary loaded with "I wills"? Or are you quick to say, "If the Lord wills"? Listen to James 4:13–17: "Come now, you who say, 'Today or tomorrow, we shall go to such and such a city, and spend a year there and engage in business and make a profit.' Yet you do not know what your life will be like tomorrow. You are *just* a vapor that appears for a little while and then vanishes away. Instead, *you ought* to say, 'If the Lord wills, we shall live and also do this or that.' But as it is, you boast in your arrogance; all such boasting is evil. Therefore, to one who knows *the* right thing to do, and does not do it, to him it is sin."

Have you seen self as the root of sin? Or have you been caught up in the doctrine of demons which twists truth, urging us to positive thinking and "the potential" which lies within?

If you are running your life rather than letting God run it, you are trying to be like the Most High. It is God's prerogative, and God's alone, to run our lives. We are the clay; He is the Potter. We are the created; He is the Creator. We are the servant; He is the Master. We are human; He is God. Are you, in any way, trying to usurp His position?

Do you aspire to be number one? Do you crave the biggest, the best? Must you be the most successful? Are you impressed with prestige, size, numbers, opulence, and money?

Although there are many godly pastors, there are some who desire to have the largest congregation and the most beautiful sanctuary. There's almost a competition among some leaders and organizations for numbers. They clamor for the largest Bible study, the largest ministry, the largest church or Sunday school, the greatest number of baptisms or decisions, the largest listening or viewing audience. Acts tells us the Lord added to the church such as were saved. Have we forgotten the scripture says that unless the Lord builds the house those that labor build it in vain (Psalm 127:1)?

In 1 Chronicles 21:1 we read, "Then Satan stood up against Israel and moved David to number Israel." Yielding to this temptation was very costly to David and the children of Israel — just as equal temptations rooted in pride and the flesh have been costly to many other leaders and their follow-ers. God will not allow the flesh to glory in His presence.

> For not from the east, nor from the west, nor from the desert *comes* exal-
> tation; but God is the Judge; He puts down one, and exalts another.
> (Psalm 75:6–7)

Let the name of God be blessed forever and ever, for wisdom and power belong to Him. And it is He who changes the times and the epochs; He removes kings and establishes kings; He gives wisdom to wise men, and knowledge to men of understanding. (Daniel 2:20–21)

Let's join the twenty-four elders before the throne of God and say, "Worthy art Thou, our Lord and our God, to receive glory and honor and power; for Thou didst create all things, and because of Thy will they existed, and were created" (Revelation 4:11). Let's acknowledge that all things have been created by Him and for Him and that He is to have the preeminence in our lives.

Write out five "I wills" for your life. Let them be a counterattack against the enemy's "I wills."

Now take all you have learned this week and turn it into a prayer of affirmation. Record it in your notebook.

CHAPTER THREE

LORD, SATAN'S ROARING — NEED I FEAR?

The day was hard. I felt unwanted, like an intruder. Everyone was in bed and asleep as I walked into the upstairs bathroom to get ready for bed. I opened my cosmetic bag and got out my cleansing cream. Being here awakened all sorts of buried hurts.

As I leaned across the sink toward the mirror, suddenly the thought was there, *Why don't you just kill yourself. Then there will be no more grief, no more pain.*

You could hang yourself like Tom did.

Then they'd find you and...

No, I shook my head, *that's too cruel. I can't do that to them — how would they live with the memory of finding me? It could ruin their lives....*

But they'd know then...and they'd hurt for you. Besides, it would be all over...you'd be home.

For a moment I entertained the thought. Then I came to my senses. The enemy had crept into the camp and, taking advantage of my pain, disguised himself as my thoughts.

What would my suicide say to all those who had listened to me proclaim the sufficiency of our Lord Jesus Christ and His Word? That His grace was *not* sufficient for all my hurts? That God couldn't possibly "work all things together for my good and His glory"? Wouldn't they then think the same when it came to dealing with their own hurts?

I was amazed that I'd allowed my thoughts to get this far! This wasn't the first time I had dealt with thoughts of suicide. I'd had them before I was saved. When my dreams of a "live-happily-ever-after marriage" had been shattered and I thought there was no hope and no way out, I went to the basement of our townhouse to find a rope. Then I thought of my sons, and I turned around and went upstairs.

I had also had these thoughts one other time when the pressures of ministry seemed overwhelming. In the bedroom of my mother's home the thought had come again, "Why don't you just kill yourself?"

Now I realized that once again the enemy was after me. However, I was not ignorant of his schemes. I knew who the murderer was! I was well aware that he was the thief who comes to kill and destroy. Yet I hadn't immediately brought my thoughts captive to the obedience of Christ. I was indulging my flesh.

It was warfare, and for a moment I was caught off guard. That's dangerous for a soldier! Many a battle has been lost when a soldier or a regiment let down for a moment or failed to recognize the enemy for who he was!

This week we are going to get a character profile on our enemy. He always acts true to character, so this information will keep you from being unaware of his devices.

1. Let's begin with John 8:44. Look up the verse in your Bible, then write it out below. By the way, when you look it up, you may want to mark your Bible so that you can spot any reference to the enemy at a glance. Before I began writing this book, I looked up every reference to the enemy and his demonic host, organized all my information, and then studied it carefully. As I looked up every reference, I marked each verse with a red pitchfork, like this: ψ

2. Read Acts 5:3 and write it out. (Can you see how this correlates with John 8:44?) Then list what you learn about the enemy. (Don't forget to add these insights to the list in your notebook.)

Now then, my friend, have you ever thought of taking your life? Where do you think that thought came from?

Who do you think is the originator of lies?

How can the truths of John 8:44 help you in warfare?

DAY TWO

I'll never forget my last six months in high school. Daddy was transferred in the middle of my senior year, so we packed up and moved from Long Island, New York, to Shaker Heights, Ohio. Immediately, as was our custom in our many moves, we found a church home and I became active in the youth group. It was either sit at home and mope because I had to leave all I'd worked to achieve in high school or try to make something of what was left of my senior year.

I got involved in every activity I could. I was also running a youth canteen in the church we joined. Something like this had been tried before but never worked. Of course, I was challenged!

I was going to make our youth canteen "the place" to be on Friday night. Shaker Heights was one of the wealthy suburbs of Cleveland, Ohio, and many of the teens could afford to do whatever they wanted. That's why many didn't think the youth canteen idea would get off the ground. But I had my own ideas. One was to throw a big dance — something with a different twist.

I was only seventeen then. I thought I was a Christian. Nobody had ever told me differently. I'd been baptized as an infant, confirmed at the age of twelve. I was allowed to take Holy Communion — didn't that make me a Christian? Of course, the Bible was boring and hard to understand, so I rarely read it.

At any rate, I needed a theme for the dance, something to draw people in. I called it a "Heaven and Hades Dance." Sure enough, the dance was a big success. One side of the parish hall was decorated like heaven with angels suspended amongst clouds hanging from the ceiling. Soft blue lighting. Heaven looked pretty, but hell was smashing — electrifying! We had flashing red lights (this was before strobes), smoke curled out of the punch bowl, but the grabber was the red devil hanging on the wall with a pitchfork in his hand. Immediately you knew who he was and where you were. That night heaven was empty. It seemed more fun to dance in hell.

I was blinded by the god of this world, and I didn't know it. As a matter of fact, my concept of the devil was simply that of the caricature on the wall. If he ever showed up, you would surely recognize him because of the way he dressed — the pitchfork would be a dead giveaway. I didn't know that he could disguise himself!

For the next twelve years, I continued to dance with the devil — and didn't even realize it.

I don't want that to happen to you, my friend. So let's go to the Word of God and gird our loins with truth. Remember, we're trying to get a character profile on our enemy. To do this, you must know truth for yourself.

Second-hand knowledge won't hold in the heat of battle. You must be trained, so be diligent to do your assignments. God's Word is truth, and when it's embraced as such, truth sets you free.

The book of 1 Peter was written to some Christians who, because of their circumstances, needed to remember that they were aliens and strangers in this world. Peter brings his epistle to a close with the following words. Read them carefully, and then I'll tell you what to do.

➤ 1 PETER 5:6–11

6 Humble yourselves, therefore, under the mighty hand of God, that He may exalt you at the proper time,

7 casting all your anxiety upon Him, because He cares for you.

8 Be of sober *spirit,* be on the alert. Your adversary, the devil, prowls about like a roaring lion, seeking someone to devour.

9 But resist him, firm in *your* faith, knowing that the same experiences of suffering are being accomplished by your brethren who are in the world.

10 And after you have suffered for a little while, the God of all grace, who called you to His eternal glory in Christ, will Himself perfect, confirm, strengthen *and* establish you.

11 To Him *be* dominion forever and ever. Amen.

1. Mark every reference to the enemy in this passage. Don't forget to include the pronouns that refer to him.

2. List what you learn about the enemy from this passage. (Also record these insights on your list in your notebook.)

3. According to this passage, what were these people going through? (This word is repeated throughout this powerful little epistle.)

4. What were they told to do? List your insights.

5. What is God going to do?

I've heard that when lions roar they throw their voice, which causes their prey to become confused and terrorized. When the lion roars, Beloved, don't run or give in. Stand firm in your faith — even if your knees are knocking. If Paul stood firm while confronting all he did in Ephesus, you can do it where you are. The same Jesus who indwelt Paul dwells within you. Remember where Jesus is seated, and remember who's in you. Then you won't become the devil's meat!

How do you stand firm? One way is to understand your position and to affirm it in prayer and in the way that you live. So apply what you've learned so far and keep studying. We haven't finished our course yet.

DAY THREE

Of all the names and titles used for the devil, none is used more than "Satan." Satan is found fifty-four times in the Old and New Testaments, while "devil" is used thirty-four times and only occurs in the New Testament. The English transliteration of the Greek word for devil is *diabolōs* and means "an accuser, a slanderer" (from *diaballō,* "to accuse, to malign").[1]

The English transliteration of the Hebrew word for Satan is exactly that — *Satan* — which means "adversary." It is from the verb which means "to attack, to accuse, to be an adversary, to resist." Don't forget these definitions, my friend, because they will help you recognize your unseen enemy.

The first time the name *Satan* is used in the Word of God is in 1 Chronicles 21:1 where Satan stands up and provokes David to number Israel. The next occurrence is found in the first and second chapters of the Book of Job, which is what we'll study today.

The Book of Job not only gives us insight into Satan's strategy, it also shows us the limits of his power.

Read Job 1:1–22, which is printed out for you. As you read, mark every reference to Satan in a distinctive way.

➤ JOB 1:1–22

1 There was a man in the land of Uz, whose name was Job, and that man was blameless, upright, fearing God, and turning away from evil.

2 And seven sons and three daughters were born to him.

3 His possessions also were 7,000 sheep, 3,000 camels, 500 yoke of oxen, 500 female donkeys, and very many servants; and that man was the greatest of all the men of the east.

4 And his sons used to go and hold a feast in the house of each one on his day, and they would send and invite their three sisters to eat and drink with them.

5 And it came about, when the days of feasting had completed their cycle, that Job would send and consecrate them, rising up early in the morning and offering burnt offerings *according* to the number of them all; for Job said, "Perhaps my sons have sinned and cursed God in their hearts." Thus Job did continually.

⁶ Now there was a day when the sons of God came to present themselves before the LORD, and Satan also came among them.

⁷ And the LORD said to Satan, "From where do you come?" Then Satan answered the LORD and said, "From roaming about on the earth and walking around on it."

⁸ And the LORD said to Satan, "Have you considered My servant Job? For there is no one like him on the earth, a blameless and upright man, fearing God and turning away from evil."

⁹ Then Satan answered the LORD, "Does Job fear God for nothing?

¹⁰ "Hast Thou not made a hedge about him and his house and all that he has, on every side? Thou hast blessed the work of his hands, and his possessions have increased in the land.

¹¹ "But put forth Thy hand now and touch all that he has; he will surely curse Thee to Thy face."

¹² Then the LORD said to Satan, "Behold, all that he has is in your power, only do not put forth your hand on him." So Satan departed from the presence of the LORD.

¹³ Now it happened on the day when his sons and his daughters were eating and drinking wine in their oldest brother's house,

¹⁴ that a messenger came to Job and said, "The oxen were plowing and the donkeys feeding beside them,

¹⁵ and the Sabeans attacked and took them. They also slew the servants with the edge of the sword, and I alone have escaped to tell you."

¹⁶ While he was still speaking, another also came and said, "The fire of God fell from heaven and burned up the sheep and the servants and consumed them, and I alone have escaped to tell you."

17 While he was still speaking, another also came and said, "The Chaldeans formed three bands and made a raid on the camels and took them and slew the servants with the edge of the sword; and I alone have escaped to tell you."

18 While he was still speaking, another also came and said, "Your sons and your daughters were eating and drinking wine in their oldest brother's house,

19 and behold, a great wind came from across the wilderness and struck the four corners of the house, and it fell on the young people and they died; and I alone have escaped to tell you."

20 Then Job arose and tore his robe and shaved his head, and he fell to the ground and worshiped.

21 And he said,

"Naked I came from my mother's womb,
and naked I shall return there.
The LORD gave and the LORD has taken away.
Blessed be the name of the LORD."

22 Through all this Job did not sin nor did he blame God.

Now list everything you learn about Satan from this passage. When you finish, remember to record your information on the list in your notebook as you have been doing. If you're thinking, "But I've just written it out once, why do it again?" let me explain. Doing it twice will help seal it in your mind — and that's where it needs to be.

D A Y   F O U R

Despite the tragedies Satan brought upon him, Job never wavered in his faith. He stood firm: "Through all this Job did not sin nor did he blame God" (Job 1:22).

But Satan wasn't through. Read Job 2:1–10, and again mark every reference to Satan. Don't forget the personal pronouns that refer to him.

➤ J O B   2 : 1 – 1 0

¹ Again there was a day when the sons of God came to present themselves before the LORD, and Satan also came among them to present himself before the LORD.

² And the LORD said to Satan, "Where have you come from?" Then Satan answered the LORD and said, "From roaming about on the earth, and walking around on it."

³ And the LORD said to Satan, "Have you considered My servant Job? For there is no one like him on the earth, a blameless and upright man fearing God and turning away from evil. And he still holds fast his integrity, although you incited Me against him, to ruin him without cause."

⁴ And Satan answered the LORD and said, "Skin for skin! Yes, all that a man has he will give for his life.

⁵ "However, put forth Thy hand, now, and touch his bone and his flesh; he will curse Thee to Thy face."

⁶ So the LORD said to Satan, "Behold, he is in your power, only spare his life."

⁷ Then Satan went out from the presence of the LORD, and smote Job with sore boils from the sole of his foot to the crown of his head.

⁸ And he took a potsherd to scrape himself while he was sitting among the ashes.

⁹ Then his wife said to him, "Do you still hold fast your integrity? Curse God and die!"

¹⁰ But he said to her, "You speak as one of the foolish women speaks. Shall we indeed accept good from God and not accept adversity?" In all this Job did not sin with his lips.

If you have learned anything new about Satan from this chapter, record it below and on the list in your notebook.

Now then, go back to the printout of Job 1:1–22 which you worked on yesterday. This time, read it through and mark every reference to Job. You could do it with a stick figure like this: J🜨b

As you read, ask our Father to give you insight into Job. Then list in the space provided everything you learn about Job and how he handled this situation.

DAY   FIVE

Satan's primary target is not those who are already deceived or lulled into a complacent, apathetic lifestyle. Such men and women are no threat to his kingdom. They are his pawns! Rather, it is the righteous, the zealous who concern him. Job was such a man.

We know from Job 1 and 2 and from Revelation 12 that for the present, God has allowed Satan access to His throne. We also saw in Job 1:7 that Satan roams about on the earth, so he is cognizant of what's happening where we live. He's aware of those who truly live for God, and he sees them as a threat to his kingdom.

However, it was the Lord who brought Job to the attention of Satan. Remember His conversation, "'Have you considered My servant Job? For there is no one like him on the earth, a blameless and upright man, fearing God and turning away from evil.' Then Satan answered the LORD, 'Does Job fear God for nothing? Hast Thou not made a hedge about him and his house and all that he has, on every side? Thou hast blessed the work of his hands, and his possessions have increased in the land'" (Job 1:8–10).

How did Satan know there was a hedge around Job? Obviously Satan had tried to get to Job but couldn't because of the hedge! How comforting that ought to be to us, Beloved! Did you realize that God can put hedges about us to protect us from the attacks of our adversary?

Although God brought Job to the attention of Satan, Satan dropped the gauntlet and challenged God's evaluation of His servant. Satan said Job was upright, blameless, feared God, and turned away from evil because God had been so good to him. After all, God had blessed him and had allowed his possessions to increase in the land. The Accuser was telling God that Job only served Him because it profited him!

With that declaration, Satan threw the gauntlet to the ground, "But put forth Thy hand now and touch all that he has; he will surely curse Thee to Thy face" (Job 1:11).

In His sovereignty, knowing that it would not be more than Job could bear, the Lord picked up the gauntlet, "'Behold, all that he has is in your power, only do not put forth your hand on him.' So Satan departed from the presence of the LORD" (Job 1:12).

Please notice, my friend, that Satan didn't challenge God's statement and tell God that he would do anything he pleased to Job! Why? Because Satan's power is limited by God. It always has been, and it always will be. God is sovereign, and Satan can't do a thing without God's permission.

How do we know this? Well, you have Ephesians 1:20–23. However, this had not been written when Job was recorded. Was God sovereign over the enemy before Jesus' death, burial, resurrection, and ascension? Yes, He has always ruled over all. Read Daniel 4:34–35 and write out verse 35 below. Then, drawing from these verses, list what God rules over.

God rules in the army of heaven, which includes both the angels who remained loyal to God and those who followed Satan.

Therefore, when Satan went out and incited the Sabeans and

Chaldeans, when He brought down fire from heaven and brought a destructive wind from across the wilderness, it was only because God allowed Satan to have that power.

Does such a statement cause you to ask, "What kind of a God is that?" The answer is, the only kind of God there is! Listen to His words: "I am the LORD, and there is no other, the One forming light and creating darkness, causing well-being and creating calamity; I am the LORD who does all these" (Isaiah 45:6–7).

As you know, in one day Job lost everything, except his wife. After the news of his losses reached him, "Job arose and tore his robe and shaved his head, and he fell to the ground and worshiped. And he said, 'Naked I came from my mother's womb, and naked I shall return there. The LORD gave and the LORD has taken away. Blessed be the name of the LORD.' Through all this Job did not sin nor did he blame God" (Job 1:20–22).

Job raised his eyes above, looked beyond the circumstances, beyond Satan, to the Sovereign Ruler of all the universe. In faith and humility he bowed his knees.

But it wasn't over! Satan wanted to strike again — harder. He knew if he could just touch Job's body, he'd win. Job would curse God.

So another gauntlet went down. Once again, God picked it up. He would permit Satan to touch Job's flesh, but he could not take his life. Once again, we see God is sovereign over life and death. Listen to what He says, "See now that I, I am He, and there is no god besides Me; it is I who put to death and give life. I have wounded, and it is I who heal; and there is no one who can deliver from My hand" (Deuteronomy 32:39).

Job's pain was great, almost unbearable. Even his friends became heavy yokes around his neck. Longing to die, he held to his integrity. He may have whispered it, but he said, "But it is still my consolation, and I rejoice in unsparing pain, that I have not denied the words of the Holy One" (Job 6:10).

Then as suddenly as his trial began, Job's test was over. Job's end was greater than his beginning. He was richer than he had ever been — not just in family and possessions, but in his knowledge of his Redeemer. His last recorded words, addressed to the Sovereign One who had given and taken away, were "I have heard of Thee by the hearing of the ear; but now my eye sees Thee; therefore I retract, and I repent in dust and ashes" (Job 42:5–6).

"And the LORD restored the fortunes of Job when he prayed for his friends, and the LORD increased all that Job had twofold. And after this Job lived 140 years, and saw his sons, and his grandsons, four generations. And Job died, an old man and full of days" (Job 42:10, 16–17).

Because God is sovereign and because He limits Satan's power, it's understandable that Paul can say, "No temptation has overtaken you but such as is common to man; and God is faithful, who will not allow you to be tempted beyond what you are able, but with the temptation will provide the way of escape also, that you may be able to endure it" (1 Corinthians 10:13).

The lion may roar and you may start to tremble, but while you're shaking, remember, "God hath not given us the spirit of fear; but of power, and of love, and of a sound mind" (2 Timothy 1:7, KJV). Fear God and God alone. Say with Job, "I know that Thou canst do all things, and that no purpose of Thine can be thwarted" (Job 42:2).

If Job could withstand the onslaught of the enemy and come forth a conqueror, how much more you and I should be able to do the same. You see, we're living on this side of our Savior's cross and ascension…and that means *power.*

If you're tempted to quit studying with me, it's the devil's prompting. Don't! He wants to keep you ignorant of your power over him. Persevere! Remember, you'll be challenged every step of the way, week in and week out, for these truths are like antiballistic missiles that will bring down the warheads aimed your way. Don't faint! Determine to stand firm.

Let me ask you this: If Satan were to stand before the Lord right now, would your character be such that God would boast of you to him? And if Satan were to throw down the gauntlet and challenge your motives for serving God, could God pick up that gauntlet in confidence? Could He know that in the midst of conflict with the enemy you would not desert the One who had enlisted you to be His soldier?

DAY   SIX

Some Saturday morning turn on the television and watch the cartoons that are mesmerizing America's children. Ask God to open your spiritual eyes to the seductive evils seeking to capture young and impressionable minds.

Walk through the toy stores. Look at the toys that have been designed for children. You'll begin to understand why illustrations like the one I'm going to share with you are not uncommon.

This letter is typical of many that parents have shared with me. It's a sign of the times, the harvest of a society that's increasingly fascinated by the supernatural. Sadly, it's not the supernatural as it relates to God, but that which belongs to Satan.

The letter is as it was written except that names, places, and times are changed so that this woman and her son can remain anonymous.

Dear 'Beloved' Kay,

Four years ago, we were living overseas. There's a military base located there. At that time we lived in base housing. My husband was not a Christian then (nor is he now), but I had been a Christian and diligently in the Word for nine years at that time. Our oldest son, Tommy, was nine years old. Tommy had always been a challenge — but around November of 1983, he started giving us more and more trouble. For four months our challenge became almost more than we could handle. He went out of his way to rebel and cause problems for the other children in our family and for us, his parents.

Each day seemed to be worse than the day before. At one point Tommy threatened to run away — and another time he said he thought seriously about hanging himself. Each night during these wretched four months, when I'd go in to say good night and try to talk to Tommy about his behavior and pray with him, he'd get a very hard look on his face and say things like, "I don't believe in God," or, "There is no God." At the time, I had the distinct feeling that it was not my son saying those things — even though it was his mouth speaking. It all scared me to death — and my husband was oblivious to the whole thing. Tommy only spoke this way to me when my husband was out of the room.

Fortunately, one of the local missionaries was a good friend of mine. I shared with her about Tommy and she encouraged me to claim the blood of Christ — and to bind Satan in the name of Jesus. So I did just that every night. Meanwhile, the Lord seemed to have me reassure my son by saying that I knew it was Satan who was having him say those things about God and that I knew that there was a boy deep inside crying that those things he was saying weren't true! This went on night after night for four months. I also kept reminding Tommy that if he wanted to be good he would have to ask Jesus for help. He refused night after night saying he didn't need Jesus — that he could be good by himself.

Finally one night, Tommy told me it was impossible for him to be good. I agreed and told him that's why Jesus died for him on the cross — and to ask Jesus to help him. So, Tommy cried out to the Lord in tears that night. Slowly but surely, his behavior got better and better. His times of disobedience became shorter and shorter — the hard look was replaced with softness…the rebellion with submission. After four years Tommy rarely has even a minute of rebellion (at least not to the same degree!) and in the past two months he seems to be consistently saying that he wants to please God.

My husband — back during those rough four months — voiced his doubts about Tommy ever being good. Now he comments on what a good kid he is!

I think in all of this the thing that makes me sad is not what we went through, but that I felt so isolated from other believers during this awful time. The average, everyday Christian is unaware of such demonic activity…and yet it's real and it's frightening and we need to understand it and know how to not only deal with it, but how to support one another through it. I hope and pray, Kay, that you will provide us with a study on spiritual warfare so that others will be equipped to deal with it — and not be ashamed or so very frightened and alone.

The battle is as real today as it was in Job's day!

Look up the following verses and record what you learn about the devil. Note how he is described, who works with him, and what he does. I've left space after each reference. I'd encourage you to write out the verse. And also mark your Bible so that you can find the verses at a later time. Don't forget to record what you learn about the enemy on the list you are keeping in your notebook.

1. 1 John 3:8

2. Ephesians 2:2; 6:12

3. John 12:31

4. Revelation 12:7 (Revelation 12:9 tells you who the dragon is.)

5. 2 Corinthians 11:14–15

6. 2 Corinthians 4:4

7. Matthew 13:19

8. 1 Timothy 4:1

If you learn all of this, you'll be able to recognize your enemy without the red outfit and pitchfork.

DAY SEVEN

It's interesting that Satan is mentioned in the first and last books of the Bible. Sin has been the habit of his life from the beginning. Since his triumph in the garden of Eden, he's sought to deceive us, to blind our eyes to the light of the one truth which can free us from his dominion — the gospel of Jesus Christ.

As the ruler of this world and of the power of the air, Satan has legions of angelic beings who serve under him in various administrative capacities as rulers and authorities. Powers and dominions are his, as are the world forces of this darkness and spiritual forces of evil in the heavenly places.

Satan often disguises himself as an angel of light. His servants do the same, even disguising themselves as servants of righteousness.

He has seduced kings, prophets, and Jewish exorcists. He has sought the downfall of righteous men such as Job by turning nature and the wisdom of men against him. Satan roams the earth, seeking to devour all he can. Seducing spirits move with him as he spreads his demonic doctrines.

He appears in the Gospels, Acts, and the Epistles. Satan plays a major role in Revelation, the prophetic book which has yet to be fulfilled in its entirety. There we learn how his wrath builds as his time grows shorter because he is aware that soon the King of kings will come and make all His enemies His footstool! We learn that Satan will be bound for a thousand years, released for a short time, and then cast into the lake of fire.

Although that time is probably closer than we realize, it is not quite upon us. Satan still continues to be Satan — the adversary of every child of God. Therefore, you must learn all you can from the Word of God about him.

Look up the following verses and do the same thing you did yesterday. Don't forget to record your insights on your list about the devil in your notebook.

1. Matthew 16:23

2. Luke 22:31

3. 1 Thessalonians 2:18

4. 1 Thessalonians 3:5

5. 2 Thessalonians 2:9

6. Matthew 13:24–30, 38–39

7. 2 Timothy 2:26; 1 Timothy 3:7

8. Luke 13:16; Acts 10:38

9. Revelation 12:12

Clearly, Satan is not interested in the things of God. You can be sure too he'll do everything he can to hinder you in your search for truth and understanding. Remember, he hates truth and will only use it when it's to his advantage, weaving it in with his lies to seduce you or to lead you astray. And if that doesn't work, he'll seek to deceive you with signs and false wonders.

Satan desires "to sift you as wheat," "to thwart" your work for God. He's known as "the tempter," and he'll set snares in the hope of taking you captive to sin or to false teaching. He even sows tares among the wheat, and the tares are hard to recognize.

The mind is the devil's primary target, but he doesn't stop there. He also attacks the body. In the Word of God we see that he bound a woman for eighteen years and threw a young boy into convulsions. He put a thorn in Paul's flesh…and God left it there because it served His higher purpose.

The day is soon coming when the devil will no longer have access to the throne of God, where he accuses us night and day. Soon he'll be cast down to earth along with his demons. When that day comes, his wrath will know no bounds because his time will be extremely short.

But those who follow God won't need to fear. The King is coming — the Kinsman Redeemer who rightly sits as the God-man above all rule, power, authority, and dominion because He has conquered sin and death.

Should you fear Satan? No, Beloved, there is only One whom you are to fear — and that is God. If you are Christ's, you're seated with Jesus in heavenly places far above all the power of the enemy. We'll study that next week.

Ask God to keep you aware of Satan's methods and devices. These should be easier to recognize now since you have better intelligence information on your enemy.

Do you know beyond a shadow of a doubt that you belong to Jesus Christ and that He belongs to you? Ask God if Jesus dwells within, if He's adopted you into His family. He'll show you.

Don't forget to write out your prayer of affirmation for this week.

LORD, I DON'T WANT TO BUY SATAN'S LIE!

DAY ONE

I still have the envelope the letter came in. It's postmarked July 22, 1985:

Precept upon precept, line upon line, bull upon bull.... Do you really think that you could establish in three weeks what I have disputed for ten years? I will not be mocked! I too answer to a higher power.

Sara is the last person on earth I would have thought would have fallen for this rhetoric with a dead shepherd for a hero.

She is special — but she is already chosen/sealed. She belongs with us.

She cannot be allowed to ingest your nonsense. She is such a fool with no knowledge of spiritual matters, no roots, no ground; even your book notes her fate. You might stand a chance — she has none. I can destroy her at will — devour as a roaring lion — this is my dominion. I will not be mocked.

Understand I wish her no harm but WE WILL NOT GIVE HER UP. She cannot be allowed to continue. You have many others — tend your flock, this one is ours.

I WILL see her removed before I WILL allow her established.

She does not understand, *you have no concept of* my *powers* — your mind cannot conceive what she will face. If you love her — SHUT UP.

I WILL see her removed before I WILL allow her established. Trust me.

This was the first of three anonymous letters that Wayne, my pastor and co-teacher, and I would receive. The final communication came with a mutilated Barbie doll, informing me that Sara would follow the doll's demise if we continued to teach her the Word of God.

Sara became involved with these people when she started attending AA meetings. The AA group had been infiltrated by some businessmen who were strong in the occult — blood sacrifices and the whole gamut. They had chosen Sara to become one of them. But when she started coming to Bible study, they knew they were in danger of losing their instrument.

As I read the first of these threatening letters (I'll share the second with you later this week), I wasn't afraid — I even chuckled. I couldn't help it. There it was in print, "You have no concept of my powers." I thought, "Oh, yes, I do. You just think I don't know where my Savior's seated — and I'm seated there with Him!"

How horribly deceived this man is! He has no idea of what the "higher power" he answers to is going to do to him! He's exactly where I was before 1963 — a slave of sin. Obviously he's entrenched in satanism. I was entrenched in religion and then immorality — but both of us belonged to the devil.

Shaken but unswayed by the threats of the enemy upon her and upon me, Sara stood firm. She understood the truths of Ephesians and walked accordingly. Jack and I recently saw Sara in a local restaurant. She still walks with the Lord.

Although you may never come face to face with something this sensational, you, too, need to understand the message of God's awesome epistle to the Ephesians. You need to know where you're seated, where to walk, how to stand, and then never, ever move from these boundaries.

Watchman Nee's commentary on Ephesians is titled: *Sit, Walk, Stand,* three key words in Ephesians. Ephesians 1–3 teaches the child of God where he's seated and why, Ephesians 4:6–9 calls the reader to the walk that is worthy of so high a calling, and Ephesians 6:10–20 instructs the believer how to stand firm in warfare.

Read through Ephesians 2:1–3 using the text printed in the back of this book. Watch for the pronouns *you* and *we* and mark them in a distinctive way, treating them as one and the same. When you finish, list below what you learn from these verses about someone who is lost.

D A Y   T W O

How did the world get so sinful? If God created it — and it was good — what happened? That's the focus of this chapter.

If you've been in the Word of God or in a Bible-teaching church for any length of time, you know how we ended up in this state of sin as described in Ephesians 2. It all started in the garden of Eden.

In our second week of study, you read Genesis 1–3 to note the first recorded appearance of Satan. Let's take another look at a part of the passage.

This time as you read pay special attention to God's instructions to Adam and then watch the serpent's tactics with Eve. Also, don't miss how Adam got into the picture. Record your insights at the end of these verses, and we'll discuss them tomorrow.

➤ SELECTED VERSES FROM GENESIS 2–3

7 Then the LORD God formed man of dust from the ground, and breathed into his nostrils the breath of life; and man became a living being.

8 And the LORD God planted a garden toward the east, in Eden; and there He placed the man whom He had formed.

9 And out of the ground the LORD God caused to grow every tree that is pleasing to the sight and good for food; the tree of life also in the midst of the garden, and the tree of the knowledge of good and evil.

16 And the LORD God commanded the man, saying, "From any tree of the garden you may eat freely;

17 but from the tree of the knowledge of good and evil you shall not eat, for in the day that you eat from it you shall surely die."

3:1 Now the serpent was more crafty than any beast of the field which the LORD God had made. And he said to the woman, "Indeed, has God said, 'You shall not eat from any tree of the garden'?"

2 And the woman said to the serpent, "From the fruit of the trees of the garden we may eat;

3 but from the fruit of the tree which is in the middle of the garden, God has said, 'You shall not eat from it or touch it, lest you die.'"

4 And the serpent said to the woman, "You surely shall not die!

5 "For God knows that in the day you eat from it your eyes will be opened, and you will be like God, knowing good and evil."

6 When the woman saw that the tree was good for food, and that it was a delight to the eyes, and that the tree was desirable to make *one* wise, she took from its fruit and ate; and she gave also to her husband with her, and he ate.

7 Then the eyes of both of them were opened, and they knew that they were naked; and they sewed fig leaves together and made themselves loin coverings.

INSIGHTS ON GENESIS 2–3

GOD'S INSTRUCTIONS   SATAN'S TACTICS

INSIGHTS ON GENESIS 2–3

GOD'S INSTRUCTIONS   SATAN'S TACTICS

DAY   THREE

The seed of all humanity was in Adam's loins. Despite what you may have learned in school, we didn't evolve from some lower form of life. We are a special creation of God! On the sixth day of creation, "God created man in His own image, in the image of God He created him; male and female He created them. And God blessed them; and God said to them, 'Be fruitful and multiply, and fill the earth, and subdue it; and rule over the fish of the sea and over the birds of the sky, and over every living thing that moves on the earth'"(Genesis 1:27–28).

God created man in His image, then man sinned.

The serpent's first recorded words were, "Indeed, has God said?" Crafty and beautiful, he deceived Eve by casting doubt on the Word of God.

Immediately he had Eve's attention. Instead of running to Adam, she dialogued with the devil. She downplayed the firm command of God's Word, indicating that if she ate *or touched the fruit* — God didn't say anything about touching it — she might die. God didn't say "lest" or "might," He said "surely"!

The serpent, picking up her hesitancy, struck quickly, "You surely shall not die!"

It was the serpent's word against God's. It's the same today: truth or a lie, God's Word or man's.

The serpent continued, "God knows that in the day you eat from it your eyes will be opened, and you will be like God, knowing good and evil" (Genesis 3:5).

There it was, one subtle accusation that cast doubts about God, His goodness, His love, His care, insinuations that God was holding out on them, depriving them of knowing good and evil. After all, with one bite of the delicious, pleasant-looking fruit, they could be like God Himself! The fruit was good for food, a delight to the eyes, and it would make them wise. It awakened the lust of her flesh, the lust of the eyes, and the pride of life.

The serpent froze, midair. Here was his chance to get back at God, to rule over those God had created for Himself. Here was his opportunity to gain control over the creation. God had His heaven, but in a moment through Adam, he could have earth. The woman reached up and touched the fruit.

"See...I didn't die." Suddenly it was in her mouth — and in Adam's, only Adam wasn't deceived. He knew exactly what he was doing (1 Timothy 2:14).

One doubt, one act of disobedience, and sin entered the world and with it, death — just as God said.

Let me ask you a question: Have you ever doubted God's Word, God's character — His love, His care, His goodness — and considered that you might be better off running your own life instead of waiting on a God you can't see?

To whom have you been listening? What do you need to tell God? Write it out.

DAY   FOUR

It looked as if the serpent had won. And he had won a battle, but not the war. The war had just begun, but God wasn't unprepared. He had a plan — a Lamb in the wings, behind the curtains of time, slain before the foundation of the world. In the fullness of time God would come, clothed in humanity, bearing the title "the last Adam."

Romans 5:12 says, "Therefore, just as through one man sin entered into the world, and death through sin, and so death spread to all men, because all sinned." Sin and death began through one man, a man named Adam.

When Adam had intercourse with Eve, the mother of all living (Genesis 3:20), sin was inherent in his sperm. They reproduced after their own kind: "Behold, I was brought forth in iniquity, and in sin my mother conceived me" (Psalm 51:5). Eve gave birth, and Adam "became the father of a *son* in his own likeness, according to his image"— a sinner was born (Genesis 5:3).

From that point on, the whole world lay in the power of the evil one (1 John 5:19). Satan became the ruler of this world (John 14:30). The creation which Adam was to subdue and govern was relinquished to Satan when Adam disobeyed God.

From that moment on, because we were all born in sin, Satan had the power of death over every human being, for the wages of sin is death (Hebrews 2:14; Romans 6:23).

Yet in the grace of God, Adam was given hope. On that fateful day, God pronounced His judgment on the serpent:

"Because you have done this,
Cursed are you more than all cattle,
And more than every beast of the field;
On your belly shall you go,
And dust shall you eat
All the days of your life;
And I will put enmity

Between you and the woman,
And between your seed and her seed;
He shall bruise you on the head,
And you shall bruise him on the heel."
(Genesis 3:14–15)

Sin had destroyed peace. Now there would be an ongoing enmity between the serpent and the woman and between the woman's seed and the serpent's seed. But God had spoken — the woman's seed, a male, would bruise the head of the serpent and the serpent would bruise his heel.

Little did the serpent realize that almost four thousand years later, as the nails pierced and bruised the heels of Jesus' feet, that his head would be bruised with the same act and that his power over us broken. The ruler of this world was cast out (John 12:31), yet Satan seemed the victor. The demons rejoiced because now they were sure they had been right in choosing to follow Satan! For three days it looked as if the war had been won.

Then the stone was rolled away!

DAY FIVE

Look at people in the shopping malls, watch them on television, read about them in the tabloids, but don't be deceived. The majority are among the living dead.

Well-dressed, beautifully groomed, highly educated…dead. Cool, punk, flaky, bashed, high…dead. Young, old, white, yellow, black, red, rich, poor…dead. In magazines, on the screens, over the headphones, in your office, at your factory, or across the breakfast table — you see them, hear them, and maybe even admire and love them, but the majority are among the living dead.

And so were you at one time, my friend — you may be even now.

The living dead are those who walk in opposition to Jesus Christ and His kingdom. They walk *kata* (according to or under the dominion of) the prince of the power of the air.

They're dead in their sins, their shortcomings, that always fall beneath God's standard for righteousness.

They're dead — doing as they please. They've tasted good and tasted evil, and they live by their appetites. They "do" what they desire. They are motivated by self, not God. They may be pillars in their church and community or junkies in a crack house, yet they are dead.

They are dead to righteousness. Controlled by an unholy spirit, they are in rebellion to God. By nature, they are children of wrath — that's how Paul describes them in Ephesians.

I want you to see for yourself what Paul says. I'm going to print out three passages that describe what we are like — or can be like — apart from God. Underline what man is like apart from God and make a list in the right-hand margin of what you see.

➤ ROMANS 1:18-32

18 For the wrath of God is revealed from heaven against all ungodliness and unrighteousness of men, who suppress the truth in unrighteousness

19 because that which is known about God is evident within them; for God made it evident to them.

20 For since the creation of the world His invisible attributes, His eternal power and divine nature, have been clearly seen, being understood through what has been made, so that they are without excuse.

21 For even though they knew God, they did not honor Him as God, or give thanks; but they

became futile in their speculations, and their foolish heart was darkened.

22 Professing to be wise, they became fools,

23 and exchanged the glory of the incorruptible
God for an image in the form of corruptible man
and of birds and four-footed animals and crawling
creatures.

24 Therefore God gave them over in the lusts of
their hearts to impurity, that their bodies might be
dishonored among them.

25 For they exchanged the truth of God for a
lie, and worshiped and served the creature rather
than the Creator, who is blessed forever. Amen.

26 For this reason God gave them over to
degrading passions; for their women exchanged
the natural function for that which is unnatural,

27 and in the same way also the men abandoned the natural function of the woman and
burned in their desire toward one another, men
with men committing indecent acts and receiving
in their own persons the due penalty of their error.

28 And just as they did not see fit to acknowledge God any longer, God gave them over to a
depraved mind, to do those things which are not
proper,

29 being filled with all unrighteousness,

wickedness, greed, evil; full of envy, murder, strife, deceit, malice; *they* are gossips,

30 slanderers, haters of God, insolent, arrogant, boastful, inventors of evil, disobedient to parents,

31 without understanding, untrustworthy, unloving, unmerciful;

32 and, although they know the ordinance of God, that those who practice such things are worthy of death, they not only do the same, but also give hearty approval to those who practice them.

➤ ROMANS 3:10–18

10 As it is written, "THERE IS NONE RIGHTEOUS, NOT EVEN ONE;

11 THERE IS NONE WHO UNDERSTANDS, THERE IS NONE WHO SEEKS FOR GOD;

12 ALL HAVE TURNED ASIDE, TOGETHER THEY HAVE BECOME USELESS; THERE IS NONE WHO DOES GOOD, THERE IS NOT EVEN ONE."

13 "THEIR THROAT IS AN OPEN GRAVE, WITH THEIR TONGUES THEY KEEP DECEIVING," "THE POISON OF ASPS IS UNDER THEIR LIPS;"

14 "WHOSE MOUTH IS FULL OF CURSING AND BITTERNESS;"

15 "THEIR FEET ARE SWIFT TO SHED BLOOD,

16 DESTRUCTION AND MISERY ARE IN THEIR PATHS,

¹⁷ AND THE PATH OF PEACE HAVE THEY NOT KNOWN."

¹⁸ "THERE IS NO FEAR OF GOD BEFORE THEIR EYES."

➤ ROMANS 5:6-8, 10

⁶ For while we were still helpless, at the right time Christ died for the ungodly.

⁷ For one will hardly die for a righteous man; though perhaps for the good man someone would dare even to die.

⁸ But God demonstrates His own love toward us, in that while we were yet sinners, Christ died for us.

¹⁰ For if while we were enemies, we were reconciled to God through the death of His Son, much more, having been reconciled, we shall be saved by His life.

As you read those verses, did you see a ray of hope at the bottom of the pit? It was the light that alone can dispel the darkness of being dead in trespasses and sins.

Let me ask you a question. Have you ever thought of people without Christ as being the living dead? What does it do to your heart? Share your thoughts.

D A Y   S I X

As the day of our Lord's coming approaches, those who are among the living dead will sink into greater depths of sin. Listen to Paul's warning to Timothy. As you read, underline the characteristics of the ungodly and again note them in the right-hand margin.

➤ 2 TIMOTHY 3:1–8

¹ But realize this, that in the last days difficult times will come.

² For men will be lovers of self, lovers of money, boastful, arrogant, revilers, disobedient to parents, ungrateful, unholy,

³ unloving, irreconcilable, malicious gossips, without self-control, brutal, haters of good,

⁴ treacherous, reckless, conceited, lovers of pleasure rather than lovers of God;

⁵ holding to a form of godliness, although they have denied its power; and avoid such men as these.

⁶ For among them are those who enter into households and captivate weak women weighed down with sins, led on by various impulses,

⁷ always learning and never able to come to the knowledge of the truth.

⁸ And just as Jannes and Jambres opposed Moses, so these *men* also oppose the truth, men of depraved mind, rejected as regards the faith.

People are not going to get better. They're going to get worse and worse. According to Revelation 9:18–21, even when God pours out His plagues upon the earth and people see a third of mankind killed by fire, brimstone, and smoke, multitudes will continue to worship demons and idols of gold, silver, brass, stone, and wood. They will not repent of their murders, of their use of drugs for magical purposes[1], of their immorality, or of their theft.

When Satan tried to convince Eve that God didn't really have their highest good at heart, little did she realize the destruction and desolation that would come if she believed the lie.

Are you a teenager? A college student? Newly married — but disappointed and disillusioned? Are you in a midlife crisis? Hitting sixty years plus? Have you bought Satan's lie? Can you see where it could end? Is this what you really want in your heart of hearts? (Note, I didn't say, is this what you deserve? I asked if this is what you want.)

We all deserve hell. We're hopeless, helpless, ungodly sinners — enemies of God (Romans 5:10). But it doesn't have to be that way for you. You could have life, righteousness, peace. You could be freed from Satan's domain. You could become God's child.

Read Ephesians 2:1–13, and then write out below how God would accomplish this…and why.

Have you, dear one, become God's child? If not, will you now? Write out your prayer to God.

DAY   SEVEN

I told you I would share the other letters I received about Sara, and I'm going to do that today. But first read through Ephesians 1 again. It will help you get a better glimpse of how the enemy takes God's truths and terms and uses them for his own purposes.

As you read these letters, keep in mind what you have just seen in Ephesians, and note how the enemy uses biblical terminology. Watch the words *power(s)* and *strength*. Also, keep in mind everything you've seen that the Bible teaches about the devil.

I don't know if you are directly involved again but let me recall to your remembrance Sara is already sealed; she belongs with us and I WILL see her destroyed before I WILL see her established in your nonsense.

She does not understand the powers she is rejecting. Among us for years, my mind is already established — My thoughts — My spirit — I AM HER FATHER — she cannot have two and My Father will not be mocked. I know from whom my powers come, my intelligence, my strength...they are centuries old. I have no need for a resurrected shepherd. My power has never died but is walking the earth — with me ever — and we can destroy her at will.

Trust me, we are her friends, we love her. She is very special and, for that reason, we cannot allow her to continue.... There is nothing you can teach her I cannot confuse — she will be blinded. Much has already been summoned against her, but the dragon has not yet been loosed — you would not want that for her. She is not a neutral person — if you persist in teaching her she will have to be destroyed. You can have all of the others in your classes, I will even call my forces from their lives and yours but do not encourage or speak with her or I WILL release my schemes upon her mind — a sheep to slaughter.

You have never seen my work directly — it isn't pretty. What have I to do with you? I will not battle with you. I WILL devour her mind — her faith — her life.

Sara has been warned....

And finally the third letter came, with the mutilated doll:

OUR *FINAL* COMMUNICATION

My thoughts are above your thoughts, my ways above your ways, your mind cannot conceive what awaits her.

Her fate is sealed. MY WORK is not part-time. How foolish of you to throw a lamb into the arena — I WILL DEVOUR HER. YOU are nearly through playing school — I have not even BEGUN.

She is so foolish — she reminds me of you and so she will be destroyed.

Trust me, I WILL NOT BE MOCKED, she belongs to us.

I CANNOT — I WILL NOT — LET HER GO.

Oh, the lion roared, but when he opened his mouth, he was toothless! We knew where Jesus Christ was seated, and we just snuggled closer. We prayed, claiming what was ours and resisting the enemy. I'll tell you how later in the study. For now, remember the thief comes to kill and destroy — and yet he calls it love.

The Good Shepherd of the sheep laid down His life, and we see His love: "My sheep hear My voice, and I know them, and they follow Me; and I give eternal life to them, and they shall never perish; and no one shall snatch them out of My hand. My Father, who has given them to Me, is greater than all; and no one is able to snatch them out of the Father's hand. I and the Father are one" (John 10:27–30).

Don't forget your prayer of affirmation, Beloved.

LORD, THE ENEMY'S ACCUSING ME!

I t was 1916, and Hattie Green was dead. Hattie's life is a sad demonstration of what it's like to be among the living dead. When Hattie died, her estate was valued at over $100 million; yet Hattie had lived in poverty. She ate cold oatmeal because it cost money to heat it. When her son's leg became infected, Hattie wouldn't get it treated until she could find a clinic that wouldn't charge her. By then, her son's leg had to be amputated. Hattie died arguing over the monetary value of skim milk.

She had money to meet her every need, but she chose to live as if the resource was nonexistent. She lived as a pauper and died as a pauper. That is the way with the living dead. They could be rich in Christ, yet they choose to live as paupers in their trespasses and sins. By an act of repentance and faith, all the wealth of Ephesians 1–3 could be theirs, but…

Read Revelation 20:11–22:21 and note on the following chart the future of the lost and of the redeemed. As you read, watch for references to the city of God and its temple.

THE FUTURE OF THE LOST AND THE REDEEMED

THE LOST   THE REDEEMED

THE FUTURE OF THE LOST AND THE REDEEMED

THE LOST   THE REDEEMED

DAY   TWO

Satan destroys. God restores.

Only God can give back what the first Adam lost in the garden of Eden. In fact, God has given us more.

How awesome our God is! What power! What love! He plunged the cross into the lowest pit of sin's degradation and provided a way out.

Read through Ephesians 2 again. As you do, note below what life is like under Satan and under God.

UNDER SATAN   UNDER GOD

"The grace of Jesus Christ rekindles the ideals which repeated falling to sin had extinguished. And by that very rekindling, life is set climbing again."[1]

DAY   THREE

From death to life. From wrath to mercy. From earth to heaven. From futility to purposefulness. From enmity to peace. From isolation to family. And all because God is rich in mercy, loving, and filled with grace.

Grace, mercy, and peace was a greeting Paul used repeatedly. Those words sum up the experience of every child of God.

Let's look at *grace, mercy,* and *peace* one by one so that we understand the meaning of these three words.

Grace is unearned or unmerited favor. Some have defined it this way:

G — God's

R — riches

A — at

C — Christ's

E — expense.

Grace is everything Jesus Christ is and has made available to us without any reason within ourselves. It is simply an act of God's love toward us. Everything you have in Christ is a gift of grace.

Because grace exists, I'm not afraid to tell you my shortcomings and my struggles. Jack is reading this as I write. It's been wonderful as we're shut up in the house alone. I cooked a big turkey for the family for Thanksgiving, and we're now surviving on leftovers. The phone is set to "make busy," and it's quiet. Every morning as I pour over and pray through Ephesians, my heart is filled with love and awe.

All that to say that when Jack got to the first page of chapter 3, he asked me if I should reveal that I had thoughts of suicide — after I became a Christian. He didn't want you to think ill of me. As a matter of fact, he didn't even know I'd gone through that battle! I explained that when many people go through similar situations they feel alone, isolated, and that it helps to realize others go through the same experiences. It's nice to know that struggling doesn't make us less spiritual, isn't it? Our spirituality shows in how we handle our circumstances of life.

Because of grace, I can share. Grace covers every sin, every failure, every need. If I didn't know this truth, I don't think I could handle my past. I'd have so much guilt I couldn't move ahead.

But grace covers. God provides it — and it doesn't cost us a thing because it cost God everything. Listen to Romans 8:31–32: "What then shall we say to these things? If God is for us, who is against us? He who did not spare His own Son, but delivered Him up for us all, how will He not also with Him freely give us all things?" Grace freely gives us all things — everything that pertains to life and godliness.

God did all of this "because of His great love with which He loved us." Remember that verse? It's Ephesians 2:4. And when did He love us? When we got our act together and cleaned up? No, He loved us when we were still sons of disobedience, children of wrath, dead in our transgressions. Remember, you are saved through faith — and even faith to believe is a gift of grace. Dr. Charles Erdman says it well: "Faith is the instrument by which the gift is received. It is not the source of the gift."[2] How we need to remember that about faith.

Paul wants you to understand you're not saved by works — works and grace are incompatible. If salvation is by works, then you can earn it. Grace is *unearned, unmerited* favor. Good works do not precede and, thus, earn salvation; good works follow and are simply the evidence of your salvation.

It's so crucial that you understand God saves you when you are still a son of disobedience because Satan is the accuser, and he loves to remind you of your sin. He will do everything he can to keep you blind to the grace of God[3], trying to convince you that God won't or can't use you, bless you, or help you because of your sin. Remember, He saved you when you were *in* sin.

Your assignment today is to read through Ephesians 1–3 again and mark every occurrence of the word *grace*. Try not to hurry through these chapters. Soak up their truths. If you will read the chapters aloud, you'll find it easier to recall what they're about. When you finish, list what you learn about grace.

"Down in the human heart, crushed by the tempter, feelings lie buried that grace can restore."[4]

D A Y   F O U R

Mercy. The word has been uttered as a whisper and a shout, as a question and a plea. But each utterance holds one meaning: "Meet my need. Give me what I need, not what I deserve."

Listen to this letter:

The example of the demonically ravaged girl lifted my spirits by show-ing your belief in the reality of demonic possession. You see, from a very early age I served as a target for almost non-ending demonic harass-ment. Because of an occult-type molestation, Satan's henchmen held a tremendous stronghold over my life that led to my years of slow self-destruction.

I believe I became a special target because of Satan's hatred of my parents' deep faith in God. Satan enjoys destroying children of Christian parents with a vengeance. Despite my training in the church, I was an alcoholic at thirteen. My chemical use spiraled into full-fledged intra-venous drug use by the time I was eighteen. My soul belonged to the hosts of demons that used my body in whatever whim of their fancy.

My parents exhausted their funds to find a cause for my extremely frightening and unusual behavior. After an EEG, my parents drew the correct conclusion — spiritual sickness of the worst kind.

To make a long story short, my nightmarish years of torment came to a close with a spectacular grand finale. My Satanist "friends" attempted to murder me by secretly slipping an overdose of PCP into my glass of orange juice. Realizing that I was dying, I cried out to the God of my parents for help. Miraculously, I escaped out of the hands of my "friends" into the safety of the County Jail.

Two weeks later, I kept my divine appointment with God. After a very rowdy deliverance, I accepted Jesus Christ's free gift of eternal salvation. God has lavishly bestowed the miraculous restoration and healing power to me since that day. Every day I long more and more for the knowledge and wisdom of my Creator and Sustainer. In my heart I hear the Holy Spirit calling me into a ministry to help victims of the occult and demonic possession. Even though the Lord didn't will my experiences, He will use my intimate knowledge of the enemy's camp in a great way.

As Paul counseled Timothy, I know it is vitally important for me to find a spiritual leader that will train me in this type of ministry. The problem comes in finding wise council that is balanced and sound. Those who see two demons behind every bush are equally as frustrating as those who ignore Satan's activity.

The letter goes on, but I will stop there.

Here is a young woman who turned her back on God and walked away in willful rebellion. He could have let her go, but He didn't.

"But God, being rich in mercy..." Mercy is "the outward manifestation of pity; it assumes need on the part of him who receives it, and resources adequate to meet the need on the part of him who shows it."[5] God is so different from us it's hard to comprehend His grace and His mercy.

Yet, if this young woman didn't understand the mercy of God, the enemy could heap guilt and condemnation on her. When you don't understand God's mercy, you are slow to run to Him in the time of need, and although the enemy cannot separate you from the love of God in Christ Jesus, once you are saved he delights in deceiving you so you don't appropriate what is yours. His strategy is to convince you that whatever you need from God you don't deserve. He wants to convince you that you shouldn't ask Him for it or expect Him to give it to you.

Don't listen to the devil's lies. Mercy is an attribute of God. God is your very present help in the time of trouble. He longs to be merciful. So run to — not from — His throne of grace. There you'll find mercy and grace to help. If you think otherwise, you've been pierced by one of Satan's fiery darts.[6]

Do you remember the Jewish exorcists in Acts 19 who went from place to place, calling on the name of the Lord Jesus as they tried to deliver people from evil spirits? Yet the evil spirits beat up the exorcists. Why? Because the exorcists were using the name of Jesus without possessing the person of Jesus. They wanted God's power, but they shunned His grace and mercy. Thus, there was no mercy for them. The spirits overpowered them, leaving them naked and wounded. But those who did believe came confessing and disclosing their occult practices. There was grace and mercy for them...even as there was for the dear one who wrote the letter you just read. God is merciful, but His mercy is only realized when we come to Jesus.

You need to remember that, my friend. Don't think you can have the benefits of salvation apart from the commitment of salvation. Otherwise the devil could easily convince you that God is not all He says He is because God didn't come through for you as He said He would. God always comes through, but it's on His terms and in His timing.

It would be profitable for you to look up some verses on the mercy of God and note what you learn about God's mercy from each verse. Some verses may be a little convicting — but they are critical in warfare. Remember, we are girding our loins with truth!

1. Titus 3:5

2. 1 Peter 1:3

3. Romans 12:1

4. 2 Corinthians 4:1

5. Matthew 5:7

6. James 2:13

7. 1 Timothy 1:12–18 (As my pastor says, "This one ought to bless your socks off!")

Remember, salvation vividly demonstrates God's mercy. Grace, mercy, and peace to you, Beloved.

D A Y   F I V E

Jesus doesn't turn the clock back on your life when you're saved by grace through faith. He doesn't change what you've done. But He does take away the guilt! When your guilt's gone, you have peace.

If peace eludes you, one or both of two things may be hampering you — unbelief (which is sin) or the devil.

If it's unbelief, you'll remain miserable and probably ineffective until you determine to believe God's Word. What more can God say, what more can He do than what He's done to blot out your sins and convince you of His forgiveness? Until you decide in faith to believe God, you're in sin: "Whatsoever is not from faith is sin" (Romans 14:23).

That's a strong statement, isn't it? Let me show you why I said it. Look up Hebrews 3:18–19, and note what is synonymous with unbelief.

The other possible explanation for your feelings of guilt is the enemy. If he can heap guilt on you, he'll flatten you with it. Remember that *Satan* means "adversary." He'll get you any way he can.

However, don't make him your focus. Don't live in fear of his attacks. Simply be aware of his devices, his schemes to get you. Remember that one of those schemes is unremitting guilt. If you will learn to live in the light of the truths of Ephesians, you can handle him attack by attack and have victory after victory "strengthened with power through His Spirit in the inner man" (Ephesians 3:16).

Since God won't turn back the clock of life and since the devil keeps discussing your guilt, condemning you, whispering accusations in your ear, reminding you of what might have been had you not gotten so messed up, what do you do?

First, remember that there is no forgiveness with Satan. He doesn't forgive. He doesn't forget. Nor does he want you to forget!

Forgiveness belongs to God and only comes from God. If you have

God's forgiveness, that's all you need to survive. God's the One you sinned against, for all sin is ultimately against God.

Remember when King David slept with Uriah's wife, Bathsheba, got her pregnant, and then strategically plotted Uriah's death? David lost a lot of sleep and was confronted by Nathan the prophet before he came face to face with his sin.

Psalm 51 is recorded for all those who, like David, want to get rid of their guilt. As you read it, you'll sense David's genuineness. His confession wasn't motivated by the fact that he got caught and messed up his life. Rather, David confessed because he was grieved: He knew that "against Thee, Thee only, I have sinned, and done what is evil in Thy sight, so that Thou art justified when Thou dost speak and blameless when Thou dost judge" (v. 4).

If you see your sin as against God, if you have a godly sorrow which leads you to repentance, and if you confess your sin to God (naming it for what it is), then God forgives. That's what God says, and God cannot lie. With forgiveness comes peace.

So whether it is guilt because of your "B.C." days or because you've sinned as a Christian, only the blood of Jesus Christ takes care of your sins.

Listen to these verses from Hebrews. They'll strengthen your shield of faith and enable you to down the enemy with the sword of the Word. As you read through this passage, mark every reference to the blood of Jesus Christ. Then, at the end of this passage, write down what takes care of an evil conscience (that's guilt!).

➤ HEBREWS 10:10, 14–22

10 By this will we have been sanctified through the offering of the body of Jesus Christ once for all.

14 For by one offering He has perfected for all time those who are sanctified.

15 And the Holy Spirit also bears witness to us; for after saying,

16 "THIS IS THE COVENANT THAT I WILL MAKE WITH THEM AFTER THOSE DAYS, SAYS THE LORD: I WILL PUT MY LAWS UPON THEIR HEART, AND UPON THEIR MIND I WILL WRITE THEM,"

He then says,

17 "AND THEIR SINS AND THEIR LAWLESS DEEDS I WILL REMEMBER NO MORE."

18 Now where there is forgiveness of these things, there is no longer *any* offering for sin.

19 Since therefore, brethren, we have confidence to enter the holy place by the blood of Jesus,

20 by a new and living way which He inaugurated for us through the veil, that is, His flesh,

21 and since *we have* a great priest over the house of God,

22 let us draw near with a sincere heart in full assurance of faith, having our hearts sprinkled *clean* from an evil conscience and our bodies washed with pure water.

If it's the enemy who parades your guilt down the main street of your mind, remind him that the blood of Jesus Christ has cleansed you from all sin. Stop the parade. Your guilt's gone.

However, if the devil doesn't stop, do what Jesus did: Command Satan to get behind you. He doesn't honor *the things* of God and the primary *thing* of God is granting forgiveness of sins. When God forgives, God forgets. But remember that the devil doesn't! So it ought to be clear where the accusations are coming from. Look up the following verses and note what they say God does with sin:

1. Micah 7:19

2. Isaiah 38:17

3. Isaiah 43:25

4. 1 John 1:9

"Therefore, having been justified by faith, we have peace with God" (Romans 5:1). Why? Because the enmity was taken care of at Calvary! You've been reconciled to God through the cross of Jesus Christ. You are now part of His holy temple, a dwelling for the Spirit of God.

What peace!

DAY SIX

And what else do grace, mercy, and peace with God bring? A seat in the heavenlies! A seat of power, of authority, of strength. Are you thinking, *That's nice? I'm looking forward to that.*

You shouldn't be looking *forward!* You should be looking *down.*

If you have been saved by grace, your feet may be on earth, but your seat's in heaven! Your legs are just kinda' dangling down on earth.

Are you picturing all this in your mind? Kinda' funny, isn't it? (I wish I could do a little body language for you at this point, but you'll have to see that on the teaching videos which accompany this series!)

You may be thinking, *How can I be living on earth and be seated with Christ in the heavenly places at the same time?* Good question. Let's see if we can understand what God is trying to show us.

If you're seated in the heavenlies now, you're seated in a place of power and authority in the spirit realm. This fact is important in the light of the historical and cultural context of this epistle. The epistle was written to saints — Christians who were living where the enemy was firmly entrenched in a stronghold of demonic activity. All sorts of magic were performed in Ephesus. People were promised that through magic they could obtain supernatural power to manipulate the spirit world.[7] As a result, many citizens of Ephesus and Asia lived in fear of these powers — a fear that governed their lives.

Well into the Christian era a prayer to the Ephesian Artemis was recorded. The prayer testifies to the respect given to Artemis's powers. It also illustrates the point I am making:

> O Great Artemis of the Ephesians, help! Display your power upon this young man who has died. For all the Ephesians know, both men and women, that all things are governed by you, and that great powers come to us through you. Give now to your servant what you are able to do in this regard. Raise up your servant, Domnos.[8]

Power, authority, and *strength* were popular words in Paul's day and are found in many of the writings of that time.[9] It's no surprise that Paul picks up the Greek equivalents of these words: *dunamis, exousia, ischus,* and *kratos* and uses them in his epistle. *Dunamis* is used in Ephesians 1:19, 21; 3:7, 16, 20; while *exousia* is found in Ephesians 1:21; 2:2; 3:10; 6:12; and *kratos* is used in Ephesians 1:19; 6:10. *Ischus* is used in Ephesians 1:19; 6:10. A combination of three of these words was found in a recipe of sorts in the magical papyri.

The Asian saints, as do the saints in every age, needed to understand there is none greater nor more powerful than their Savior. Jesus, made flesh, crucified, and resurrected, sits at the right hand of the Sovereign Ruler of all the universe. He sits far above all rule and authority and power and dominion and every name — even the names the Ephesians conjured up as they pled with their gods for deliverance and aid.

But that's not all Paul wants the Christians at Ephesus to understand. He wants them to know that God the Father placed Jesus there in accordance with the strength (the *ischus* of His might — the *kratos*) which raised Him from the dead. Now everything is in subjection under His feet. They need not fear. They need not cower. They only need to stay seated!

Oh yes, at one time they had been under the power of the evil one, but no longer. God, the One enthroned above all, made them alive together with Christ. Jesus is the head; they are the church, His body. And if the Head is seated in the heavenlies, the body's there, too (Ephesians 1:22–23; 5:30). The same power (*dunamis*) that resurrected Jesus Christ from hell is not only in them (Ephesians 1:19; 3:20), but it has resurrected them with Jesus above all the power (*dunamis*, 1:21) of the enemy.

So, although we still walk on earth, we need to remember that we're seated in the heavenlies, and we need to live accordingly. "Seated in the heavenlies" is not a dimensional position but a position of authority and power. If we hold our position, victory is assured despite the fierceness of the battle or the power of the enemy.

Paul prays that first we might know the hope of His calling — that we might know He who has begun a good work in us will complete it. In other words, heaven is a surety. This is not an "I hope so" kind of hope. It is an "I know so" kind of hope, a confident hope which says, "Absent from the body, present with the Lord" (2 Corinthians 5:8). Included is the confidence of 1 John 3:2–3: "Beloved, now we are children of God, and it has not appeared as yet what we shall be. We know that, when He appears, we shall be like Him, because we shall see Him just as He is. And everyone who has this hope *fixed* on Him purifies himself, just as He is pure."

Do you have this hope?

Paul then prays that we might realize what are the riches of the glory of His inheritance in the saints. Did you see "His"? It's Christ's inheritance, not ours! We are redeemed and are members of His body, part of His holy temple, part of our Lord's riches, His inheritance — the fruit of His obedience. We are the harvest of the grain of wheat that fell into the ground and died so that He would not abide alone (John 12:24). Jesus rejoices over us!

As other saints are our crown and joy of rejoicing at His appearing (1 Thessalonians 2:19), so we are His. When we believe in Jesus Christ and receive Him as our Lord and Savior, Jesus sees the travail of His soul and He is satisfied (Isaiah 53:11). We who have believed bring Him glory. What an incredible privilege! Do you realize how your salvation has enriched and pleased your Lord?

Paul also prays that we might know the surpassing greatness of His power (*dunamis*) toward us who believe. With faith comes power: power to be all that God ever intended man to be, power that equips us for service (Ephesians 3:7), power that strengthens us in the inner man (Ephesians 3:16), power that works within us (Ephesians 3:20), power that seats us in the heavenlies.

It's a very real power. I've used it in hand-to-hand combat with the enemy as he has sought to keep people bound by demons. I've seen him lift up a human fist in my face as he spit these words from a person's mouth: "If I could just touch you...." To which I replied, "But you can't; you're under the authority of Jesus Christ."

O Beloved, you may never find yourself in this type of battle with demons, but if you belong to God, you'll find yourself in some sort of conflict — one that may be more subtle and more insidious. But the question is the same, "Will you fight the good fight of faith from your position of power?"

The three things that Paul prayed we'd know are all in accordance with (are all possible because of) the working of the strength of God's might. This same might raised Jesus from the dead and seated Him at God's right hand above all the power of the enemy and above every name named in this age and in the one to come.

That age is soon to come. Stay seated, Beloved!

DAY SEVEN

One of the enemy's tactics is to isolate people, to cut them off from fellowship with one another, to convince them that they are alone and that no one really cares about them. (I believe that's one reason families are under such attack today.)

The latter portion of Ephesians 2 stresses our oneness in Him and with

Him…and with the whole household of faith. On Day Two of this week, you read through Ephesians 2 and listed what we were or had under Satan and then under God. Go back and take a look at what you wrote down. Then read through Ephesians 2:11–22, and make sure you didn't miss anything. If you did, add it.

Belonging is a basic need. We each need to be part of something beyond ourselves. Ephesians 2:11–22 tells you that once you have been saved by grace you are in Christ Jesus. You belong! You'll never be alone again. If you are a Gentile, like most of the citizens of Ephesus were, you have been brought near to God through the blood of Jesus Christ. God is not some distant, supreme sovereign you can never communicate with. Jesus has brought you into peace with the Father, and now through the gift of the indwelling Holy Spirit you have access to Him. You are no longer an alien or a stranger. You are part of God's forever family. You've come home. You are in Christ, and He's in you. You're His dwelling place.

You'll never, ever be alone again. You are bone of His bone — an indispensable member of His body.

God chose you! Can you imagine that! You didn't choose Him. In fact He chose you before the foundation of the world. Nothing you did before you believed on His Son changed His mind. He adopted you as His very own child. He redeemed you through the blood of His only begotten Son so that you became His very own possession. He sealed you with the Holy Spirit. Do you think He's ever going to let you go or turn His back on you? If you think so, you're listening to your flesh or to the enemy, and you cannot trust either one.

God says, "I WILL NEVER DESERT YOU, NOR WILL I EVER FORSAKE YOU." So then you may confidently say, "THE LORD IS MY HELPER, I WILL NOT BE AFRAID. WHAT SHALL MAN DO TO ME?" (Hebrews 13:5–6).

If you want to put a hedge of protection around your family, or any believer, teach these truths…and pray, pray, pray they'll believe them and never forget them.

And when the adversary parades your guilt, reminds you of your failures, or tells you no one cares or wants you, take him to Calvary and remind him that God so loved you that He gave His only begotten Son to die in your place. Tell the devil you are now bone of Jesus' bone, a member of His body, seated with Him in the heavenlies. Then, from your heavenly seat of authority, command him to be gone.

When you feel all alone, Beloved, look at Calvary and remember the nail prints in His hands; they're His for eternity, and so are you. "But Zion said, 'The LORD has forsaken me, and the Lord has forgotten me.' 'Can a woman forget her nursing child, and have no compassion on the son of her womb? Even these may forget, but I will not forget you. Behold, I have inscribed you on the palms *of My hands*'" (Isaiah 49:14–16).

Write out your prayer of affirmation.

LORD, I NEED A KINSMAN REDEEMER!

D A Y   O N E

S ean, a high school sophomore, was looking for power. Fascinated by the martial arts, Sean found that Ninjutsu mysteriously connected him with the spiritual world and introduced him to the power he longed for. After learning Ninjutsu, he began to play "Dungeons and Dragons." Compelled to know even more, Sean decided to do some research on dragons. About that time he saw the enticing advertisement of the Time/Life Series on the occult. After reading about wizards and witches, he looked up demons, Salem, voodoo, and whatever else he could find. "There was power in the supernatural world, and I wanted to learn how to harness and use it," he told reporters.[1]

Sean moved into satanic worship — blood sacrifices and all. His story hit the headlines around the United States when he murdered his parents and a convenience store clerk. Why? Because Satan directed his actions. Sean was incarcerated on death row at the Oklahoma State Penitentiary...*BUT GOD HAD A PLAN.*

Katherine was chosen to be a special instrument of Satan's. From childhood she was subjected to ritualistic sexual abuses. Eventually she was recognized in athletics, yet lurking in the shadows was the awareness that her father had dedicated her for another purpose...*BUT GOD HAD A PLAN.*

Chris had been a Christian for years, but the church did little to challenge him in the areas of commitment and sacrifice. Then came the invitation to attend a "Divine Principle Seminar." The love, authority, and call to commitment he found with the Moonies caused him to resign his position as president of his fraternity and move in with others from the Unification church. From that point it was all downhill for Chris — as long as he suppressed some nagging doubts. Because he was intelligent and personable, Chris moved to a key position in the organization of Rev. Sun Myung Moon[2]...*BUT GOD HAD A PLAN.*

Joel's sexual appetites were awakened by a perverted pedophile. From there Joel was introduced to homosexuality. Hating homosexuality because of his Christian environment, yet drawn by his fleshly desires, Joel would give in. Joel was saved. At last he thought he'd be free. Still the enemy pursued him, and his flesh tormented him[3]...*BUT GOD HAD A PLAN.*

All these are true stories, stories of men and women created by God, made in His image. Yet these people became pawns of evil, entrenched in deception, headed for destruction. However, for each one there was a turn of events. God checkmated the devil.

God has a plan — a plan for redemption. Through Sean, Katherine, Chris, Joel, and through every other person who receives the Lord Jesus Christ, God's wisdom is made known to the rulers and authorities in the heavenly places (Ephesians 3:10).

Twice in Ephesians Paul uses the word *administration* which is a significant word in our study of spiritual warfare. "He made known to us the mystery of His will, according to His kind intention which He purposed in Him with a view to an administration suitable to the fulness of the times, *that is,* the summing up of all things in Christ, things in the heavens and things upon the earth" (Ephesians 1:9–10).

Then in Ephesians 3:8–10: "To me, the very least of all saints, this grace was given, to preach to the Gentiles the unfathomable riches of Christ, and to bring to light what is the administration of the mystery which for ages has been hidden in God, who created all things; in order that the manifold wisdom of God might now be made known through the church to the rulers and the authorities in the heavenly *places.*"

Peter was right when he said Paul wrote things which were hard to understand, wasn't he? Although what Paul is saying in these passages may be difficult to grasp, it's worth wrestling with. Stick with me, and you'll get the big picture of the worldwide war that has been escalating since the Garden of Eden.

The English transliteration of the Greek word for *administration* is *oikonomia*. It refers to the administration of a house or property. It is a mode of dealing, an arrangement or administration of affairs.[4] That's why in the introduction to this week's study, I kept repeating the phrase "but God had a plan."

He does! Not only for the people I mentioned, but for you, Beloved. So if you have "known the depths of Satan" or of sin, do not despair. Your story's not finished. The enemy has not triumphed...*GOD HAS A PLAN.!*

Paul tells us that even before man sinned God had a plan to bring all things *in the heavens and on the earth* back under His authority. However, the administration of this plan would remain a mystery until God was ready to unfold it. When that time came, the church would be God's statement to all of the angels, good and bad, including Satan, that Satan had not blindsided God. It would be clear that God was never out of control!

Follow me carefully. All of this I'm sharing now will be backed up with scripture later. Let me simply give you an overview of God's plan.

Before the foundation of the world God knew that Adam and Eve would disobey Him. He knew that as a result of Adam and Eve's transgression all mankind would become sinners. So, before He even created the world, God had a plan of redemption, a way to administrate our salvation. In the fullness of time, Jesus would leave heaven, take on flesh and blood, and become the Son of Man so that He could pay the penalty for our sin. Jesus would be our Kinsman Redeemer.

When the serpent deceived Eve, God was not taken by surprise. This anointed cherub who had defected and taken a third of the angelic host with him in his rebellion, did not blindside God...*GOD HAD A PLAN.*

However, because the devil is not omniscient, he didn't know about God's plan. God gave him a broad overview of the plan though in Genesis

3:14–15. God revealed to Satan that the woman would have a seed and that although the serpent would bruise the heel of the woman's seed, the woman's seed would crush his serpent head. God told Satan what would happen, but He did not tell him when it would happen.

Through Adam's one sin, all Adam's offspring came under the serpent's power and authority. Mankind moved into the domain of darkness. It "looked" like the enemy was victorious. But he wasn't! *GOD HAD A PLAN.* Its administration was set. The plan was partially revealed to a man whom God would name Abraham.

Out of a world of Gentiles, God called a man named Abram from the Ur of the Chaldees and made a covenant with him. From Abram, whom God would rename Abraham, He raised up a nation, a separate people for His own possession. From Abraham came Isaac; from Isaac, Jacob; and from Jacob came twelve sons who became the heads of the twelve tribes of Israel.

This nation would bring forth the One who would bruise the serpent's head. And in Abraham's seed — the Lord Jesus Christ — all the nations of the earth would be blessed. Yet the details of the administration of the plan were a mystery.

Then, in the fullness of time, God sent forth His Son, born of a virgin. Had Jesus been born of an earthly father, He would have been of Adam's seed and, thus, born in sin. Had Jesus been born of an earthly father, He would not have been able to redeem Himself or anyone else. However, Jesus was born, not of corruptible seed, but of God. God was the Father of Jesus, and Jesus was born outside of the slave market of sin.

Jesus was the last Adam. He was sent to be the federal head of a new class of men, men who would be born again of incorruptible seed by the Word of God.

Because the last Adam was without sin, He was not under the dominion of "the prince of the power of the air, of the spirit that is now working in the sons of disobedience" (Ephesians 2:2). Jesus was the one and only human being over whom Satan had no power. But if Satan could get Jesus to sin...

Satan tempted Him, but Jesus would not sin. Jesus had come for the express purpose to seek and to save lost mankind. He would not exchange God's cross for Satan's crown. This time Satan failed.

Jesus came to His own people, Israel, but, for the most part, they would not recognize Him for who He was — God incarnate (in the flesh), their Kinsman Redeemer. Instead, the Jews became pawns of Satan, bent on killing Jesus.

Jesus was "hanged upon a tree." Then according to His plan, the administration of His mystery, God took all the sins of the world from eternity past to eternity future and put them on His Son. He was God's Passover Lamb, the scapegoat of the day of atonement. His cry was heard from Golgotha, "MY GOD, MY GOD, WHY HAST THOU FORSAKEN ME?" (Matthew 27:46).

Satan had delivered his death blow. Jesus was crucified, His heel bruised. Death opened her arms. Hell received Him. The demons danced. The Son of God was dead.

One day passed. Two days. It looked as if Satan had triumphed again...*BUT GOD HAD A PLAN.*

On the third day the stone was rolled away. The tomb was empty! God's holiness was satisfied with the offering of Jesus' blood. Jesus crashed through the gates of hell. In power, God raised Jesus Christ from the dead, crushing the head of the serpent! Satan's grip on death was gone. Jesus had paid the wages for our sin — in full. Satan's power was broken. The administration of the summing up of all things in Christ was unfolding for all to see.

Look at His hands! His feet! It is your Kinsman Redeemer!

Jesus offered forgiveness of sins and eternal life to all who would believe in Him.

He ascended to the Father to sit at His right hand as the Son of Man. However, before He ascended, He told His disciples to wait for the promise, the Holy Spirit who would indwell and seal them until the day of their full redemption. The Spirit of God within was part of the administration of the mystery, planned before the foundation of the world.

After Jesus ascended, God sent the Holy Spirit to indwell those whom He had chosen to adopt as sons *before* the foundation of the world. These became members of the body of Jesus Christ, the Church — a church composed of

Jews and Gentiles from every tribe and tongue and people and nation; a church, redeemed from among mankind, seated with Him in the heavenlies, *far above all the power of the enemy*, no longer to be slaves of sin.

Freed from sin's slavery and Satan's dominion, the church would reveal to the demonic and angelic hosts the manifold wisdom of God's plan. Then, all the rulers and authorities in the heavenly places would know that Satan never once had God cornered or disarmed. God was always in charge, carrying out the administration of the mystery of His will. Now all could see that before time began, God knew He would triumph over the devil through His church.

Satan would do all he could to destroy Sean, Katherine, Chris, Joel, and even you...*BUT GOD HAS A PLAN!* And as He has planned, so shall it be. No one can thwart God. And that's what the angels see every time a child of God is set free!

Battles may be fought, but victory is assured. "Then *comes* the end, when He delivers up the kingdom to the God and Father, when He has abolished all rule and all authority and power" (1 Corinthians 15:24). The war will be over, and all things will be turned over to the Father, *the one and only true God.*

Hallelujah, hallelujah, hallelujah, hallelujah, hallelujah! (Can you hear the music of Handel's *Messiah* in the background?)

DAY TWO

The young woman standing in front of me looked pitiful. Her dark eyes contrasted starkly with the whiteness of her skin. She showed no energy or emotion. I knew she was there because she wanted to talk to me, but she wouldn't say a thing. A lifeless, barely audible yes or no was about all I could get out of her. Finally, I said, "Honey, I cannot do a thing to help you if you won't talk with me."

My bluntness evoked slightly more responsiveness, at least enough for me to hear what I already knew — the girl was hurting. When we finished our brief, one-sided conversation, I put my arms around her and hugged her. If I couldn't do anything else, at least I could give her one thing I knew she desperately needed.

Although I asked her to spend time with our staff counselor, I still saw a lot of Rachel. Invariably she'd drop by on Tuesday mornings even if she couldn't come to class. She'd just stand there until I finished talking with people. She had come for her hug.

For the next two years we came alongside Rachel in her struggles. Sometimes her heaviness would lift and she'd smile, but her progress was slow.

Rachel was learning more about God and about herself as her feelings were brought face to face with "thus saith the Lord." Finally, Rachel was ready to forgive.

Like over a fourth of all women in America, Rachel was a victim of sexual abuse. It was easy to understand why Rachel was the way she was, except for one thing. Rachel professed to know the Lord Jesus Christ. She had done my *Lord, Heal My Hurts* study, she had been counseled by a number of godly people, and she had been loved unconditionally. Over and over she'd been confronted with the Word. But just when we'd think we were getting someplace, there'd be another defeat. Those working with her questioned her to be sure she had a true understanding of salvation, but Rachel was convinced she belonged to Jesus. And she did, in "the mystery of His will." The only problem was that it was still a mystery!

Just recently I received one of Rachel's precious letters. She's living in another city and state now and is doing well because of two things: her understanding of salvation and her knowledge of warfare. Let me share what she wrote.

I remember when I came to Precept. I was so full of hurt and anger and I so longed to be loved. I couldn't talk much (now I can't stop talking!) but you'd just hug me and tell me you loved me. I wanted what you had. I knew all about the Bible in my head, but not in my heart. Then I took the Precept course on Colossians. I couldn't understand what it meant when it said, "You are complete in Him."

Lynda prayed for me and loved and encouraged me. And then I realized I was lost. I met Jesus personally. Things haven't been the same since! The empty longing for love is gone, and every day I marvel that a person could be so loved. I want others to know the same love I've found.

Then on my birthday, Judy and a pastor and I prayed through all those strongholds the enemy had erected in my life, and the Lord set me free. I'm finding He *has* given me all I need for life and godliness. It's exciting — and what a neat thing to finally have a Father.

Rachel was set free because she had a Kinsman Redeemer, One who could be touched with her pain, who could heal her hurts. She had cried, "Heal me, O LORD, and I will be healed; save me and I will be saved" (Jeremiah 17:14). And that's exactly what God did!

Oh, how God's wisdom is being revealed through Rachel to the rulers and authorities in heavenly places! She has triumphed through the Lord Jesus Christ and is no longer under the power of the enemy. For "if therefore the Son shall make you free, you shall be free indeed" (John 8:36).

Yesterday, and then again today, you saw that I used the term "kinsman redeemer." "Kinsman redeemer" is a title full of truth — invaluable truth — when it comes to holding your position in Christ Jesus and to standing firm. Therefore, my friend, we're going to spend the rest of this week looking in detail at the teaching of the "kinsman redeemer."

Although God didn't bring to light the administration of the mystery of how He would redeem mankind and place him above all the power of the enemy until He formed His church, His plan was seen in seed form in the Old Testament teaching of the kinsman redeemer.

A kinsman redeemer or *gōʾēl* was a person who had the right to redeem, to purchase, to buy back either a blood relative or family inheritance where it had been lost either through debt or death.

There are three Old Testament words for redeem: *pādâh, gāʾal* (verb form of *gōʾēl*), and *kōper*. Each of these three words "is cast against the background of helplessness. Each finds human beings captured, held captive by the power of forces they cannot overcome. Only by the intervention of a third party can bondage be broken and the person freed."[5] The third party is the kinsman redeemer.

Kōper is translated "ransom" and comes from the word *kāpar,* which means to make atonement. Therefore *kōper* means "to atone by making a substitutionary payment."[6]

Pādâh was originally used "to indicate a transfer of ownership through payment or some equivalent transaction."[7]

"The verb *gā'al* appears 118 times in the Old Testament. In each case, persons or objects are in the power of another, and the one whose person or possessions are held is unable to win release. Then a third party appears, and this person is able to effect release.

"The verb *gā'al* places the emphasis on the relationship between redeemer and redeemed. Because of his close kinship, the redeemer had the privilege and the duty of coming to the relative's aid."[8]

My precious friend Rachel has a Kinsman Redeemer who bought her out of her difficulties and dangers. His name is Jesus Christ. Have you recognized Christ as your Kinsman Redeemer? If you'll call upon His name, He can deliver you just as He delivered Rachel. He came for one purpose: to act on your behalf and to set you free from anyone or anything which enslaves you.

DAY THREE

Today we're going to look at the law of the kinsman redeemer as explained in Leviticus 25:47–55. As you read this passage, mark every occurrence of the words *redeem* and *redemption.* Keep in mind the meanings of the three words for redeem.

➤ LEVITICUS 25:47–55

47 "'Now if the means of a stranger or of a sojourner with you becomes sufficient, and a countryman [literally, a brother] of yours becomes so poor

with regard to him as to sell himself to a stranger who is sojourning with you, or to the descendants of a stranger's family,

48 then he shall have redemption right after he has been sold. One of his brothers may redeem him,

49 or his uncle, or his uncle's son, may redeem him, or one of his blood relatives from his family may redeem him; or if he prospers, he may redeem himself.

50 'He then with his purchaser shall calculate from the year when he sold himself to him up to the year of jubilee; and the price of his sale shall correspond to the number of years. *It is* like the days of a hired man *that* he shall be with him.

51 'If there are still many years, he shall refund part of his purchase price in proportion to them for his own redemption;

52 and if few years remain until the year of jubilee, he shall so calculate with him. In proportion to his years he is to refund *the amount for* his redemption.

53 'Like a man hired year by year he shall be with him; he shall not rule over him with severity in your sight.

54 'Even if he is not redeemed by these *means,* he shall still go out in the year of jubilee, he and his sons with him.

55 'For the sons of Israel are My servants; they are My servants whom I brought out from the land of Egypt. I am the LORD your God.'"

1. According to this passage, why would a person need redeeming?

2. Who has the right of redemption?

3. Could a man redeem himself? How?

According to the Law, the redeemer had to be a blood relative of the one sold into slavery. But how does all this relate to you and me and our warfare? Listen to John 8:34–36, and then write out how these verses correspond to the teaching on kinsman redeemer. "Jesus answered them, 'Truly, truly, I say to you, everyone who commits sin is the slave of sin. And the slave does not remain in the house forever; the son does remain forever. If therefore the Son shall make you free, you shall be free indeed.'"

Now, Beloved, are you beginning to see why God had to send His Son? The more you know about your Kinsman Redeemer and what He has purchased for you, the greater your ability to stand against Satan's devices! He won't be able to catch you off guard as easily.

DAY   FOUR

We were late, and it was my fault. Jack was being his usual sweet and patient self, but I felt guilty. As we clipped down the hallway from the hotel elevators to our meeting, Jack stopped without putting on his brake lights. I almost tripped over him.

"We're going the wrong way."

"Honey," I replied as I suddenly reversed direction, "I'm sure we're supposed to go to the right."

"Nope, that's some other group's meeting place."

"But, Sweetheart," I was a little frustrated and confused, "this only leads to the restaurant."

"Well, then, we're on the wrong floor."

Before I knew it, we were headed back to the elevators. I couldn't stand it. I knew we had to be on the right floor. So while Jack punched the button, I ducked around the corner to the right to look down the hall. I laughed. No wonder "Sweetheart" thought we were in the wrong place. There was a big sign announcing "Moonlight and Roses," the Georgia Romantic Writers Convention.

Our regional meeting of the National Religious Broadcasters was lost in a maze of women who had come to learn how to tap more successfully one of the biggest markets in the publishing world. Love stories, from those lining the shelves in Wal-Mart to the libraries of our nations, are a dime a dozen. They usually hold to a common theme of love desired, discovered, and requited in one way or another. Then comes the grand and usually obvious finale.

If you want a love story with an unusual twist, don't look for it at the Georgia Romantic Writers Convention. Look in the world's oldest book, the Bible. It's the story of Ruth and Boaz. No other book portrays more clearly how the law of redemption, described in Leviticus and Deuteronomy, is lived out.

In a few short verses we're caught in the pathos of three widows — a mother-in-law and her two daughters-in-law. Naomi dutifully followed her husband, Elimelech, to Moab in an attempt to flee the famine in Bethlehem, but she lost him through death. Soon after, Naomi's sons married Moabite women. Ten years later her sons were dead, leaving Naomi alone, far from her land and her people. She wanted to go home, but her heart would not allow her to force Orpah and Ruth to go with her. In tears, Naomi told them to stay in Moab and find new husbands. She knew she was too old to bear more sons for them to marry. (That's a different twist, wouldn't you say? It was Jewish law.) Read on, but don't forget our goal is not romance but an understanding of the role of the kinsman redeemer. Of course, we might find some romance along the way!

Orpah agreed to return to her Moabite people, but Ruth protested. "Do not urge me to leave you *or* turn back from following you; for where you go, I will go, and where you lodge, I will lodge. Your people *shall be* my people, and your God, my God. Where you die, I will die, and there I will be buried. Thus may the LORD do to me, and worse, if *anything but* death parts you and me" (Ruth 1:16–17).

When they returned to Bethlehem, they had to eat, so Naomi urged Ruth to glean in the fields of Boaz. Boaz was a kinsman of Naomi's husband and a man of great wealth (Ruth 2:1, 20).

Now comes the really different twist. Pay attention!

What does the Law say about raising up a seed when a man died and left his wife without an heir? Read Deuteronomy 25:5–10 which follows. Although the word *redemption* or *kinsman redeemer* is nowhere to be found in this passage, we will see it clearly pictured in the Book of Ruth tomorrow.

> When brothers live together and one of them dies and has no son, the wife of the deceased shall not be *married* outside *the family* to a strange man. Her husband's brother shall go in to her and take her to himself as wife and perform the duty of a husband's brother to her. And it shall be that the first-born whom she bears shall assume the name of his dead brother, that his name may not be blotted out from Israel. But if the man does not desire to take his brother's wife, then his brother's wife shall go up to the gate to the elders and say, "My husband's brother refuses to

establish a name for his brother in Israel; he is not willing to perform the duty of a husband's brother to me." Then the elders of his city shall summon him and speak to him. And *if* he persists and says, "I do not desire to take her," then his brother's wife shall come to him in the sight of the elders, and pull his sandal off his foot and spit in his face; and she shall declare, "Thus it is done to the man who does not build up his brother's house." And in Israel his name shall be called, "The house of him whose sandal is removed."

1. Why was a widow not to remarry outside the family?

2. What was a kinsman to do if he did not want to marry the widow?

Now that you've seen the law instituted by God we'll return tomorrow to our love story in the Book of Ruth.

DAY FIVE

As Boaz walked through his fields, he immediately noticed Ruth. He knew she was a faithful daughter-in-law to Naomi. Boaz didn't want her gleaning in anyone else's fields! He told his harvesters to leave handfuls of grain for her purposefully.

Naomi was thrilled; this was a kinsman worthy of her Ruth. So Naomi gave Ruth her instructions. While Boaz was sleeping, Ruth was to uncover his feet, lie down there, and wait.

When Boaz awoke and found Ruth lying at his feet, that was it! He wanted to redeem this blood relative. But there was a problem. There was one who was of closer kinship than Boaz!

Chapter 4 of the Book of Ruth records the next occurrence. As you read, keep in mind what you have learned in Deuteronomy. Mark every reference to *close* or *closest relative* in a distinctive way or color. Then mark every use of the word *redeem* and its synonyms in another distinctive manner.

➤ RUTH 4:1–10, 13–14

1 Now Boaz went up to the gate and sat down there, and behold, the close relative of whom Boaz spoke was passing by, so he said, "Turn aside, friend, sit down here." And he turned aside and sat down.

2 And he took ten men of the elders of the city and said, "Sit down here." So they sat down.

3 Then he said to the closest relative, "Naomi, who has come back from the land of Moab, has to sell the piece of land which belonged to our brother Elimelech.

4 "So I thought to inform you, saying, 'Buy *it* before those who are sitting *here,* and before the elders of my people. If you will redeem *it,* redeem *it;* but if not, tell me that I may know; for there is no one but you to redeem *it,* and I am after you.'" And he said, "I will redeem *it.*"

5 Then Boaz said, "On the day you buy the field from the hand of Naomi, you must also acquire Ruth the Moabitess, the widow of the deceased, in order to raise up the name of the deceased on his inheritance."

6 And the closest relative said, "I cannot redeem *it* for myself, lest I jeopardize my own inheritance. Redeem *it* for yourself; you *may have* my right of redemption, for I cannot redeem *it.*"

7 Now this was *the custom* in former times in Israel concerning the

redemption and the exchange *of land* to confirm any matter; a man removed his sandal and gave it to another; and this was the *manner of* attestation in Israel.

8 So the closest relative said to Boaz, "Buy *it* for yourself." And he removed his sandal.

9 Then Boaz said to the elders and all the people, "You are witnesses today that I have bought from the hand of Naomi all that belonged to Elimelech and all that belonged to Chilion and Mahlon.

10 "Moreover, I have acquired Ruth the Moabitess, the widow of Mahlon, to be my wife in order to raise up the name of the deceased on his inheritance, so that the name of the deceased may not be cut off from his brothers or from the court of his *birth* place; you are witnesses today."

13 So Boaz took Ruth, and she became his wife, and he went in to her. And the LORD enabled her to conceive, and she gave birth to a son.

14 Then the women said to Naomi, "Blessed is the LORD who has not left you without a redeemer today, and may his name become famous in Israel."

The name of Boaz did become famous in Israel. From the line of Boaz would come our Kinsman Redeemer. Oh, the manifold wisdom of God! How awesome it is to trace His ways as He executes his plan!

To Ruth and Boaz would be born Obed. Obed was the father of Jesse, the father of David, of the genealogy of our Lord, God's "Son, who was born of a descendant of David according to the flesh" (Romans 1:3).

Doesn't that make you want to join Naomi's friends and say, "Blessed is our Lord who has not left us without a kinsman redeemer"?

Thank you, Precious Lord, for not taking off your shoe but for redeeming us that we might be your bride and be seated with you far above all the power of the enemy. Amen and Amen.

D A Y   S I X

When God created us, He created us lower than the angels, crowned us with glory and honor, appointed us over the works of His hands, and put all things in subjection under our feet (Psalm 8:5–6; Hebrews 2:7–8).

But, it didn't last long. In Adam, we believed a lie. We thought we could become like God. Instead, we became captives of sin under the domain of Satan and, in the process, lost the privilege of ruling over the works of God's hands.

Mankind was lost — dead in transgressions and sins, seemingly without hope or help because there was no one left untouched by sin and its awful wages of death. "But God, being rich in mercy, because of His great love with which He loved us…when the fulness of time came…sent forth His Son, born of a woman, born under the Law, in order that He might redeem" mankind through the law of the *gō'ēl* (Ephesians 2:4; Galatians 4:4–5).

In Paul's letter to the Ephesians, he stresses our position in Christ. Why? Because victory in warfare is assured as long as you hold your position and don't move from what you've gained through redemption.

Because our position is so important, we're going to study what I'll call "the law of the *gō'ēl* as described in the Old Testament. As we read about kinsman redeemers, we'll discuss six qualifications or responsibilities that a kinsman redeemer had to consider in order to redeem his relative.

First, the redeemer had to be a blood relative. If all mankind is born in a state of sin, who is there to redeem him? Angels can't redeem us. The blood of bulls and goats can't! We can only be redeemed by another human being, and there was no one born outside the slave market of sin to come to our rescue.

It looked as if the devil would have mankind under his power forever.

BUT GOD HAD A PLAN…

Follow me closely because I am about to "string pearls" of scripture together into a priceless chain of truth — truth which will show you why you can live as more than a conqueror over all the wiles of the evil one. Ask

the Father to open the eyes of your understanding so that you can comprehend the height, depth, and breadth of these liberating truths and live
accordingly.

> Since then the children share in flesh and blood, He Himself likewise
> also partook of the same, that through death He might render powerless
> him who had the power of death, that is, the devil; and might deliver
> those who through fear of death were subject to slavery all their lives.
> For assuredly He does not give help to angels, but He gives help to the
> descendant of Abraham. (Hebrews 2:14–16)

There was no redemption for angels. When a third of the angels made a
choice to follow Satan, they sealed their destiny. But not so with us. Adam's
choice did not seal our fate! God had a plan for our redemption. He would
send a Kinsman Redeemer made of flesh and blood just like us, yet without
sin. "Now the birth of Jesus Christ was as follows. When His mother Mary
had been betrothed to Joseph, before they came together she was found to
be with child by the Holy Spirit" (Matthew 1:18).

When Mary asked how this was to be, "the angel answered and said to
her, 'The Holy Spirit will come upon you, and the power of the Most High
will overshadow you; and for that reason the holy offspring shall be called
the Son of God'" (Luke 1:35).

God would provide our Kinsman Redeemer by incarnating His Son.
Jesus would then be a blood relative of mankind, born of the seed of God,
made flesh and blood. That was the first step, but to be a blood relative was
not enough to redeem man.

*Second, the kinsman redeemer had to have the ability to pay the price of
redemption.* There are two New Testament words for redeem: *Lutroō* means
"to release on receipt of ransom" and *exagorazō* means "purchasing a slave
with a view to his freedom."9

What price would redeem man from the slave market of sin? You need
to search the scriptures for the answer. It is what delivers you from Satan's
grip and gives you authority over him.

1. Look up the following verses. Note what you learn about sin and what atones or pays for sin. Write out enough of the verse to remember what it says.

  a. Leviticus 17:11 (Remember what you learned several days ago about atonement and redemption.)

  b. Hebrews 10:4–10 (If all it took was blood to redeem man, why not the blood of animals?)

  c. 1 Peter 1:18–19

  d. Ephesians 1:7–8a

2. Look up Colossians 1:13–14. According to these verses, what does redemption bring us?

It was one thing to have a blood relative who could act as a kinsman redeemer and pay the price of redemption, but it was another for the kinsman to be willing to do so. Thus, we come to the *third* responsibility: *The*

kinsman had to have the desire to redeem his fellow kinsman. Listen to Hebrews
10:4–10…and tell me, did Jesus desire to redeem you?

> For it is impossible for the blood of bulls and goats to take away sins.
> Therefore, when He comes into the world, He says, "SACRIFICE AND
> OFFERING THOU HAST NOT DESIRED, BUT A BODY THOU HAST PRE-
> PARED FOR ME; IN WHOLE BURNT OFFERINGS AND *sacrifices* FOR SIN
> THOU HAST TAKEN NO PLEASURE. THEN I SAID, 'BEHOLD, I HAVE
> COME (IN THE ROLL OF THE BOOK IT IS WRITTEN OF ME) TO DO THY
> WILL, O GOD.'" After saying above, "SACRIFICES AND OFFERINGS AND
> WHOLE BURNT OFFERINGS AND *sacrifices* FOR SIN THOU HAST NOT
> DESIRED, NOR HAST THOU TAKEN PLEASURE *in them*" (which are
> offered according to the Law), then He said, "BEHOLD, I HAVE COME
> TO DO THY WILL." He takes away the first in order to establish the sec-
> ond. By this will we have been sanctified through the offering of the
> body of Jesus Christ once for all.
>
> For the Son of Man has come to seek and to save that which was
> lost. (Luke 19:10)

May I suggest, Beloved, that you close today's study with a time of worship and thanksgiving to our Father God and His Son for their willingness to
pay the price to redeem you. Your redemption cost our Father His Son, and
it cost the Son His life. "Greater love has no one than this, that one lay down
his life for his friends" (John 15:13). "See how great a love the Father has
bestowed upon us, that we should be called children of God" (1 John 3:1).

DAY   SEVEN

Jesus came for one purpose — to redeem us. But, like every kinsman
redeemer, He had to realize that in the redemptive process He could mar or
jeopardize His own inheritance. The *fourth* qualification was *the willingness to
do so.*

Remember what we studied in the story of Ruth and Boaz? The man who had the immediate right of redemption in respect to Ruth said, "I cannot redeem *it* for myself, lest I jeopardize my own inheritance. Redeem *it* for yourself; you *may have* my right of redemption, for I cannot redeem *it*" (Ruth 4:6).

Although Jesus came with the express purpose of being the Lamb who would shed His blood for our redemption, He asked the Father "with great tears and loud crying" if there were some other way to redeem His kinsmen.

Oh, how our Lord wrestled with the weakness of His flesh that night in the Garden of Gethsemane! "His sweat became like drops of blood, falling down upon the ground," as He beseeched the Father, "Father, if Thou art willing, remove this cup from Me; yet not My will, but Thine be done" (Luke 22:44, 42). Not once, but three times He asked God if it were not possible to let the cup of Calvary pass from His lips. Why?

Let me take you to Matthew 26:36–44 and then to Hebrews 5:7–9. Read and see if you can discover why.

> Then Jesus came with them to a place called Gethsemane, and said to His disciples, "Sit here while I go over there and pray." And He took with Him Peter and the two sons of Zebedee, and began to be grieved and distressed. Then He said to them, "My soul is deeply grieved, to the point of death; remain here and keep watch with Me." And He went a little beyond *them,* and fell on His face and prayed, saying, "My Father, if it is possible, let this cup pass from Me; yet not as I will, but as Thou wilt." And He came to the disciples and found them sleeping, and said to Peter, "So, you *men* could not keep watch with Me for one hour? Keep watching and praying, that you may not enter into temptation; the spirit is willing, but the flesh is weak." He went away again a second time and prayed, saying, "My Father, if this cannot pass away unless I drink it, Thy will be done." And again He came and found them sleeping, for their eyes were heavy. And He left them again, and went away and prayed a third time, saying the same thing once more. (Matthew 26:36–44)

The author of Hebrews gives us deeper insight into this time in Gethsemane.

In the days of His flesh, He offered up both prayers and supplications with loud crying and tears to the One able to save Him from death, and He was heard because of His piety. Although He was a Son, He learned obedience from the things which He suffered. And having been made perfect, He became to all those who obey Him the source of eternal salvation. (Hebrews 5:7–9)

If God were not satisfied with Jesus' sacrifice, Jesus would remain in hell and, thus, lose His inheritance.

Of course, we realize from other passages that Jesus already knew He would die, be buried, and rise the third day. He told His apostles of his death, burial, and resurrection several times. However, they didn't seem to understand Him. Jesus was God, and He never laid His deity aside. He only set aside His prerogative to act as God. When he became a man, He lived as a man was supposed to live — in complete dependence on God.

When we see Jesus agonizing in the Garden of Gethsemane, we see Him in all His humanity — wanting to do the will of the Father, but battling with the weakness of the flesh. Hebrews 5 shows this same struggle, thus, the loud crying and tears to the One able *to save Him out of death.* There are several ways to interpret this phrase, yet no one can say exactly how it should be interpreted.

Vincent in *Word Studies in the New Testament* says, "*To save him from death* may mean to deliver him from the fear of death, from the anguish of death, or from remaining a prey to death. In any case, the statement connects itself with the thought of Christ's humanity. He was under the pressure of a sore human need which required divine help, thus showing that he was like unto his brethren. The purport of the prayer is not stated."[10]

If the purport of Jesus' cry was that He would not *remain a prey to death,* or in other words that death would not hold him in its clutches, its prison, then we would see the parallel to the kinsman redeemer's willingness to jeopardize His inheritance for our sake.

Either way, His cry "not my will, but Thine be done" is evidence that our redeemer was willing to forsake His intimacy with the Father in order to become sin for us so that we might be forgiven all our sins and regain what we lost in Adam. Hebrews tells us that God heard the cry of His Son asking if He might be delivered *ek thanatou,* — *ek* meaning "out of," *thanatou* meaning "death."

Yes, in His humanity Jesus asked the Father three times for an alternative — and there was none. Only His blood, only His death would do. And so he became "obedient to the point of death, even death on a cross" (Philippians 2:8).

What kinsman redeemer would be willing to pay such a price, to humble himself so greatly, to leave a throne in glory, to redeem people who were otherwise without hope — helpless, sinners, ungodly, and, on top of all that, enemies?

Only Jesus, Beloved, only Jesus — Jesus, who, "although He existed in the form of God, did not regard equality with God a thing to be grasped, but emptied Himself, taking the form of a bond-servant, *and* being made in the likeness of men. And being found in appearance as a man, He humbled Himself by becoming obedient to the point of death, even death on a cross" (Philippians 2:6–8).

So many times we forget the cost our Lord paid to buy our redemption. Instead, the cross simply marks time. It is viewed as a pivotal event in history, moving man from B.C. to A.D. instead of from death to life.

We forget that flesh and bone held together by sinews and joints, strung with nerves, hung by nails on a felled tree.

We forget that every nerve in our Lord's body was intact, excruciatingly aware of every move His flesh made against the rough bark. He dehydrated. His tongue began to swell.

We forget that the beatings at the house of Caiaphas and the scourging of Roman soldiers marred His form more than any man, leaving Him unrecognizable as a human being (Isaiah 52:14).

We forget that the only One who could again breathe life into man could breathe only as He pushed against the spike, piercing His feet.

We forget the incomprehensible horror of bearing the sins of *all* mankind — past, present, and future.

We forget that it must have been hell to have His Father turn His back on Him as He cried, "MY GOD, MY GOD, WHY HAST THOU FORSAKEN ME?" and as He heard no answer.

We forget that, in silent but vivid testimony, blood and water poured from His side. He died of a broken, ruptured heart.

We forget that our Kinsman endured all this and more.

In His sacrifice we see His willingness to jeopardize His inheritance for us. If God was not satisfied, if His holiness was not propitiated, Jesus would lose what He once had with the Father.

For three days, there was silence. Then an angel rolled away the stone.

Hallelujah! God was satisfied with the substitutionary death of His Son! Thus, He raised Him from the dead, never to die again. Through His death, those who believe in Jesus become "heirs of God and fellow heirs with Christ" (Romans 8:17).

There are two more responsibilities of the Kinsman Redeemer, but we will look at them next week. You have enough to meditate upon, dear one. Let these truths fall softly like rain on the soil of your heart until they soak deep into your being and a harvest of righteousness springs up.

"Only the Scriptures, of all the world's great religious writings, so portray the relation between human beings and God in terms of redemption. Redemption reveals a helpless humanity; and redemption affirms a God whose love drives him to take the part of the near kinsman. At his own expense, he paid the price needed to win our release"[11] from the powers of darkness and sin.

Hallelujah!

What is your prayer of affirmation this week, Beloved?

CHAPTER SEVEN

LORD, KINSMAN REDEEMER, HOW CAN SATAN BE DEFEATED?

DAY ONE

"My children were murdered...."

We were in Texas doing a Precept Training Workshop. I had just done an evening teaching session, and there was a long line of people waiting to talk with me. Michele said she just wanted to thank me for writing *Lord, Heal My Hurts*. "If you hadn't taken the time and effort to write such a wonderful study, I would still be trying to make things happen and trying to fix all my problems. You see, my children were murdered by our babysitter."

Suddenly I wanted the people behind her to walk away so that Michele and I could talk. Michele wasn't falling apart. Peace permeated her countenance. Obviously she knew the sufficiency of our Father's grace, and I was eager to hear her story.

Her story is tragic, unbearable apart from the grace of God and His promises. God has been her sanity, her shield, her rock of refuge.

When Max and Michele moved to their little Texas town, their real estate lady found a house for them right across the street from hers. It was only natural for her teenage son, Bruce, to babysit four-year-old Donnie and

137

two-year-old Carol for Max and Michele. Donnie loved Bruce because they could do all sorts of neat things together, like playing with trucks.

Oh, from time to time Bruce got into a little trouble, like when he fiddled with the television, trying to get pay channels on cable although they didn't have that service. But all in all, both families enjoyed being neighbors. What Max and Michele didn't realize was Bruce was an avid player of "Dungeons and Dragons."

As Michele looks back now, things happened that night which were not "typical." When Bruce came to babysit at 5:50 P.M., Max and Michele were running late. As they hurried out the door, Michele was giving last-minute instructions, telling Bruce not to fiddle with the TV and not to let Donnie make a mess. Usually after Bruce babysat, Donnie's room was a royal mess.

As Donnie ran out to the car for a last good-bye kiss, Bruce yelled from the house, "What time will you be home?" He'd never asked that question before, but Michele didn't think a thing about it until she later rehearsed every last precious moment she'd had with her children. One of the things Michele and Max treasure is the memory of little Carol standing at the door waving good-bye. And Michele vividly remembers the feeling of Donnie's wet kiss on her check.

When they got home at 11:20, the house was unusually dark. Only a hallway light was on. Even the TV screen was black. Suddenly Bruce came down the hall with a gun in his hand.

When Max asked Bruce what was wrong, Bruce said, "I've flipped out." Max asked him where the kids were. "I killed them." His words shot through their hearts.

Bruce pointed the gun at Michele and pulled the trigger three times, but the gun didn't fire. Throwing it down, he swooped up a rifle and pulled the trigger. It didn't fire either.

By then Max had pushed Michele out the garage door. As she ran frantically across the street to Bruce's house, all she could think was, *If I can just reach their door, they'll know something's wrong.*

She thought the heavy footsteps behind her were Bruce's. As she banged on the door, Max ran up behind her shouting, "Don't knock; just go in."

Bruce's mom began crying hysterically as Bruce's dad, Tom, and Max went back across the street to Bruce. Tom insisted Max stay outside as he went in, shouting, "What in the hell do you think you're doing?" He was met by a bullet.

Bleeding, Tom ran from the house just as the police drove up. Bruce shouted at them from the garage, "I'm the terminator. I've killed twice. I'll kill again." Then he started barking like a dog and chirping like a bird. When they put handcuffs on him, he proudly stated, "Success, success at last. But wait. I didn't kill myself, so I have failed."

Max and Michele believe that there was a warfare going on that night. Besides playing "Dungeons and Dragons," Bruce listened to rock groups that have been charged with having suicidal and satanic messages. On the night Bruce killed Donnie and Carol a movie was on in which a little boy and girl were supposed to be sacrificed in a satanic ritual, but they were rescued by a man who had an eagle and tiger for his friends.

Max and Michele had a bird that they never let out of his cage. When they came home, the bird was out, and little Donnie's body was wearing a tiger Halloween costume. They believe ritualistic things happened that night. All of Donnie's baby souvenirs were on the bed where Bruce had shot the children. The TV had been tampered with, and Donnie's room was a disaster.

Max and Michele don't know much more because the case was never brought to trial. They only know the district attorney believes that "Dungeons and Dragons" played a big part in what happened that night.

A fourteen-year-old girl was to testify against Bruce about his D&D playing. She received a phone call and was told that if she testified she would find herself in the same position. A detective told Max and Michele that Bruce had told a girl at school he was going to kill someone that night.

I know, Beloved, that this is a hard story to read. It was hard for me to type it, but it's something we need to know. Sometimes when we read biblical accounts of conflicts with the enemy, especially in the Gospels, it seems as if those events belonged only to a past age. Don't be deluded! As our Lord's coming draws closer and closer, the warfare's escalating.

Just remember, precious one, the same Kinsman Redeemer that was and is there for Michele is there for you. He is able to be touched with the feeling of your infirmities and able to save forever those who draw near to Him since He lives to make intercession for them (Hebrews 7:25). Think on Him and tomorrow we'll learn about our Kinsman Redeemer's triumph over the enemy.

DAY TWO

When it seems as if the enemy has brutally afflicted the child of God, we need to remember that we have a Kinsman Redeemer who will ultimately triumph over the enemy and bring him into account for all he has done. This brings us to the *fifth* responsibility: *The kinsman had to serve as the judicial executioner of the murderer of his relative.* Let me explain this and have you do a little work. Then we'll apply it to spiritual warfare.

If a person murdered another human being, what redemption price could he pay to the family for the loss of their loved one?

Because we were made in the image of God, life is sacred. This is why capital punishment was instituted by God and never revoked! It was to be a life for a life![1]

Listen to what God said to Noah and watch for the word *brother:* "And surely I will require your lifeblood; from every beast I will require it. And from *every* man, from every man's brother I will require the life of man. Whoever sheds man's blood, by man his blood shall be shed, for in the image of God He made man" (Genesis 9:5–6).

1. You may feel like this is a simple question with an obvious answer, but I don't want you to miss it because it is so important! *Bear with me!* Why was an animal or a man to be put to death if either killed a person?

2. Look up Exodus 20:13. The English transliteration of the Hebrew word for *murder* is *rāsah*, which means to murder intentionally. You might want to write this Hebrew word in your Bible next to this verse. What does it say? Does it contradict Genesis 9:5–6?

3. Look up Exodus 21:12–14 and record what you learn.

4. Now read Deuteronomy 19:10–13 and mark any use of the word *avenger*. The English transliteration of the Hebrew word for *avenger* is *gā'al*. From what you know, who then would become the avenger?

The main passage from which we can learn more about this rather difficult responsibility of the kinsman redeemer is Numbers 35. As you read the portion of Numbers 35 that is printed here for you, mark the word *avenger* in a distinctive way, and remember it is the Hebrew word for kinsman or redeemer, *gā'al*.

➤ NUMBERS 35:15–25, 30–31, 33

15 "'These six cities shall be for refuge for the sons of Israel, and for the alien and for the sojourner among them; that anyone who kills a person unintentionally may flee there.

16 "'But if he struck him down with an iron object, so that he died, he is a murderer; the murderer shall surely be put to death.

¹⁷ "'And if he struck him down with a stone in the hand, by which he may die, and *as a result* he died, he is a murderer; the murderer shall surely be put to death.

¹⁸ "'Or if he struck him with a wooden object in the hand, by which he may die, and *as a result* he died, he is a murderer; the murderer shall surely be put to death.

¹⁹ "'The blood avenger himself shall put the murderer to death; he shall put him to death when he meets him.

²⁰ "'And if he pushed him of hatred, or threw something at him lying in wait and *as a result* he died,

²¹ or if he struck him down with his hand in enmity, and *as a result* he died, the one who struck him shall surely be put to death, he is a murderer; the blood avenger shall put the murderer to death when he meets him.

²² "'But if he pushed him suddenly without enmity, or threw something at him without lying in wait,

²³ or with any deadly object of stone, and without seeing it dropped on him so that he died, while he was not his enemy nor seeking his injury,

²⁴ then the congregation shall judge between the slayer and the blood avenger according to these ordinances.

²⁵ "'And the congregation shall deliver the manslayer from the hand of the blood avenger, and the congregation shall restore him to his city of refuge to which he fled; and he shall live in it until the death of the high priest who was anointed with the holy oil.

³⁰ "'If anyone kills a person, the murderer shall be put to death at the evidence of witnesses, but no person shall be put to death on the testimony of one witness.

[31] "'Moreover, you shall not take ransom for the life of a murderer who is guilty of death, but he shall surely be put to death.

[33] "'So you shall not pollute the land in which you are; for blood pollutes the land and no expiation can be made for the land for the blood that is shed on it, except by the blood of him who shed it.'"

According to what you have just read:
1. What does murder do to the land?

2. What is the only expiation (full payment) that can be made when someone is murdered? What did God forbid in this respect.?

In explaining the word *gā'al,* the *Theological Wordbook of the Old Testament* states, "The root is used to refer to the next of kin who is the 'avenger of blood'...for a murdered man. The full phrase 'avenger of blood' is almost always used (cf. Numbers 35:12ff). Apparently the idea is that the next of kin must effect the payment of life for life. As a house is repurchased or a slave redeemed by payment, so the lost life of the relative must be paid for by the equivalent life of the murderer. The kinsman is the avenger of blood. This system of execution must be distinguished from blood feuds for the *go'el* was a guiltless executioner and not to be murdered in turn."[2]

Now, how does our Lord Jesus Christ fulfill this fifth responsibility as our blood avenger? Satan led Adam and Eve into sin — and death. Satan deceived Eve. Eve believed his lie, ate of the fruit of the tree, and gave it to Adam. Adam ate it and died. With him all mankind died because mankind was in the loins of Adam.

Who instigated Adam's death? Satan. And what does Jesus say Satan is? In John 8:44 Jesus refers to Satan as a murderer — a murderer from the beginning. Therefore, shouldn't our Kinsman Redeemer avenge our blood by executing our murderer?

Remember Numbers 35:17, 19: "And if he struck him down with a stone in his hand, by which he may die, and *as a result* he died, he is a murderer; the murderer shall surely be put to death.... The blood avenger himself shall put the murderer to death; he shall put him to death when he meets him."

When our Kinsman Redeemer returns to earth, He'll meet the destroyer face to face, bind him for a thousand years, loose him for a short time, and then complete His duty as our blood avenger. Satan will be cast into the lake of fire lake prepared for the devil and his angels where he will be tormented forever and ever.

Yes, Beloved, God is just. The guilty will not go free, nor will their father, the devil. God will avenge us, but we are not to avenge ourselves.

As we read through the New Testament, we are told a number of times that we are not to take vengeance on another, nor are we to return evil with evil. God tells us instead to love our enemies, to do good to those who despitefully use us, and to turn the other cheek.

Does this mean that people, like Bruce, who become tools of Satan are to go free without punishment or judgment? Absolutely not. The law was made for "those who are lawless and rebellious, for the ungodly and sinners, for the unholy and profane, for those who kill their fathers or mothers, for murderers and immoral men and homosexuals and kidnappers and liars and perjurers, and whatever else is contrary to sound teaching, according to the glorious gospel of the blessed God, with which I have been entrusted" (1 Timothy 1:9–11).

We are to have laws in our land which deal with such transgressions. Laws should restrain man's ungodly behavior. However, as you know, such men and women are many times allowed to go free, often to the jeopardy of the innocent. Will justice never be executed in their lives? Oh, yes! Our Kinsman Redeemer is a righteous judge. The Lord will "execute judgment

upon all, and…convict all the ungodly of all their ungodly deeds which they
have done in an ungodly way, and of all the harsh things which ungodly sinners have spoken against Him" (Jude 15). His day of judgment is coming, a
day when He will judge the world in righteousness and truth.

That's what we must — and can — rest in.

> Never pay back evil for evil to anyone. Respect what is right in the sight
> of all men. If possible, so far as it depends on you, be at peace with all
> men. Never take your own revenge, beloved, but leave room for the
> wrath *of God,* for it is written, "VENGEANCE IS MINE, I WILL REPAY,"
> says the Lord. "BUT IF YOUR ENEMY IS HUNGRY, FEED HIM, AND IF HE
> IS THIRSTY, GIVE HIM A DRINK; FOR IN SO DOING YOU WILL HEAP
> BURNING COALS UPON HIS HEAD." Do not be overcome by evil, but
> overcome evil with good. (Romans 12:17–21)

> …but to those who are selfishly ambitious and do not obey the truth,
> but obey unrighteousness, wrath and indignation. *There will be* tribula-
> tion and distress for every soul of man who does evil, of the Jew first and
> also of the Greek, but glory and honor and peace to every man who
> does good, to the Jew first and also to the Greek. For there is no partial-
> ity with God. (Romans 2:8–11)

1. Have you been wounded, hurt, abused, mistreated, or destroyed by
someone's murderous tongue? How have you responded to your enemy?
Write it out.

2. How does God say you are to respond? List your observations.

3. What would keep you from doing this?

4. What is God's assurance in regard to your enemies?

5. How are you going to live?

Rest, Beloved, your Kinsman Redeemer is coming soon to fulfill His responsibility — a responsibility He will fulfill in absolute righteousness.

DAY   THREE

We now come to the sixth responsibility for the kinsman redeemer: *the kinsman's responsibility and authority to redeem the land and remove all squatters and invaders.* The significance of this in spiritual warfare is enlightening.

Read Leviticus 25:23–25 and mark any reference to the kinsman redeemer.

23 The land, moreover, shall not be sold permanently, for the land is Mine; for you are *but* aliens and sojourners with Me.

24 Thus for every piece of your property, you are to provide for the redemption of the land.

25 If a fellow countryman of yours becomes so poor he has to sell part of his property, then his nearest kinsman is to come and buy back what his relative has sold.

When Adam and Eve sinned, the serpent gained not only dominion over mankind but rulership over the earth. The power and authority which rightfully belonged to Adam and Eve was forfeited to the one who now ruled over them (Genesis 1:26–28). That's why Satan is referred to as the god and ruler of this world, as you'll see in the following verses. You may want to mark them in your Bible with that symbolic red pitchfork.

"I will not speak much more with you, for the ruler of the world is coming, and he has nothing in Me" (John 14:30). "Now judgment is upon this world; now the ruler of this world shall be cast out" (John 12:31).

"And even if our gospel is veiled, it is veiled to those who are perishing, in whose case the god of this world has blinded the minds of the unbelieving, that they might not see the light of the gospel of the glory of Christ, who is the image of God" (2 Corinthians 4:3–4). "World" in this passage could be translated "age."

Yes, Satan is the ruler of this world, but know this, it's a temporary position. We have a Kinsman Redeemer who has the power and authority to remove and clean out all squatters and invaders from the land that once belonged to his kinsman. If it was the responsibility of the kinsman redeemer to repossess an inheritance sold because of debt, it would only be assumed that once the *gō'ēl* took back the land, he would also have the necessary power and authority to rid the land of all invaders or squatters.

Follow me closely. We need to go back to Genesis 3 again. Remember the prophecy of Genesis 3:15? Not only was the serpent to bruise the heel of the woman's seed, but the woman's seed was to crush Satan's head. When did this crushing take place, or is it yet to happen?

Although we have not yet seen the full ramifications of the crushing of the serpent's head, I believe the death blow was delivered at Calvary. You may disagree, but bear with me for a few minutes while I tell you why I believe Satan's head was crushed at Calvary. If his head was crushed at Calvary, you and I have a mighty weapon at our disposal in this warfare with our enemy.

A blow to the head is a strike at the place of authority and power. Throughout His ministry, Jesus said, "My hour has not yet come." However, six days before the final Passover, Jesus said to His disciples,

> "The hour has come for the Son of Man to be glorified. Truly, truly, I say to you, unless a grain of wheat falls into the earth and dies, it remains by itself alone; but if it dies, it bears much fruit. He who loves his life loses it; and he who hates his life in this world shall keep it to life eternal. If anyone serves Me, let him follow Me; and where I am, there shall My servant also be; if anyone serves Me, the Father will honor him. Now My soul has become troubled; and what shall I say, 'Father, save Me from this hour'? But for this purpose I came to this hour. Father, glorify Thy name." There came therefore a voice out of heaven: "I have both glorified it, and will glorify it again." The multitude therefore, who stood by and heard it, were saying that it had thundered; others were saying, "An angel has spoken to Him." Jesus answered and said, "This voice has not come for My sake, but for your sakes. Now judgment is upon this world; now the ruler of this world shall be cast out. And I, if I be lifted up from the earth, will draw all men to Myself." But He was saying this to indicate the kind of death by which He was to die. (John 12:23–33)

1. Why did Jesus use the illustration of the grain of wheat? What do you think He was telling His disciples?

2. What hour was Jesus talking about?

3. When Jesus talked about being lifted up and all men being drawn to Him, what was He speaking of?

4. Write down everything you learn about the "ruler of this world" from this passage.

What your Blood Avenger began at Calvary, He will fully execute when He reclaims the earth, rids it of all its squatters, and casts Satan into the lake of fire!

<hr>

DAY FOUR

Colossians tells us that all the fullness of Deity dwelt in bodily form in Jesus Christ, that He is the "head over all rule and authority," and that we are complete in Him. After Paul made this statement in Colossians 2:9–10, he went on to explain what Christ accomplished in His death, burial, and resurrection and what it means to those who are "in Him."

Quickly review what you saw yesterday in John 12 so that you can compare it with Colossians 2:11–15 which follows.

And in Him you were also circumcised with a circumcision made without hands, in the removal of the body of the flesh by the circumcision of Christ; having been buried with Him in baptism, in which you were also raised up with Him through faith in the working of God, who raised Him from the dead. And when you were dead in your transgressions and the uncircumcision of your flesh, He made you alive together with Him, having forgiven us all our transgressions, having canceled out the certificate of debt consisting of decrees against us *and* which was hostile to us; and He has taken it out of the way, having nailed it to the cross. When He had disarmed the rulers and authorities, He made a public display of them, having triumphed over them through Him.

Besides revealing the mystery of the church, Jew and Gentile in one body, Paul was also given the awesome privilege of understanding and explaining another mystery hidden from past ages and generations — the mystery of "Christ in you, the hope of glory" (Colossians 1:26–27).

In the revelation of this mystery, Paul assures us that when Christ died on the cross, all our sins were forgiven. This truth is critical because it's through sin that Satan gains power over us.

Until Calvary, Satan had the power of death. Remember Hebrews 2 tells us that Jesus became flesh and blood in order to die for us so "that through death He might render powerless him who had the power of death, that is, the devil" (Hebrews 2:14b). The power of death was the authority to hold us in sin's consequence, which is eternal punishment and separation from God.

Our Kinsman Redeemer is capable of recovering all that we lost because He took care of that which gave Satan control over us — *sin!* At the moment Jesus cried, "MY GOD, MY GOD, WHY HAST THOU FORSAKEN ME?" all the sins of mankind were transferred to the head of the sinless Lamb of God. Jesus was made sin for you. Your sin separated Him from God. God sacrificed His Lamb and shed His blood. Through Jesus' one sacrifice, our sins were covered once for all time (Hebrews 10:8–12).

When you take God at His Word and accept Jesus' sacrifice for your sins and, in faith, confess with your mouth Jesus as Lord and believe in your heart that God raised Him from the dead, you are saved. Jesus' death takes away Satan's power of death over you because you have received forgiveness of sins and, thus, eternal life. At that moment you pass from death to life. "But now having been freed from sin and enslaved to God, you derive your benefit, resulting in sanctification, and the outcome, eternal life. For the wages of sin is death, but the free gift of God is eternal life in Christ Jesus our Lord" (Romans 6:22–23).

Colossians 2:13–14 says that at that moment God forgave "us all our transgressions, having canceled out the certificate of debt consisting of decrees against us *and* which was hostile to us; and He has taken it out of the way, having nailed it to the cross."

And what does this mean to you? Your sin was paid for in full at Calvary! Satan's power over you has been destroyed! Satan no longer has legitimate authority over you. Why? *Your debt of sin has been paid for in full!*

Now, let me take it one step further. Remember that we are looking at the work of our Kinsman Redeemer. When the kinsman redeemer buys back the family property, he has the power and authority to remove and clean out all squatters and invaders from the land! Colossians 2:15 says, "When He had disarmed the rulers and authorities, He made a public display of them, having triumphed over them through Him."

O Beloved, do you see it? Not only did Jesus pay for your sins in full, but He also triumphed over Satan and all his demonic rulers and authorities. The enemy is defeated…and he knows it.

Throughout the Gospels, the demons recognized Jesus as "the Son of the Most High God." When they came face to face with Jesus, they cried out from the bodies they inhabited, "'What do I have to do with You, Jesus, Son of the Most High God? I implore You by God, do not torment me!' For He had been saying to him, 'Come out of the man, you unclean spirit'" (Mark 5:7–8). They were squatters, holding captive men and women Jesus had come to set free. So He cast them out. Why? How? Hear His words, "But if I cast out demons by the Spirit of God, then the kingdom of God has come upon you" (Matthew 12:28).

The demons knew the time was coming when Jesus would remove *all* demonic squatters and usurpers from God's creation and all His enemies would become a footstool for His feet (Psalm 110:1; 1 Corinthians 15:25–28). The mention of being under someone's feet was symbolic of total conquest. When His enemies are His footstool, the devil and his angels, *along with death,* will all be cast into the lake of fire (Matthew 25:41; Revelation 20:10, 14) and the kingdom will be delivered up to God the Father!

Satan and his host recognize the power and authority of Jesus Christ.

The question is, Do we? Do the demons believe and tremble before God while we doubt His Word and tremble before demons? If so, what shame!

What are we as members of Christ to do when we meet the demons of hell? We're to remember that they're squatters and that our Kinsman Redeemer has come. Remember that their power has been broken. Don't fear. Remember where you're seated, and simply ask Jesus what to do. He'll show you.

DAY FIVE

Have you ever wondered what it will be like when our Kinsman Redeemer stands as the just Avenger of His kinsman and begins His final cleansing of the earth? Revelation gives us an account of the finish of Satan and sin.

Revelation 5:1–14; 6:1 is printed out for you. As you read it carefully, you might want to mark in distinctive ways every reference to *Lamb* and every reference to *book*, which could be translated *scroll*.

➤ REVELATION 5:1–14; 6:1

¹ And I saw in the right hand of Him who sat on the throne a book written inside and on the back, sealed up with seven seals.

² And I saw a strong angel proclaiming with a loud voice, "Who is worthy to open the book and to break its seals?"

³ And no one in heaven, or on the earth, or under the earth, was able to open the book, or to look into it.

⁴ And I *began* to weep greatly, because no one was found worthy to open the book, or to look into it;

⁵ and one of the elders said to me, "Stop weeping; behold, the Lion that is from the tribe of Judah, the Root of David, has overcome so as to open the book and its seven seals."

⁶ And I saw between the throne (with the four living creatures) and the

elders a Lamb standing, as if slain, having seven horns and seven eyes, which are the seven Spirits of God, sent out into all the earth.

7 And He came, and He took *it* out of the right hand of Him who sat on the throne.

8 And when He had taken the book, the four living creatures and the twenty-four elders fell down before the Lamb, having each one a harp, and golden bowls full of incense, which are the prayers of the saints.

9 And they sang a new song, saying, "Worthy art Thou to take the book, and to break its seals; for Thou wast slain, and didst purchase [*agorazo* — buy at a marketplace, to redeem] for God with Thy blood *men* from every tribe and tongue and people and nation.

10 "And Thou hast made them *to be* a kingdom and priests to our God; and they will reign upon the earth."

11 And I looked, and I heard the voice of many angels around the throne and the living creatures and the elders; and the number of them was myriads of myriads, and thousands of thousands,

12 saying with a loud voice, "Worthy is the Lamb that was slain to receive power and riches and wisdom and might and honor and glory and blessing."

13 And every created thing which is in heaven and on the earth and under the earth and on the sea, and all things in them, I heard saying, "To Him who sits on the throne, and to the Lamb, *be* blessing and honor and glory and dominion forever and ever."

14 And the four living creatures kept saying, "Amen." And the elders fell down and worshiped.

6:1 And I saw when the Lamb broke one of the seven seals, and I heard one of the four living creatures saying as with a voice of thunder, "Come."

1. List everything you learn about the Lamb from this passage.

2. Now list everything you learned about the book or scroll.

3. Finally, compare this scroll or book with Jeremiah 32:6–15, 44, which is printed out below. Mark every reference to the *deed* or *deed of purchase* and every use of the word *redemption*.

➤ JEREMIAH 32:6–15, 44

6 And Jeremiah said, "The word of the LORD came to me, saying,

7 'Behold, Hanamel the son of Shallum your uncle is coming to you, saying, "Buy for yourself my field which is at Anathoth, for you have the right of redemption to buy *it*."'

8 "Then Hanamel my uncle's son came to me in the court of the guard according to the word of the LORD, and said to me, 'Buy my field, please, that is at Anathoth, which is in the land of Benjamin; for you have the right of possession and the redemption is yours; buy *it* for yourself.' Then I knew that this was the word of the LORD.

9 "And I bought the field which was at Anathoth from Hanamel my uncle's son, and I weighed out the silver for him, seventeen shekels of silver.

10 "And I signed and sealed the deed, and called in witnesses, and weighed out the silver on the scales.

11 "Then I took the deeds of purchase, both the sealed *copy containing* the terms and conditions, and the open *copy;*

12 and I gave the deed of purchase to Baruch the son of Neriah, the son of Mahseiah, in the sight of Hanamel my uncle's *son,* and in the sight of the witnesses who signed the deed of purchase, before all the Jews who were sitting in the court of the guard.

13 "And I commanded Baruch in their presence, saying,

14 'Thus says the LORD of hosts, the God of Israel, "Take these deeds, this sealed deed of purchase, and this open deed, and put them in an earthenware jar, that they may last a long time."

15 'For thus says the LORD of hosts, the God of Israel, "Houses and fields and vineyards shall again be bought in this land."'

44 "'Men shall buy fields for money, sign and seal deeds, and call in witnesses in the land of Benjamin, in the environs of Jerusalem, in the cities of Judah, in the cities of the hill country, in the cities of the lowland, and in the cities of the Negev; for I will restore their fortunes,' declares the LORD."

What similarities do you see, if any, in Jeremiah and Revelation? Note them, and we'll take up from here tomorrow.

D A Y   S I X

As I read Revelation 4 and 5, I'm enthralled by the glimpse of our Father and the cry of worship as the twenty-four elders cast their crowns at His feet. Once again I am reminded of the purpose of my existence. "Worthy art Thou, our Lord and our God, to receive glory and honor and power; for Thou didst create all things, and because of Thy will they existed, and were created" (Revelation 4:11).

Yet praise is followed by pathos. As you see the scroll in the right hand of God, you hear the angel's cry of anguish, "Who is worthy to open the book [scroll] and to break its seals?" (Revelation 5:2).

What is sealed in the scroll? What difference does it make that it can't be opened? I believe that the scroll is the title deed, or as Jeremiah puts it, "the deed of purchase" to the earth. Remember, "the earth *is* the LORD's and the fulness thereof" (KJV). Thus, it is God's prerogative to give it to whomever He wishes, and that's what He did when He created man. Mankind was given custody of the earth, even as God later gave the Israelites custody of the land of Canaan.

Let's look at Israel's custody of Canaan in order to see a beautiful picture of the Kinsman Redeemer's relationship to His inheritance.

Because of repeated sin and rebellion, God expelled Israel from their land. Assyrians, Babylonians, Medes, Persians, Greeks, Romans, Crusaders, Turks, Arabs, and British usurpers would at one time or another occupy the land which once belonged to the nation of Israel.

Yet, we know from the Bible that God is going to redeem Canaan and give it back to Israel, just as He covenanted with Abraham. That's what God was confirming to Jeremiah when his uncle gave him the right of redemption. God told Jeremiah to exercise his right as kinsman redeemer and purchase the land even though he knew the Babylonians were going to capture Judah and Jerusalem.

"'Buy for yourself the field with money, and call in witnesses' — although the city is given into the hand of the Chaldeans [Babylonians].... For thus says the LORD of hosts, the God of Israel, 'Houses and fields and vineyards shall again be bought in this land'" (Jeremiah 32:25, 15).

But that was not all. Listen! "Behold, I am the LORD, the God of all flesh; is anything too difficult for Me?" (Jeremiah 32:27) No, Lord, no! Nothing is too difficult for Thee.

The deed was signed, sealed, and put in an earthenware jar so it would last a long time. God was showing Jeremiah that He would eventually bring His people back to the land that was His and theirs. And, when He brought them back, He would clean out all the squatters and invaders. Further, He would punish those who had murdered the people of His chosen nation.

What we see in Jeremiah is just a foretaste of what our Kinsman Redeemer, the Lord Jesus Christ, is going to do when He returns as King of kings and Lord of lords. O Beloved, are you distressed at the seeming victories of the evil one and all his satanic host? Are you distressed because of stories like the one we read at the first of the week?

Do you ever have thoughts like *If God is all powerful and sovereign, why doesn't He put a stop to all the rebellion, crime, and bloodshed?* Do you wonder why He doesn't call a halt on drugs, alcohol, and all sorts of immorality and perversion? Do you have a hard time understanding why He allows evil men to rule and ungodly nations to persecute His people?

Do you weep over history? Do you fear what is yet to come and wonder where it all will end?

Weep not, Beloved! Look! There is One standing in the midst of the Throne of God, in the midst of the living creatures and the twenty-four elders. It's the Lion from the tribe of Judah, the root of David. It's your Kinsman Redeemer who has overcome!

The Lion is the Lamb, bearing in His body the marks of Calvary — marks which give eternal testimony that through redemption in His blood, He has crushed the head of the serpent. The deceiver who usurped man's dominion is about to be evicted from the heavens and earth with all his demonic host because the Lamb is approaching the throne to take the title deed of the earth and break the seals.

Worthy is He to take the scroll and to break its seals because He was slain, and He redeemed for God, with His blood, men from every tribe and tongue and people and nation. And those He has redeemed, He has made to be a kingdom of priests unto our God; and they will reign on earth (Revelation 5:9–10).

O Beloved, put away your questions, your doubts. Weep not. Your redemption draweth nigh. The scroll will soon be opened, and the earth will be cleansed from all the ungodly deeds of ungodly men. Jesus, our Blood Avenger, will come to execute vengeance upon those who "do not know God and...who do not obey the gospel of our Lord Jesus. And these will pay the penalty of eternal destruction, away from the presence of the Lord and away from the glory of His power, when He comes to be glorified in His saints on that day, and to be marveled at among all who have believed" (2 Thessalonians 1:8–10).

How will He rid the earth of its usurpers and squatters? It is all recorded in Revelation 6–20. The breaking of the seals begins the cleansing process.

Then "the devil who deceived them [will be] thrown into the lake of fire and brimstone, where the beast and the false prophet are also; and they will be tormented day and night forever and ever" (Revelation 20:10). Our Kinsman Redeemer will have fulfilled His last two responsibilities as our *gō'ēl!* He will avenge the death of the saints, and He will cast all those who rejected Him into the lake of fire with the devil and his angels.

Hallelujah to the Lamb! Our Blood Avenger has triumphed!

·D A Y   S E V E N

Jesus was worthy to open the title deed to the earth for one reason: Although He was a man, He never sinned.

Redemption, with all its benefits, could not be ours until the son of Man was tempted by the devil, just as Adam was. How crucial that we understand this truth!

There are two fundamental doctrines that the enemy seeks to twist because they are so critical to salvation: the deity of Jesus Christ and the humanity of Jesus Christ.

Satan hates the deity of Jesus Christ because it places Jesus outside and above the realm of created man. However, the incarnation of Deity makes our redemption possible. Of course, for this reason, Satan did all he could to annihilate the woman's seed. When man sinned, only a sinless man could redeem man.

Yet, as I've shared, there existed no man outside of the realm of sin. Every human being could trace his genealogy to Adam. Therefore, all lived under the federal headship of Adam until God, in His grace, sent His Son. The Son who was fully God came to earth to become fully man!

When Jesus became fully man, He too had to be tempted by the devil just as Adam was. If Jesus never yielded, He would remain without sin and, thus, be offered as the Lamb of God, unblemished and spotless, to redeem us from sin — and, if from sin, then from death. If man was redeemed from sin and death, then man would be delivered from Satan's power and kingdom!

Since the temptation of Jesus is critical to man's redemption, we need to examine it carefully. Besides establishing a correct doctrine on Jesus' temptation, there are principles in this passage which the Lord will use to teach us more about standing victoriously in warfare.

The devil first tempted Jesus after He was baptized by John the Baptist in the Jordan River and the Spirit of God descended on Him in the form of a dove. Let's look at it and see what we can learn about the devil and his tactics.

➤ MATTHEW 4:1–11

1 Then Jesus was led up by the Spirit into the wilderness to be tempted by the devil.

2 And after He had fasted forty days and forty nights, He then became hungry.

3 And the tempter came and said to Him, "If You are the Son of God, command that these stones become bread."

4 But He answered and said, "It is written, 'MAN SHALL NOT LIVE ON BREAD ALONE, BUT ON EVERY WORD THAT PROCEEDS OUT OF THE MOUTH OF GOD.'"

5 Then the devil took Him into the holy city; and he had Him stand on the pinnacle of the temple,

6 and said to Him, "If You are the Son of God throw Yourself down; for it is written,
'HE WILL GIVE HIS ANGELS CHARGE CONCERNING YOU';
and
'ON *their* HANDS THEY WILL BEAR YOU UP,
LEST YOU STRIKE YOUR FOOT AGAINST A STONE.'"

7 Jesus said to him, "On the other hand, it is written, 'YOU SHALL NOT PUT THE LORD YOUR GOD TO THE TEST.'"

8 Again, the devil took Him to a very high mountain, and showed Him all the kingdoms of the world, and their glory;

9 and he said to Him, "All these things will I give You, if You fall down and worship me."

10 Then Jesus said to him, "Begone, Satan! For it is written, 'YOU SHALL WORSHIP THE LORD YOUR GOD, AND SERVE HIM ONLY.'"

[11] Then the devil left Him; and behold, angels came and *began* to minister to Him.

1. Now go back and mark the following words and their pronouns, each in a distinctive way, so you can easily note their repeated use:
   a. Jesus and every term and/or pronoun used for Him
   b. THE LORD YOUR GOD
   c. devil and every term and/or pronoun used for him
   d. It is written

2. In what ways did the devil tempt Jesus? What kind of motive or action would be behind yielding to each of these temptations?

3. When the devil tempted Jesus in these ways, were they far-fetched temptations, unrealistic, or could they really happen? Explain your answer.

4. If Jesus had yielded to any of these three temptations, would there have been temporal benefits? Explain the benefit for each temptation.

5. If Jesus had yielded to any or to all three, how would it have affected His relationship with God?

6. How did Jesus handle the devil in each of these situations? Can you learn anything from His example that you could apply to your own life? Explain your answer.

7. How did Jesus finally get rid of the devil?

Just as Satan tried to get Adam and Eve to act independently of God, so he tried the same thing with the Son of Man. When he told Jesus to turn the stones into bread in order to satisfy His hunger, the devil was suggesting that Jesus could be like God, that He did not need to be dependent upon the Father. He was tempting Him to satisfy His own hunger, by His own power.

It was almost as if the devil was once again accusing God as he did with Eve — "God knows that in the day you eat from this tree." In other words, he was telling Eve: "God is holding out on you!" The devil was implying the same thing when he tempted Jesus. He insinuated that God was denying Him the staple of life. He suggested that Jesus ought to make His own bread.

Jesus could have done it. He was God. He had the power. The problem was Jesus knew He could not act independently of the Father. He was always and only to do those things which pleased the Father. He was to live by every word which came from the mouth of God. He was to walk by the Spirit, even as man is to walk by the Spirit. The flesh with its desires was never to control Him, rather He was to control the flesh, just as man is to control his flesh by the spirit. Adam was supposed to behave in this same way, but he didn't. Jesus did!

Sin has its roots in independent action. When we choose to walk independently of God and His Word, we fall into sin. And, when we fall into sin, we are headed for the snare of the devil, unless we repent and confess our sin (2 Timothy 2:26). O Beloved, if only we understood that it is unforsaken sin in the life of the believer that gives Satan a "hold!" If we could truly comprehend the truth of that reality we would quickly flee our youthful lusts!

Satan wants his throne above God's and above the host of heaven. If the Son would worship him, his throne would be above the Most High's. When Satan offered Jesus all the kingdoms of this world, he wasn't making an empty offer. Satan's fallen angels influenced earthly kingdoms as rulers, authorities, and powers. As Satan pointed out in what he said in Luke 4:6, the kingdoms of the world were handed over to him. He could give them to whomever he wished. Now he was offering them to Jesus. If the Son worshiped him, Satan would finally have what he wanted — a throne above God's.

Satan was not lying or exaggerating, nor did Jesus accuse him of such. Jesus knew that when Satan snared Adam, he gained rulership of the world. But Jesus would get it back — not for himself, but for His kinsmen.

In order to win the rulership of earth, Jesus had to submit to God. He had to resist the devil and draw near to God. That He would do! The last Adam would win back what the first Adam lost. There would be a new federal head for all who wished to be set free from sin and death. Our Kinsman Redeemer would see to that (1 Corinthians 15:45–49). Jesus used the one and only offensive weapon He needed — the sword of the Word of God.

Yet the enemy was not to be outdone! He drew the sword also. You could hear the clash of metal on metal, until with one final thrust the devil was sent on his way — until another time.

No appeal to the flesh and its ego would trap Jesus. He knew who He was. He did not have to prove His identity to Satan by throwing Himself off the high pinnacle of the temple. God would justify who He was when the time came. His faith was in His Father. And there it would remain, even when men would say that God had forsaken Him by abandoning Him to Calvary's tree.

The federal head of a new race had not yet yielded. For the time being the temptation was done. Jesus was the Conqueror, and as the Conqueror, He said, "Begone Satan." And Satan had to leave!

That same Jesus with that same authority is in you, Beloved. Do you believe that? Then live as He lived, do as He did. Walk in His authority!

Write out your prayer of affirmation in light of what your Kinsman Redeemer has done in regard to the enemy.

LORD, HOW DO I PUT ON THE ARMOR? BELT ON TRUTH?

M any times beneath surface appearances an unseen, but very real, spiritual battle rages. If you've moved in Christian circles, you've heard we have three enemies: the world, the flesh, and the devil. And this is true. However, the three form a coalition, and Satan is the mastermind.

This coalition was formed when Adam and Eve listened to the serpent in the Garden of Eden. As we discussed, the kingdoms of this world and their glory were handed over to Satan when Adam and Eve disobeyed. The world became our enemy — an enemy that wants to squeeze us into its mold. Thus, God says we're not to be "conformed to this world, but be transformed by the renewing of your mind" (Romans 12:2). Remember that you deal with the world by knowing God's Word and refusing to conform to the world's pressures.

And what about the flesh? The minute Adam bit the fruit, the flesh became Satan's cohort. Before we were saved, we walked according to our flesh, indulging its desires (Ephesians 2:1–3). However, when the Holy Spirit takes up residence within us, the battle begins. How is the battle won?

Galatians 5:16 says if we walk by the Spirit, we will not fulfill the lusts of the flesh. Please note that it does not say that the flesh will *not* lust. The flesh is the flesh! It has not been redeemed. It will always lust. However, when the Holy Spirit is in control, He enables us to override the desires of our flesh.

As I said, the brain behind this coalition is Satan. He governs the world and, as the tempter, appeals to the desires of our flesh. When you meet the devil, you must resist him. We'll see the how of all this in detail as we move through these last critical chapters of our study. (By the way — the study just gets better and better and more and more practical. Press on! You'll be so thankful you persevered.)

At this point you need to read Ephesians 4–6 printed in the back of the book. It will give you a context for what we'll study next.

Now let me recap Ephesians. In the first three chapters, Paul explains the relationship and position of a person saved by grace. When we are saved, each of us becomes a member of Christ's body, forged with resurrection power, and seated with Him in heavenly places above all rule, power, and authority. Nothing can alter our position. It is set forever in heaven. But position is one thing; living accordingly is another.

In the last three chapters of Ephesians, Paul tells us how we are to "flesh out" these positional truths in the daily arena of life. Although we're seated in the heavenlies, we still live on earth in bodies of flesh — bodies with very real appetites that we're not to succumb to. We are to walk in a manner worthy of God's calling upon our lives.

We are members of a new family, composed of Jews and Gentiles. This family adds new members daily and, therefore, is at various levels of maturity and Christlikeness. Unity in the midst of diversity is crucial, and, thus, Paul urges us to walk in a love that covers.

We must remember we've put off the old self. We are not to participate in its unfruitful deeds of darkness. The days are evil — and short. We must be careful how we walk. As husbands, wives, children, parents, employers, and/or employees who belong to the Lord Jesus Christ, we should be filled with the Spirit and treat one another properly.

And finally, although we are seated above the enemy, we're in an ever-present warfare. Some skirmishes are worse than others. So, we need to stand firm in the Lord and put on the whole armor of God so that we can resist the devil.

D A Y   T W O

We long for peace, for tranquillity. Yet if there has to be war, we'll do anything to avoid hand-to-hand combat. Better an air battle than a ground war! Just bomb the enemy forces, destroy their weapons, and get out of there. Make it short! Although this type of combat may be our hope in spiritual warfare, it's not realistic.

Until Jesus comes, we'll be in a relentless struggle. This struggle is summed up by Paul's use of the Greek word *palē*. This word indicates a hand-to-hand fight, wrestling. Paul says, "we wrestle not against flesh and blood but against principalities." We are in a hand-to-hand combat with the enemy. "Wrestling was a fight characterized by trickery, cunningness, and strategy."[1] The enemy has three objectives in this combat.

First, he wants to destroy our unity with God, with the body of Christ, and with our families. If Apollyon, the destroyer, can persuade us that we are cut off from the Father, where is our hope, our power? If God has abandoned us, we might as well give up.

How often I have seen the demoralizing effects of these devilish tactics! People write to me in anguish, feeling that they have blasphemed the Holy Spirit and are cut off from God forever. They disregard His promise that the One who comes to Him will never be cast away but will be raised up in that last day to live with Him forever (John 6:37, 39, 44). They buy a lie from the enemy. Instead of clinging to the whole teaching of the Word, they take this one verse on blaspheming the Holy Spirit and run with it — right into the arms of despair. And Satan shrieks with delight. He has them right where he wants them — in unbelief.

Satan also uses a lack of assurance of salvation to "separate" us from God. I'm not saying you don't need to examine yourself to make sure that you are really in the faith. A changed life testifies to this reality. I'm talking about people who have repented and believed in Jesus Christ and whose lives give evidence that they have become new creatures. Yet they are plagued with doubts — doubts about their sincerity, doubts about God's mercy and grace in their situation. They depend on their feelings — and they don't feel saved.

Beloved, if you are being tormented in these areas, do what James 4:5–7 says: *Submit to God.* Verbalize your desire to belong to His kingdom of righteousness. Agree with Him regarding your sinfulness and inability to please Him. Thank Him for His mercy and grace. Tell Him how grateful you are that He's not willing that any should perish but that all should come to repentance. Tell Him that you have repented, that you want to belong to Him, that you live to do His will. Confess these things audibly.

Then, *resist the devil.* Command him aloud in the name and authority of Jesus Christ to be gone. Jesus said, "Begone, Satan." Do the same. Then draw near to God. Read Ephesians 1–3, and turn it into a prayer of thanksgiving. Pray those chapters aloud to God, and thank Him in faith that these truths are "yea and amen." If any doubts come to you later, simply refuse them in the name of Jesus Christ. Resist the devil, and he will flee from you.

If the enemy is attacking you in the area of your oneness with other believers or with family members, keep studying because we will touch on these areas later as we look at Paul's command to put on the sandals of peace.

Satan's *second* objective is to entice you to sin so that he can gain a place in your life as a child of God. We'll talk more about this wile of the enemy when we study the breastplate of righteousness. Simply remember that 1 John 3:8 says the devil has sinned habitually from the beginning. He wants you to do the same. Don't!

Satan's *third* objective is to lead you into false teaching. He will do everything he can to keep us from the light of truth and to lure us into greater darkness. We see him escalating his efforts to capture the minds of our children.

While I was writing this book, I received a call from Nancy Schaeffer, the head of Moral Concerns in Atlanta, Georgia. She called to tell me that I'd been on her heart and that the Lord had her interceding for me. As she learned of the warfare involved in writing this book, she understood why she had called. She, too, had been in the midst of battle. At the time she called, Georgia's textbook committee was considering using a reading series called "Impressions" as required reading for kindergarten through sixth grade. Moral Concerns played a major role in opposing "Impressions." Twenty-two of the 822 stories in this series mention things related to witchcraft. I am horrified as I see the enemy's strategy to teach these children lies and lead them into the occult. Each of these reading series has a teacher's project book. In the *Fourth Grade Teacher's Project Book* the teacher is told to "form small groups of sorcerers."

The project book for "Cross the Golden River" gives instructions on page seventy-nine for casting a spell. "There are some spells that a sorcerer might need to get out of difficulties or overcome opponents.... Zan, for example, is an extremely powerful weapon. This spell creates a blast of lightning that shoots from the caster's hand which must be pointed in the desired direction. It is effective against virtually all living creatures that have no magical defenses but it takes great strength and concentration to use."

Among the second graders' stories is "The Hairy Toe," which tells of an old woman who finds a hairy toe in her garden, boils it, and eats it. Then while she's sleeping, a creature comes into her house looking for its toe. There's also "The Seven Ravens," which tells of a little girl who takes a knife, cuts off her finger, and sticks it into a key hole to open a door.

Satan is after the children — the future of our nation. Satan is a liar who doesn't abide in truth. He doesn't want you to either! We'll look at this when we study the belt of truth next week. However, let me simply remind you that the devil would either like to keep you blind regarding his existence and activity or take you to the other extreme where he becomes your focus rather than the Lord Jesus Christ. He loves it when you see him in everything, when you credit him with all your problems, and when you ascribe to him all of your defeats. He likes you to attribute all sorts of power to him so that you live in fear of him rather than in reverence and awesome respect of God. That's why Jesus told us not to fear the one who is able to kill the body but to fear Him who is able to cast both body and soul into hell.

There's one thing I want you to do, and then we'll call it a day. Read through Ephesians 6:10–18 and then list below Paul's specific instructions in regard to warfare.

DAY   THREE

When Paul instructs us to be strong in the Lord and in the strength of His might, he takes us full circle in his warfare terminology. Remember when we looked at Ephesians 1:19 where Paul used the Greek words *dunamis, kratos,* and *ischus* in reference to God's resurrection power? Again in Ephesians 6:10 he uses the same trio of words. "Be strong" is the word *empowered* which contains *dunamis,* while *kratos* is translated *strength* and *ischus* is translated *might.* Paul was using the same terms the magicians used to describe their power. If Christians understand their source of true power, they won't have to fear any secondary power.

As Paul closes his epistle, he reminds us of our inevitable warfare. He doesn't want us to think we're to operate in our own might or power.

Paul prays earnestly in Ephesians 1:15–23 and 3:14–21 that we would recognize the resurrection power that is ours. He then goes on to command us to act accordingly, to be strong in the Lord. He also instructs us to put on the full armor of God and to stand firm.

Paul wrote Ephesians while he was a prisoner of Rome, chained to a Roman soldier. Although the soldier assigned to him was probably not dressed in his full armor, Paul knew what battle dress was like and used those images to describe the Christian armor.

The English transliteration of the Greek word for "full armor" is *panoplia.* The armor consists of individual pieces collectively referred to as *hopla.* The minute you entered the kingdom of God, you were outfitted for battle. Each piece of your armor was provided in salvation. And although ultimate victory is secure, you must put on each piece of the armor if you're going to win the battle. Not a piece can be missing. Then, you must stand firm!

"Stand firm" was a military term which meant to hold one's position. Rienecker and Rogers say, "the word could be used in a military sense indicating either 'to take over,' 'to hold a watch post,' or it could also mean 'to stand and hold out in a critical position on a battlefield.'"[2] The term is used successively in chapter six verses 11, 13, and 14.

True to style, Paul first lays out doctrine and then follows it with duty. In order to study the meaning of "stand firm," I went back to the first three chapters of Ephesians, intent on discovering what Paul had to say about our position in Christ. I saw that I could describe our position with six S's that remind us of the essence of the position we hold.

1. We have been *selected* by God. We didn't volunteer to become His children. He chose us. That reality ought to put a "wow" in your heart! Look at Ephesians 1:4 and write it out. It will be good to rehearse the truth of it!

Now, whenever the enemy seeks to persuade you that you've been cut off from God, cut him down with the sword of this truth.

2. God not only selected you, He *saved* you. Write out Ephesians 1:7.

Because God redeemed you with the blood of His Son, you have for-giveness of sins. So if Satan threatens your life, you need to remind him that because you have been redeemed he no longer has the power of death over you (Hebrews 2:14). Remember that the devil can't do a thing to a child of God without God's permission. The same God who had a hedge around Job is able to keep one around you. And if He takes it away, it will be for your good and His glory. Rejoice, redeemed one, and stand firm!

3. You're *sealed.* Twice in Ephesians, God reminds you that you're sealed by the Holy Spirit. Look up 1:13 and 4:30, and write each out below.

Satan wants to demoralize you, to take away your hope of spending eternity with God. He wants you to doubt the security of your relationship to God. Don't forget, Beloved, "He who began a good work in you (salva-tion) will perfect it until the day of Christ Jesus" (Philippians 1:6). The day of Christ is the day you get your new, glorified body. Wrestle with him from this vantage point. The Holy Spirit is your source of the life of Jesus Christ. He's sealed you, guaranteeing your redemption.

4. Positionally, you are *seated.* You can probably tell me where by now without even looking it up. Write out Ephesians 2:6.

That's a good vantage point in war, isn't it!

5. You're *secure*. You'll always be seated "there"! Why? What are you that entitles you to this security? Look up Ephesians 2:19 and 3:6, and then write out these verses.

God's not going to amputate Jesus' arms, legs, or any member of His body, so hold that tiger — lion — at bay with this truth.

6. Your position is always one of *strength*. Strengthened by what? Look up Ephesians 3:16 and write it out.

You are to stand firm in these truths. Now, my friend, do you see why you don't have to give in, run away, or be pinned to the ground? Put on the full armor of God so that you will be able to resist and taste victory as you stand firm.

And if you don't resist, what can the devil do to a Christian? There's much debate about that — even division. The enemy loves it. And for this reason and because the Word of God is not definite on the subject, I refuse to allow this issue to separate me from fellowship with any member of the body of Christ. If we part company on the issue, it will be your decision, not mine.

The Word of God is not clear or dogmatic on the Christian's relationship to the devil. It is clear though regarding our position, and you will see too that there is definition as to the areas which he attacks. We'll see these as we look at the armor.

We have seen that practice does not always match position. The Word teaches that we are dead to sin; that we are freed from slavery to sin; and that if we walk in the Spirit, we will not sin. Yet, we sin. If we are truly His, sin is not a total habit of life. Yet Christians can get into some mighty nasty sins and stay in them for quite a while. Ephesians 4–5 spells out some of the things we can become involved in.

The Bible does present a tension between position and practice. The extent to which a Christian can be oppressed, tormented, or deceived by Satan is not defined. So I suggest you simply deal with the devil and his host as instructed in the Word of God or as modeled by Christ. Watch how He dealt with the enemy and remember His words: "He who believes in Me, the works that I do shall he do also; and greater *works* than these shall he do; because I go to the Father" (John 14:12). Operate within your realm of faith, and don't go beyond your measure of faith (Romans 12:3).

Let me hasten to add that although I teach people how to study the Word of God inductively — which is a skill not specified in the Word of God — I still believe truth is revealed. Interpretation cannot be reduced to a science!

We all have theological kinks in our armor. So be very careful in being dogmatic where God's Word isn't. And be careful of negating the experiences of others. Doctrine is never to be based on experience, but God's Word should speak to our experiences, either affirming or discrediting them.

DAY FOUR

He was a young pastor, determined to tell his church that there was nothing wrong with horoscopes and fortune-telling.

"I'll prove it to you. I'll have someone chart out my course according to my horoscope and tell my fortune. You'll see then."

In his zeal the pastor forgot his warfare was not with flesh and blood.

Even as the fortune-teller told him his future, he didn't believe what she was saying. But in the days which followed, he felt an oppression come over him. What he was told would come to pass began happening. In a short time he was a wreck.

Confused and not knowing what to do, he sought the counsel of an older and godly pastor who opened the Word and showed him what God had to say. The young pastor had opened the door to the enemy, and the world forces of darkness had moved in. Astrology is demonic. As he wept and confessed his sin, the oppression lifted as the enemy fled.

In Ephesians 6 Paul warns his readers that among Satan's hierarchy are "world forces of this darkness." Such a phrase would convict those enslaved in astrology.

> The word *kosmokratōres* was used in astrology of the planets which were thought to control the fate of mankind, in the Orphic Hymns of Zeus, in rabbinical writings of Nebuchadnezzar and other pagan monarchs, and in various ancient inscriptions of the Roman emperor. All these usages exemplify the notion of a worldwide rule.
>
> When applied to the powers of evil they are reminiscent of the devil's claim to be able to give Jesus 'all the kingdoms of the world', of the title 'the ruler of this world' which Jesus gave him, and of John's statement that 'the whole world is in the power of the evil one.' These texts do not deny our Lord's decisive conquest of the principalities and powers, but indicate that as usurpers they have not conceded defeat or been destroyed. So they continue to exercise considerable power.[3, 4]

Can you understand that when you get involved in astrology in any form — in horoscopes, in wearing astrological jewelry, in having signs of the zodiac on any object — you are giving ground to the enemy?

"But," you may say, "I read my horoscope, but I don't take it seriously. It's just for fun." To which I would reply, "But do you know for whose fun?" It's for the devil's, dear one. And I believe it opens the door to oppression from the enemy.

Look up Deuteronomy 17:2–7. List what God says about astrology and the consequences of participating in it.

Aren't you thankful that we live under grace? God's not going to have you stoned, but what should you do, my friend, if you have been involved in any form of astrology? (Of course, if you're not a child of God, you must first repent of your sin and receive the Lord Jesus Christ as your Savior and your God.)

1. Get rid of any books or articles that have anything to do with astrology. Don't give them to anyone else. Burn them or dispose of them as they did in Acts 19. It doesn't matter how valuable they may be, don't keep them. The value of the books that were burned in Ephesus was very great. Many in Ephesus would have purchased them or gladly received them as a gift, but instead they burned them.

2. Confess your sin to God. Name it for what it is. Tell God you repent — which is obvious if you have carried out the first step.

3. Thank God for the blood of the Lord Jesus Christ which cleanses you from all unrighteousness. Claim 1 John 1:9.

4. Refuse any work or influence the enemy may have gained in your life through this sin. From your position of authority seated above the enemy with Christ in you and you in Christ, command the enemy and all his host to leave you alone in the name of the Lord Jesus Christ and by His blood (1 John 4:4; Revelation 12:11).

5. Ask the Holy Spirit to fill your being. Tell your heavenly Father you want everything in your earthly temple to glorify Him.

6. Spend some time praising the Father. He inhabits the praises of His people (Psalm 22:3).

Let me close today with this reminder. While the "world forces of this darkness" refers to astrology, the "spiritual *forces* of wickedness" are those who instigate evil in our societies and cultures. They encourage and empower people like Hitler. They support and applaud Saddam Hussein, whose aspiration is to be another Nebuchadnezzar, the king of Babylon. Spiritual forces of wickedness are just that — spirit beings with maligning influence. From MTV to pornography to horror movies. From crime to brutality to sexual perversion. When you see wickedness in operation, know that spiritual forces are behind it.

"'The wiles of the devil' take many forms, but he is [the most insidious] when he succeeds in persuading people that he does not exist. To deny his reality is to expose ourselves the more to his subtlety."[5]

. D. Lloyd-Jones expressed his conviction on this matter in the following statement: "I am certain that one of the main causes of the ill state of the Church today is the fact that the devil is being forgotten. All is attributed to us; we have all become so psychological in our attitude and thinking. We are ignorant of this great objective fact, the being, the existence of the devil, the adversary, the accuser, and his 'fiery darts.'"[6]

Part of our problem is that many who acknowledge the existence of the devil only think of him as the devil or as the source of evil when he boldly identifies himself and/or when something is openly touted as being satanic. Remember that even though they belong to the pit of darkness, Satan's angels can cloth themselves as angels of light.

When one thinks of television programming, it may seem to be more flesh than demonic. We forget, however, that Satan's rulership is over the sons of disobedience who walk according to the lusts of their flesh, *indulging* the desires of their flesh and their mind.

When Satan has access to the mind, he has an inroad to the flesh. Don't forget that, my friend! Remember that he already has the world. Satan wants what he doesn't have — you!

Thus Paul's sharp command: Take up the full armor of God that you may be able to resist. Stand firm. *Take up* "was a military term describing the last preparation and final step necessary before the actual battle begins."[7] It's a call to immediate action.

With this command comes the reaffirming assurance that you will be able to quell the enemy and hold your position. No ground will be taken by him.

Obedience guarantees victory. In warfare there's nothing to fear but your unbelief or disobedience — and those you determine.

Think about it.

D A Y   F I V E

Satan's first tactic was to cast doubt on God's Word, and it was effective. He hasn't altered his battle plan. That's why, before Paul enumerates the various pieces of armor, he tells us to stand firm, "having girded" our loins with truth. The verb tense Paul uses here indicates completed action because in Ephesians 6:11 he has already commanded us to put on the armor. We are not to be passive but to take action and arm ourselves! The armor was not automatically put in place when we "put on Christ." I disagree with those who equate the armor of God with the person of Jesus Christ. The armor is something we have because we have Christ, but we are commanded to put it on. If we are saved, we have put on Christ. We are in Him, and He is in us. Yet we are told to put on specific pieces of armor, pieces which cover or protect us in the areas where our enemy attacks.

As you look at the individual pieces of armor, you will better understand the significance of each if you will focus on the word which follows — for instance, "the breastplate *of righteousness.*" Then as you connect the word with the particular piece of armor mentioned, you'll have a better understanding of what Paul is telling us to put on — the shield of faith, the helmet of salvation, etc. It is each individual's responsibility to put on the armor; it is not a passive claiming of something which happened at salvation. We are told to take up the full armor! It is an act of doing — believing, embracing, responding. Remember that as Paul prepares to discuss the armor, he first tells us to stand firm, "having girded" our loins with truth. We've put on truth, now we're to stand firm. Why does Paul begin with the belt of truth? Let's look at the belt of a Roman soldier, and I think you'll see why.

According to Rienecker and Rogers: "The Roman soldiers wore one of at least three wide belts or girdles. [1] The breech-like leather apron worn to protect the lower abdomen, [2] or the sword-belt which was buckled on together with the sword as the decisive step in the process of preparing one's self for battle and [3] the special belt or sash designating an officer or high official."[8] The belt that was of absolute necessity when going into battle held the sword. No sane soldier will go to war without his weapon!

You could tell by the way a Roman soldier wore his belt whether or not he was on duty. If his belt was tight, he was prepared for action. If it hung loose, he was off duty. Look around you. Do you see a lot of Christians with their belts hanging down around their knees?

The belt was essential to the soldier. Not only did it hold the scabbard for his sword, it kept his tunic in place so he wouldn't get entangled in it in the midst of a battle. It also secured the breastplate which protected him from the opponent's sword. Obviously the belt was essential and foundational to the armor because it kept everything in its proper place. Truth performs the same function! It wraps up things which get in the way. It keeps righteousness in its proper place. How can you know what is truly right or wrong apart from truth?

All our lives we were subjected to the father of lies. We believed a lie. We lived a lie. We told lies. Then in the grace of God, our eyes were opened to see the Truth…and the Truth set us free. Jesus is Truth, and His Word is truth.

It was the truth which sanctified you — set you apart unto God. And it is the truth which continues that sanctification. Read John 17:14–17 and write out what you learn from this passage regarding the world, the devil, and the Word. Also, note any relationship you see between these three things. As you look up this passage, remember that John 17 is Jesus' prayer to the Father on your behalf on the night of His arrest.

"I have given them Thy word; and the world has hated them, because they are not of the world, even as I am not of the world. I do not ask Thee to take them out of the world, but to keep them from the evil one.

They are not of the world, even as I am not of the world. Sanctify them in the truth; Thy word is truth." (John 17:14–17)

D A Y   S I X

In all the course of history never has one book been so hated, so maligned, so ridiculed, so attacked as the Word of God. Kings, philosophers, statesmen, and governments have tried to rid the earth of it, yet the Bible has endured each assault. And the Word of God has covered the earth.

Thwarted in his attempts to extinguish the Bible's light, there was another tact the enemy could take: He would sow seeds of doubt in the minds of those who taught it.

In the late 1800s from a group of German rationalists Satan would raise up Julius Wellhausen, an Old Testament scholar, an intellectual, and a theologian. Wellhausen would be used to give the Christian community a new and "better" way to understand the Bible. He would become the father of modern criticism.

Only those who tightened their belt of truth and stood firm would survive this battle. The following is taken from Dave Breese's book *Seven Men Who Rule the World from the Grave*. It tells more about Wellhausen.

LORD, HOW DO I PUT ON THE ARMOR? BELT ON TRUTH?   181

Before Wellhausen came on the scene the Bible was generally accepted as the revealed, true, and inerrant Word of God. Christians everywhere believed that all of Scripture was given by inspiration of God; it was breathed by the Lord Himself and was therefore totally dependable and useful for all matters of doctrine, reproof, correction, and instruction in righteousness. In the Bible we had a book we could trust. Man's reason may be incorrect at certain points, but the Bible was infallible.

Wellhausen, along with other German rationalist theologians, turned all of that around. He held instead that human reason was totally dependable and insisted that it was the Bible that could not seriously be trusted. He presented the idea that the Bible, far from being the Word of God, was in fact a sublime collection of human documents. For instance, he insisted that we must not hold that Moses wrote the Pentateuch. Rather, this history of early man was given to us by a number of writers, whose views were compiled to form what we now call the Pentateuch. Therefore, the story of Adam and Eve is a lovely myth that can illustrate certain truths, but it surely does not represent the actual story of people whom God called Adam and Eve.

Wellhausen also insisted that the subsequent account of various events given to us in the Old Testament was a product of evolutionary thinking, rather than divine inspiration. Until the advent of Wellhausen and the German rationalists, the answer to the question, Can I trust my Bible? was yes, a thousand times yes! After that, the answer was of course not. You can trust human reason, but certainly not the Bible, to be the sole dependable source of divine revelation.

Wellhausen presented his views to the world in *Prolegomena to the History of Israel,* calling for a new understanding of the nature of the revelation of God in the Bible. At this point, 1878, a new wind began to blow through the churches, the schools, and the homes of Germany and Europe. It was the cold wind of doubt, distrust of God, and spiritual disquiet, and it has continued to blow from then until now....

From that point, the advent of anti-revelational liberalism, Christianity ceased to be a religion based on *divine revelation* but rather became a set of composite religious views anchored in *human reason*. Revelation was doubted and then denied, and rationalism took its place. So fundamental was the change, and so long standing and deadly were the results, that Wellhausen can be regarded as one of the seminal thinkers who rule the world from their graves.[9]

Is it no wonder that the Apostle Peter urged us to "gird your minds for action" (1 Peter 1:13)? The metaphor could easily be understood by his readers. In Peter's day men wore long robes which would easily get tangled up in their legs if they moved swiftly. So it was not uncommon for someone to reach between his legs, grab the back of his robe, pull it up, and stick it in his belt. With his loins girded in this way, the robe turned into baggy pants and he could run unencumbered.

In 1 Peter 5:8–9, Peter warns that our adversary goes about as a roaring lion, and he encourages us to "resist him, firm in *your* faith." You must be convinced of the truthfulness, the veracity of God's Word to be firm in your faith.

My friend, what do you believe about the Word of God? Look up the following verses and note what you learn about the Bible.

1. 2 Peter 1:19–21

2. 2 Timothy 3:16–17

3. Matthew 5:17–18

4. Luke 24:25–27

5. Matthew 12:40; 19:4–6 (Just wanted you to see what Jesus confirmed!)

Do you think Jesus, Peter, and Paul can be trusted? Are they liars? Do you think God is strong enough, wise enough, and sovereign enough to see that man, whom He created, and the devil, whose power He limits, do not alter His Word?

It's imperative that you have a settled conviction that the Word of God is just that, the God-given, God-breathed, God-protected, and God-preserved Word of God. You must settle in your heart that it is without error and that it contains all you need in order to live righteously before Him. If you are not convinced of these things, then the rest of the armor will be useless.

If you aren't actively reading the Bible, absorbing it, studying it, you won't be convinced of its truth. Truth must become at home in you, and you must be at home in it. Otherwise you'll find it easy to diminish it or to add to it.

Tighten your belt, or you could be taken captive.

DAY SEVEN

You have a choice. God grants you that. You can walk in the futility of your mind, or you can walk in truth. But know, dear one, that if you walk according to your thoughts, your understanding, your feelings, you'll become lion's meat!

When we meet the Lord Jesus Christ, we encounter truth, pure unadulterated truth. Jesus is the way, the truth, the life (John 14:6). His Word is truth (John 17:17). We have come to know the truth, and the truth has set us free (John 8:32).

However, the one who once ruled over us does not stand in the truth. There is no truth in him (John 8:44). And he doesn't want us to stand in truth. So what does he do?

Read 2 Corinthians 11:2–15, typed out here for you, and mark every reference to the enemy.

➤ 2 CORINTHIANS 11:2-15

2 For I am jealous for you with a godly jealousy; for I betrothed you to one husband, that to Christ I might present you *as* a pure virgin.

3 But I am afraid, lest as the serpent deceived Eve by his craftiness, your minds should be led astray from the simplicity and purity *of devotion* to Christ.

4 For if one comes and preaches another Jesus whom we have not preached, or you receive a different spirit which you have not received, or a different gospel which you have not accepted, you bear *this* beautifully.

5 For I consider myself not in the least inferior to the most eminent apostles.

6 But even if I am unskilled in speech, yet I am not *so* in knowledge; in fact, in every way we have made *this* evident to you in all things.

7 Or did I commit a sin in humbling myself that you might be exalted, because I preached the gospel of God to you without charge?

8 I robbed other churches, taking wages *from them* to serve you;

9 and when I was present with you and was in need, I was not a burden to anyone; for when the brethren came from Macedonia, they fully supplied

my need, and in everything I kept myself from being a burden to you, and will continue to do so.

10 As the truth of Christ is in me, this boasting of mine will not be stopped in the regions of Achaia.

11 Why? Because I do not love you? God knows *I do!*

12 But what I am doing, I will continue to do, that I may cut off opportunity from those who desire an opportunity to be regarded just as we are in the matter about which they are boasting.

13 For such men are false apostles, deceitful workers, disguising themselves as apostles of Christ.

14 And no wonder, for even Satan disguises himself as an angel of light.

15 Therefore it is not surprising if his servants also disguise themselves as servants of righteousness; whose end shall be according to their deeds.

1. According to this passage, what is Paul's concern? Or to put it another way, what does the enemy want to do?

2. According to this passage, what would Satan's strategy be? How would he try to accomplish this?

3. What do you see the enemy doing today to lead us away from truth? Be as specific as you can.

Never forget, Beloved, your warfare is not with flesh and blood. Satan has a host of deceitful spirits whose assignment is to seduce us from the truth.

4. Read 1 Timothy 4:1–3. What can happen to people who do not keep on the belt of truth?

5. According to 1 Timothy 4:6–8, what is the value of a study like this one? What does it take to keep from being seduced?

Are you careful to see that your body gets exercise while neglecting the essential spiritual disciplines that have eternal ramifications?

It is one thing to stand in truth, to believe it, and embrace it, yet there's more to girding our loins with truth. We are to walk in truth. You'll find two other references to truth in the practical segment of Ephesians. Look up each reference and record what you learn. Make sure you are careful to look at each word in its context.

6. Ephesians 4:15

7. Ephesians 4:25

Establishing Christians in the Word of God has been a challenge through the periods of church history. In Ephesians 4, Paul commands believers to keep the unity of the Spirit until we come to the unity of the faith and to spiritual maturity. Much error can be spread by zealous new Christians who step into positions of leadership or teaching before they have a solid understanding of truth.

If you look at the context of Ephesians 4:15, you'll see that Paul is saying if we're properly equipped, we won't be like "children, tossed here and there by waves, and carried about by every wind of doctrine, by the trickery of men, by craftiness in deceitful scheming." Who's behind such tactics? Isn't it our enemy who wants to lead us away from the simplicity and purity of devotion to our Lord? That's why he disguises his servants and himself as angels of light.

When a believer is led astray, what should we do? Ephesians 4:15 tells us to speak the truth in love. It could also be translated "holding to or walking in truth in love."

Here is our clue. When people are doctrinally wrong, we are not to go along with error. But we are to keep the unity of the Spirit in the bond of peace and "truth it in love." Peace and love are the keys. We must stand with the belt of truth tight about us and wait, holding to the truth. But while we wait for our brothers and sisters to come to maturity, we hold to it in love! If we take this stance, the enemy will not steal sheep from the fold.

Many young people have been seduced into a cult because they did not know truth, and/or did not experience the unconditional love of the body of Jesus Christ. The cult provided what they needed — love and acceptance. Truth was overruled, and they believed a lie.

There's another essential verse related to truth we need to talk about. Read Ephesians 4:25.

Can you imagine, my friend, what would happen if the body of Jesus Christ stopped lying to one another, and spoke the truth — in love? If we were very careful not to gossip, to check out rumors, tracing them back to the source? I'll never forget when one of our Precept leaders and an associate staff member of a large church in the same city contacted us because both had been told that Jack and I had started a church on our property. The story went that I was the pastor and that we required every staff member to attend our church. I laughed because it was all so contrary to our theology.

Personally, I don't even believe that the Word allows women to be elders or pastors. Secondly, we had vowed from the inception of our ministry that we'd never become a church. We're here to support the local church, not start one. Third, it has always been our policy not to become ingrown doctrinally but to bring in teachers from the outside so that we don't come to think we have a corner on the truth. We need to stay teachable and open. Can you understand now why I laughed? It was so ridiculous.

The rumor had been spread by a godly and well-known Bible teacher and conference speaker, a man we admired. I called the man's home. He wasn't there, but I asked his wife to have him call me. He got right back to me. As we talked, I found out he had heard the rumor from someone else. He said he simply mentioned it to others to see if it was true. "But," I replied, "why didn't you call us and ask us." He apologized and said he'd go back and straighten it out and have the person call me. He was true to his word. I so appreciated that, and I also learned a great lesson: "Kay, check out the rumors with the person they're about."

Amazing, isn't it? And yet we're more ready to believe a lie and discuss it with a third party or to spread an untruth than we are to go to the source and confront it.

I want us to look at one last sobering passage. Read Acts 4:32–5:11; mark the reference to Satan and every occurrence of the word *lie* and its synonyms. Then answer the following questions.

➤ ACTS 4:32–5:11

32 And the congregation of those who believed were of one heart and soul; and not one *of them* claimed that anything belonging to him was his own; but all things were common property to them.

33 And with great power the apostles were giving witness to the resurrection of the Lord Jesus, and abundant grace was upon them all.

34 For there was not a needy person among them, for all who were owners of land or houses would sell them and bring the proceeds of the sales,

35 and lay them at the apostles' feet; and they would be distributed to each, as any had need.

36 And Joseph, a Levite of Cyprian birth, who was also called Barnabas by the apostles (which translated means, Son of Encouragement),

37 and who owned a tract of land, sold it and brought the money and laid it at the apostles' feet.

5:1 But a certain man named Ananias, with his wife Sapphira, sold a piece of property,

2 and kept back *some* of the price for himself, with his wife's full knowledge, and bringing a portion of it, he laid it at the apostles' feet.

3 But Peter said, "Ananias, why has Satan filled your heart to lie to the Holy Spirit, and to keep back *some* of the price of the land?

4 "While it remained *unsold*, did it not remain your own? And after it was sold, was it not under your control? Why is it that you have conceived this deed in your heart? You have not lied to men, but to God."

⁵ And as he heard these words, Ananias fell down and breathed his last; and great fear came upon all who heard of it.

⁶ And the young men arose and covered him up, and after carrying him out, they buried him.

⁷ Now there elapsed an interval of about three hours, and his wife came in, not knowing what had happened.

⁸ And Peter responded to her, "Tell me whether you sold the land for such and such a price?" And she said, "Yes, that was the price."

⁹ Then Peter *said* to her, "Why is it that you have agreed together to put the Spirit of the Lord to the test? Behold, the feet of those who have buried your husband are at the door, and they shall carry you out *as well.*"

¹⁰ And she fell immediately at his feet, and breathed her last; and the young men came in and found her dead, and they carried her out and buried her beside her husband.

¹¹ And great fear came upon the whole church, and upon all who heard of these things.

8. What happened to Ananias and Sapphira? Why?

9. What role did the enemy play in it all?

Some theologians would say Ananias and Sapphira weren't saved. I won't get in a debate over it. It seems to me they were. If they weren't saved, lying would have been expected. After all, they were sons of disobedience and their father was the devil, a liar. If they were believers, then the Holy Spirit indwelt them, and if they told a lie, they would be lying to the Holy Spirit. Does what happened to Ananias and Sapphira show you the value God places on truth — even in the inward parts?

Tighten that belt of truth, Beloved.

Write out your affirmation of faith in your notebook.

LORD, TEACH ME ABOUT THE BREAST-PLATE AND SHOES

I listened to Robert tell me about the young man who came to our February men's conference — a man I'll call Mike. Saturday evening Mike asked Robert if they could talk. At ten o'clock they got together in Mike's room. As they sat on the floor, Mike shared about the problems he'd had with drugs and alcohol, and about his time in a rehabilitation center. When it was all out, they began to pray.

Robert said, "As we prayed, I sensed a heaviness in that room, a deep despair. I would pray and then wait for him. When he didn't speak, I looked over at him. He sat with his legs crossed, his arms out with the palms of his hands open as if to receive something. He wanted to speak, but all he could do was mutter and groan. He was in such agony. His breathing was like shallow panting. Finally, he told me that there was something else he needed to share. He said that he had struggled with homosexuality for as long as he could remember. He said that he had not practiced it for many years but that he still struggled with it. So we prayed and asked the Lord for deliverance and for strength for him to go on with his life.

"Again, as I prayed, I waited for him. I could sense his agony and despair, and the heaviness seemed to increase. I knew we were in no ordinary battle. This was serious business. In futility and exasperation he muttered that there was something else he needed to share. At this point I didn't know what to

193

expect. He struggled, but the words wouldn't come. On the second try, in utter frustration and despair he said that he was HIV positive."

Mike died in August. The sin of homosexuality had taken him farther than he wanted to go. And sin, tasted, tolerated, and indulged, will take you farther than you intend to go.

O Beloved, once you put on the breastplate of righteousness, you must keep it on. If you don't, you will fall prey to the roaring lion who longs to devour you.

Have you been tolerating sin in your life? What is it? Name it. Are you harboring bitterness and unforgiveness? Against whom? Why? Didn't you know that it's sin? Write it out. It helps to see things in black and white, to bring them out in the open.

Cry out to God. Tell Him you want to walk in His righteousness, to stand with your feet "shod with the preparation of the gospel of peace." Ask Him to minister to you this week as we study the breastplate of righteousness and the shoes of peace. Tell God you'll have ears to hear — a will to obey. If you'll do this, He will hear. And He will answer because you have asked according to His will.

DAY TWO

There's much debate today about what is right and what is wrong. Without the breastplate (righteousness), you can be wounded by sin. As a society, we have passed from morality to immorality to amorality. Many have abandoned absolutes, making truth relative. Thus, Satan's grip is destroying us. No nation need conquer us because sin already has.

Look up the following scriptures and note what each says about immorality and about its physical and/or spiritual consequences. Also, note any instructions as to how we should deal with immorality.

1. Romans 1:22–27

2. 1 Corinthians 6:9–11

3. 1 Corinthians 6:18 (Please note that this is a command given to those who are indwelt by the Holy Spirit: 6:19–20.)

4. Ephesians 5:1–13

5. 1 Corinthians 5:1–5

6. What do you think Paul means when he says they're "to deliver such a one to Satan for the destruction of his flesh, that his spirit may be saved in the day of the Lord Jesus"?

7. Leviticus 20:10–22 (I'm using this Old Testament passage so you will understand God's heart and mind from the beginning.)

What would happen if our society adhered to God's commands in respect to our sexuality? AIDS would eventually cease, and God would not have to judge us and other countries who tolerate and protect immorality. Do you realize that what we once condemned we now condone? Yet the acts themselves have not changed! We have adjusted our standards to cover our unrighteousness, and the flames of hell are licking the earth.

In the early 1990s, *The Los Angeles Times* carried an article by Marshal Alan Phillips entitled, "Bible Doesn't Say What We Thought It Did." The article states, "New Biblical discoveries move toward acceptance of gays. The law should do the same." The article attempts to justify a lifestyle that the Bible clearly states is a sin — a sin that the Bible says brings its own judgment.

The word *sodomy* from the biblical city of Sodom is popularly thought to be synonymous with homosexuality, but since the 1955 publication of Derrick Sherwin Bailey's "Homosexuality and the Western Christian Tradition," scholars agree that Sodom was destroyed for inhospitable treatment of visitors sent from God and not for anything to do with homosexuality. Indeed, the word *homosexual* nowhere appears in the Bible. Sodomy today has a variety of meanings and most states have voided laws against it.

The AIDS plague and its staggering economic cost have so drastically affected our society that legal recognition of gay marriage should be explored. The virus thought to cause the fatal disease hit gay males disproportionately in part because society does not support and promote stable couples among them. The enormous psychological, social, religious, and legal contempt heaped on gays discouraged them from settling down with one partner. As the sexual and social revolutions of the 1960s and 1970s encouraged gays to seek their own civil and human rights, many embraced promiscuity as a rebellious act without knowing about AIDS.

Just as past plagues altered society, gay people now realize that sexual fidelity in committed relationships can be a matter of life and death. Public policy, it follows logically, should support gay couples. Constitutionally, gays should have the same rights to privacy, personal liberty and societal stability as non gays. This would benefit all.[1]

A friend recently told me that she was in the children's section of a large bookstore and opened a book entitled *Daddy's Roommate*. Its first words were "My Mommy and Daddy got a divorce last year. Now Daddy has a new roommate, Frank." The pictures show Frank and Daddy doing all sorts of things together, including sharing the same bed. And in most of the pictures you see the son having a wonderful time doing what Frank and Daddy do together. At the close of the book the little boy tells what fun he has with them. Then comes the explanation: "Mommy says Daddy and Frank are gay. Mommy said, 'Being gay is just one more kind of love, and love is the best kind of happiness.'"

Beloved, can you see where we'd be if we didn't put on our belt of truth and breastplate of righteousness? We'd follow the pack, believe a lie, walk in sin, and be held captive by the devil to do his will (2 Timothy 2:26).

How are you standing? Are you living righteously? If you ask, "What is righteousness?" I would reply, "It is doing what God says is right." And if you asked, "How do we know what God says is right?" I would say, "The Bible tells you what God says is right and wrong. Heed its words carefully, for it will be your judge" (John 12:48).

What will be God's verdict?

DAY THREE

The Roman soldier's breastplate covered all his vital organs, protecting his body front and back, and was usually made of metal. Let's look at this breastplate from every angle.

The breastplate — righteousness — is a gift given to every child of God. Without the Holy Spirit you could never be righteous, let alone walk in righteousness. Look up 2 Corinthians 5:21, and note below what you learn about sin and righteousness from this verse.

When you were nothing but a sinner — helpless, ungodly, and without hope — God justified you. Even though you were His enemy, when you repented and believed that Jesus Christ was God and that He died for your sin, God immediately transferred you from Satan's domain of darkness into His glorious kingdom. Instantly, you were pardoned and declared righteous in the eyes of God. All your sins — past, present, and future — were forgiven. You were given the promise of the Holy Spirit, the Spirit who would indwell you and cause you to walk in God's statutes and keep His commandments so that you would no longer live a life of habitual sin.

And, as I said before, because your sins were absolutely forgiven, Satan no longer has the power of death over you. Sin and death are not like oil and water — they mix. Death follows sin. One combines with the other in full partnership. Therefore, if your sins had not been paid for in full, if you had not been made righteous, you would die and be eternally separated from God.

One of Satan's most effective strategies is to keep our sin before us. He'll remind us of sins we've already confessed or convince us that because of them, God can't use us. Sometimes he tries to convince us that our sin is so terrible God will never forgive us. If you fall for any of these tactics, you'll go into battle without your breastplate. So when condemnation comes, you must recognize who's the instigator of those accusations.

Romans 8:31–39 is always a comfort and help to me. Read it carefully and mark the word *condemn* and its synonyms. Also watch for and mark words which refer to Satan's emissaries, i.e. principalities, powers, angels.

➤ ROMANS 8:1–2, 31–39

1–2 There is therefore now no condemnation for those who are in Christ Jesus. For the law of the Spirit of life in Christ Jesus has set you free from the law of sin and of death.

31 What then shall we say to these things? If God is for us, who *is* against us?

³² He who did not spare His own Son, but delivered Him up for us all, how will He not also with Him freely give us all things?

³³ Who will bring a charge against God's elect? God is the one who justifies;

³⁴ who is the one who condemns? Christ Jesus is He who died, yes, rather who was raised, who is at the right hand of God, who also intercedes for us.

³⁵ Who shall separate us from the love of Christ? Shall tribulation, or distress, or persecution, or famine, or nakedness, or peril, or sword?

³⁶ Just as it is written, "FOR THY SAKE WE ARE BEING PUT TO DEATH ALL DAY LONG; WE WERE CONSIDERED AS SHEEP TO BE SLAUGHTERED."

³⁷ But in all these things we overwhelmingly conquer through Him who loved us.

³⁸ For I am convinced that neither death, nor life, nor angels, nor principalities, nor things present, nor things to come, nor powers,

³⁹ nor height, nor depth, nor any other created thing, shall be able to separate us from the love of God, which is in Christ Jesus our Lord.

Stand with the breastplate of righteousness on, and remember that "there is therefore now no condemnation" because God's righteousness has been put to your account. It is imputed through His death and imparted to your life through His Spirit. God does not condemn. God does not accuse. God convicts of sin and seeks to lead us to repentance. Satan is the accuser of the brethren. He accuses you night and day before the throne of God (Revelation 12:10). But do not fear because Jesus sits at the right hand of the throne of God where He lives to make intercession for you (Hebrews 12:2; 7:25).

D A Y   F O U R

There is more to understanding the breastplate of righteousness than accepting the fact that we have been declared righteous. We are also expected to
live righteously day in and day out. When we don't choose to live in this
way, we must confess our sins so that the devil has no opportunity to get us
in our vital organs.

After stating the Christian's position in Christ in the first segment of his
letter to the Ephesians, Paul exhorts the saints not to walk any longer as the
Gentiles walked. He wants us to understand that the old self is laid aside and
that the new self is put on.

The old man, the old self, is all you were before you were saved. The
new man, the new self, is what you become once you are indwelt by the
Spirit of God. Find the fourth chapter of Ephesians in the back of this book
and then do the following assignments:

1. Read Ephesians 4:17–19 and note below how the Gentiles walked.

2. What do you learn about the old self versus the new self in Ephesians
4:22–24?

3. The old man and new man are mentioned in only two other passages in the New Testament: Romans 6:6 and Colossians 3:9–11. Look up these verses and record what you learn simply from observing the text.

4. Ephesians 4:25 begins with the word *Therefore* — therefore, what? Therefore, since as children of God we have laid aside the old man and have put on the new man, we are to live righteously. Read Ephesians 4:25–32. List what we are to do and what we're not to do. Also as you read, watch for the devil — mark him.

5. Do you think a person who gets involved in these things has taken up the full armor of God — the breastplate of righteousness? Why?

According to Ephesians 4:27, sin in the life of a Christian gives Satan a place of occupation, an opportunity. That's a significant statement, and we need to look at it.

The Greek word *topos* is translated as *opportunity*. It is used eighty-four times in the Word of God in regard to a place of occupancy. It is used of a region, a locality, or a place which persons or things occupy. It is also used metaphorically of a condition, an occasion, an opportunity.

Paul uses the word nine times in his writings (if we assume that he did not write Hebrews), and in every case the word is used to designate a place. In Romans 12:19 he uses it in a slightly different way when he says "leave room for the wrath *of God*." I haven't found that Paul uses *topos* as a metaphor.

Warren Wiersbe in his book *The Strategy of Satan* says,

> If the believer cultivates in his life any known sin, he is giving Satan an opportunity to get a foothold, a beachhead in his life. Satan will then use this opportunity to invade and take over other areas. Paul warns in Ephesians 4:27, "And do not give the devil an opportunity." The word translated 'opportunity' simply means a place such as a city or a building. But it carries the idea of *a foothold or opportunity, a chance to operate.*"[2]

Sin in a believer can become an open door to the enemy. Wiersbe continues, using the term *beachhead* for the Greek word *topos*.

> Any sin that we harbor in our lives, that we know is there and yet we refuse to acknowledge and confess, will give Satan a beachhead for further attacks. It has been my experience that this includes material objects that are definitely related to Satanism and the occult. No Christian has any right to possess such objects because they give Satan the foothold he is looking for. When the Ephesian Christians burned their magic books (Acts 19:18–20), they were taking a giant step forward in defeating Satan.

Finally, we must never look upon any sin or questionable object as a "little thing." Nothing is "little" if Satan can use it to attack you! I recall counseling a Christian student who had an obsession for food. She was ruining her health and her studies, and her anxiety was only making the problem worse. I asked her if she had anything in her possession that was related to the occult. She confessed that she did, and I urged her to get rid of it, confess her sin to the Lord, and claim the victory of Christ over whatever demons were using that object as a beachhead. She did all of this, and the Lord gave her wonderful victory. Illustrations of this kind of victory can be multiplied by pastors who have confronted occult powers.[3]

Take heed, my friend. If you tolerate sin in your life, you'll open the door to the one who has sinned from the beginning. And you'll find that sin will not only take you farther than you wanted to go, it will keep you longer than you wanted to stay, and it will cost you more than you ever thought you'd pay.

Listen and learn.

I became a Christian at the age of nine and was active as a teenager in the church youth department. Throughout those years and into my adult years I have had one major stronghold in my life — stealing and shoplifting.

A final confrontation with the devil occurred about four months ago — I am now free! I have gotten on with my life having confessed my sin and accepted God's wondrous forgiveness.

My guilt was gone until I read Exodus 22:14–15. It states that what is taken by robbery must be repaid in order to be forgiven. Kay, there is no way I could possibly account for everything I have taken through the years. Even if I could, I could never repay it. We live from paycheck to paycheck and then we only make it with help from God (our house payment and utilities are a month past due). To top this off, I have been ill since July and though we have insurance my part has been very expensive.

I never took extravagant items; only things we needed and couldn't afford. This wasn't meant to be a hard-luck letter. I just want to know your opinion of where I stand with God. Now, my prayer time, Bible study, and devotional time are definitely hindered.

I cried out to God and have felt like God has told me that my salvation is safe although my relationship to Him may be hindered. Then I thought maybe that was Satan telling me that to trick me. Or is this whole thinking Satan's attempt to make me think I have to earn my way by doing what is impossible — making restitution?

I'm very confused. I love my Lord. My relationship with Him is far better than ever and I don't want this to get in the way of my growth. I also should mention, *no one* knows or suspects my previous problem. If you asked anyone who knows me, they'd say that I was honest, trustworthy, a good Christian example.

And I am, except I had that one stronghold in my life. *Please,* I don't want my Christian walk to be hindered. I want to be obedient to God. Is my salvation or my forgiveness conditional? I would appreciate your help in working through this. Please let me know your opinion.

How did I answer this dear woman? I suggested she tell God she's willing to make restitution if that is what He wants — not as a work, but out of obedience. Yes, she had sinned against God, but she has also stolen other people's possessions. Because she had confessed, she could face God without shame. But what about those whom she robbed? Could she have a clear conscience before them if she had not made right what was wrong?

Of course not. Therefore, I suggested she should wait before God in prayer and ask Him to reveal to her what she had stolen. As He revealed something, I told her to write it down and then ask God what she should do to make restitution.

If it is her sincere desire to be obedient to her Father, then I knew He would reveal what He wanted her to do. He would put it in her mind, and she would know it was Him. When He showed her, He would also supply her with what she needed in order to make restitution. If her heart's goal is to obey and walk righteously before Him, then I knew He would meet her at her point of obedience. That's the kind of Father He is. Where God leads, God provides. He promised, and His Word is truth.

Such a response will enable her to withstand the attacks of the enemy. With her belt of truth tightened, her breastplate of righteousness on, she'll be at peace because she is right with God — and with those she's stolen from.

Now, Beloved, what about you? What must you do in order to tighten your breastplate of righteousness?

1. Make sure you are a true child of God — make sure you have it on!

2. Ask God to show you any place in your life where you have tolerated sin or opened yourself to sin. Wait on Him, listen, and He will show you. Write it down.

3. Read 1 John 1:9 and confess your sin *aloud*. The word confess is *homologeō* and means to say the same thing. In other words, name your sin for what it is. Say the same thing God says about it. Don't cover it up.

4. Thank God aloud for being a God of His Word and for doing what He said He would do — forgiving your sin *and* cleansing you from *all* unrighteousness.

5. Then if you have taken something which is not yours, make restitution. You know how I advised the dear woman who wrote. Take those principles and apply them to yourself.

6. When the enemy comes to accuse you, take the sword of the Spirit and command him aloud to be gone.

DAY   FIVE

Peace, peace wonderful peace. Peace with God. Peace with others. Who can buy the well-being peace brings? If you're at peace with God and others, then you can withstand almost anything. But let that peace be disturbed, and you're in torment.

Because peace is so vital to our being able to withstand circumstances, Paul uses the illustration of the soldier's shoes when he tells us: "shod your feet with the preparation of the gospel of peace." Even the best equipped, highly skilled soldier cannot win the battle if he isn't able to stand on his feet.

Thus, Paul shows the necessity of the believer's participation in putting on shoes which will enable him to stand firm when the enemy attacks. The word *shod* means "to bind under" or "to strap on." It is possibly a reference to the *caliga,* a shoe worn in battle.

"The Roman soldier wore sandals which were bound by thongs over the instep and around the ankle, and the soles were thickly studded with nails."[4] John MacArthur points out that "in the time of Roman wars, there was a common military practice (similar to the land mines of today) of planting sticks in the ground which had been sharpened to a razor-point, and concealing them so that they were almost invisible. This was a very effective tactic because, if the soldier's foot was pierced, he wouldn't be able to walk; and if he couldn't walk, he was totally debilitated."[5]

It's clear we need to wear proper shoes in warfare. But the question now remains: How do we put on "the preparation of the gospel of peace"? If we are familiar with the Book of Romans, our minds immediately turn to Romans 10:15: "And how shall they preach unless they are sent? Just as it is written, 'HOW BEAUTIFUL ARE THE FEET OF THOSE WHO BRING GLAD TIDINGS OF GOOD THINGS!'"

However, the context of Romans 10:15 is salvation, sharing the gospel. In Ephesians 6, the context is warfare. Granted, when we bring the gospel to people, we are going to war against the enemy who holds them captive. But I do not believe that this is the primary meaning of shodding our feet with the gospel of peace. Note, I did say "primary." The English transliteration of the word for *preparation* is *hetoimasiai,* which means preparation or readiness. "The word may however in this context have the meaning 'firmly' and express solidity, firmness, solid foundation (Barth)."[6] A. T. Robertson says it is a "readiness of mind that comes from the gospel whose message is peace."[7]

You will remember that this isn't the first time Paul uses the word *peace* in his epistle. Let me remind you of the other occurrences so you can look them up and record what you learn. Also note Paul's use of *enmity,* which is the opposite of peace.

1. Ephesians 2:14–17

2. Ephesians 4:3

3. Ephesians 6:23

According to these verses, our position with God is one of peace — peace with God and with those in the body of Christ. I believe Paul is pointing out that to stand firm in warfare we must be convinced that we are at peace with God. As much as is possible, we are to be at peace with others. If I have done everything I can to walk in peace with God and others, I will be able to *stand* against the enemy's accusations. I won't be used as his pawn.

Remember Satan is a murderer — a destroyer. Jesus is the Prince of peace, the Giver of life. We'll talk more tomorrow. The next two days could be the most freeing, victorious days you've experienced to this point because we're going to look at anger, unforgiveness, bitterness, and depression — four tactics of the enemy to rob you of peace.

DAY SIX

As we studied the breastplate of righteousness, you read Ephesians 4:25–32 and listed things which are not to have any place in the life of a child of God.

Today read through Ephesians 4:25–32 again and mark any reference to anger, bitterness, and forgiveness. Then, list below exactly what God says about each of these.

According to this passage, anger is not a sin. It can even be righteous. As a matter of fact, the majority of references to anger in the Bible refer to God's anger. God hates sin. His righteousness and holiness don't leave Him passive in respect to our unbelief and disobedience. Nor should sin leave us passive. If God gets angry over sin, then so should we. I believe the more we become like Him, the more we will abhor sin.

Anger is an emotion. But when anger rules, you're in trouble! According to Galatians 5:19–20, an outburst of anger is one of the works of the flesh, and when the flesh controls you rather than the Spirit, that's sin.

Harboring anger is also sin. Anger, justified or not, must be given to God. He can handle it righteously and justly, you can't. (For the purposes of this book, I've chosen to talk specifically about harboring anger. If you'd like to know more about what the Bible says about anger, you need to read my book *Lord, Heal My Hurts* by Questar Publishers.)

If you harbor anger and don't deal with it biblically, then you can know for certain, Beloved, that you are giving the devil an opportunity or place in your life. Mark it down and never forget it: When you harbor sin, it wears away at you and at your relationships, and it opens the door to the enemy.

How does harboring anger give ground to the enemy? In the Greek the tense of the command "do not give the devil an opportunity" is present active imperative — a command that forbids or prohibits something from continuing or becoming an action. Robertson says, "Either stop doing it or do not have the habit."[8] "The day of anger should be the day of reconciliation."[9]

The *Linguistic Key to the Greek New Testament* explains anger as "an angry mood, a violent irritation is meant, expressed by either hiding one's self from others or by flaming looks, harmful words, inconsiderate actions."[10] Interesting definition, isn't it?

Ask God to show you if there is any unresolved anger in your heart. If there is, write it down. Put down who or what you're angry about. Then tell God how you feel about letting go of your anger. If you want to be at peace with God and with others, tell Him. If you don't, tell Him why. Be honest. Say it aloud. He'll listen. And He'll help, if you genuinely want His help, His release.

Beloved, I've seen how anger consumes and destroys. People who harbor anger are like hyenas, who when caught in a trap eat their own flesh. Forgiveness, faith, and obedience would spring anger's trap. A child of God doesn't have to live this way! Don't listen to any psychologist, psychiatrist, or counselor who tells you differently. They are denying the truthfulness and power of God's Word. They're speaking a lie from the father of lies. You can be set free from anger and bitterness. God's made every provision — you're without excuse.

Healing begins when we are willing to forgive. Remember what you just read in Ephesians 4? Let's look at it again. "And be kind to one another, tender-hearted, forgiving each other, just as God in Christ also has forgiven you" (Ephesians 4:32). If you and I are unwilling to put away bitterness, anger, wrath, malice, if we are unwilling to forgive, we can't put on the sandals of peace. Our feet will be pierced by those barely visible, sharpened spears, and we'll find ourselves immobilized, our feet infected.

When Paul tells us to put away bitterness, anger,...and to forgive as Christ forgave us, we must realize that it is possible to do so because the old man has been put off and because we've put on the new. Therefore, if these things are not put away, if we don't forgive, we're to blame! God's done everything necessary for you and me to have victory over our flesh and over the devil.

Listen to Paul's words to the Colossians. As you read, mark any reference to *peace, unity,* or *forgiveness.* Also, watch for the word *love.*

➤ COLOSSIANS 3:12-15

12 And so, as those who have been chosen of God, holy and beloved, put on a heart of compassion, kindness, humility, gentleness and patience;

13 bearing with one another, and forgiving each other, whoever has a complaint against anyone; just as the Lord forgave you, so also should you.

14 And beyond all these things *put on* love, which is the perfect bond of unity.

15 And let the peace of Christ rule in your hearts, to which indeed you were called in one body; and be thankful.

What did you learn from this passage? Did God speak to your heart in any way? Write it out in your own words.

Look at 2 Corinthians 2:5–11, and again mark references to *forgiveness* and *love.* Also, identify the reference to Satan with a red pitchfork.

➤ 2 CORINTHIANS 2:5–11

5 But if any has caused sorrow, he has caused sorrow not to me, but in some degree — in order not to say too much — to all of you.

6 Sufficient for such a one is this punishment which was *inflicted by* the majority,

7 so that on the contrary you should rather forgive and comfort *him,* lest somehow such a one be overwhelmed by excessive sorrow.

8 Wherefore I urge you to reaffirm *your* love for him.

9 For to this end also I wrote that I might put you to the test, whether you are obedient in all things.

10 But whom you forgive anything, I *forgive* also; for indeed what I have forgiven, if I have forgiven anything, I *did it* for your sakes in the presence of Christ,

11 in order that no advantage be taken of us by Satan; for we are not ignorant of his schemes.

1. What is Paul telling the Corinthians to do? Why?

2. According to this passage, how could Satan take advantage of "us"?

To be unwilling to forgive anyone is sin, and sin gives your adversary the advantage. Is that what you want?

If you are God's child and have been set free because God graciously forgave you, why would you come back under Satan's "power"? Put on the shoes of the gospel of peace. Be willing to be at peace with everyone. Put on the breastplate of righteousness; forgive out of obedience. Put on the belt of truth; believe what God says rather than following your feelings or your reasonings. God says He will judge those who sinned against you. You are not the judge; God is. Do you want mercy? Be merciful.

I have a friend who committed adultery and confessed it to her husband, who was a godly man. I said "was" because now he is verbally and physically abusing his wife. He has become like a Dr. Jekyll and Mr. Hyde. One moment he is kind and repentant, and the next moment his countenance changes and vile, filthy words come out of his mouth like machine-gun fire.

What's happened? He refuses to forgive his wife as Jesus Christ forgave him a long time ago. He has allowed anger, resentment, and bitterness to fester within his soul, and the enemy has taken great advantage of him. He's even come at her at times in such a way that she feared for her life.

When he reacts this way, she goes to a room, rebukes the enemy aloud, and exercises her authority in Christ. Using her authority in prayer has been her only protection. (We'll talk about rebuking the enemy in our last week of study.)

Why is this man behaving like this? He's sinned by allowing anger to control him. The enemy has gained an advantage in his life, a place, a base of operation because he didn't stand firm in the Lord, in the strength of His might, clothed in the full armor of God.

Remember this, dear one, the best defense a Christian can have against the enemy is a righteous lifestyle — doing what God says is right, no matter how you feel, no matter what you think. We are to walk in a manner worthy of the calling with which we have been called. Matthew 5:9, 44–48 describes this walk in respect to the shoes of peace.

Blessed are the peacemakers, for they shall be called sons of God.... love your enemies, and pray for those who persecute you in order that you may be sons of your Father who is in heaven; for He causes His sun to rise on *the evil* and *the* good, and sends rain on *the* righteous and *the* unrighteous. For if you love those who love you, what reward have you? Do not even the tax-gatherers do the same? And if you greet your brothers only, what do you do more *than others?* Do not even the Gentiles do the same? Therefore you are to be perfect, as your heavenly Father is perfect.

3. What do you learn from these verses that you can apply to your own life?

4. Read Matthew 18:21–35, and note below what happens to those who don't forgive.

5. Doesn't this describe what has happened to this husband who has refused to forgive his wife?

6. What have you learned? What will you do?

If you're bitter, you don't have peace. You haven't let go of your anger and disappointment. And, in all probability, you're angry and bitter with God.

You're probably thinking that if God is sovereign, He should have done something to stop whatever it was that has made you bitter. Maybe it was your parents — maybe they didn't love you or raise you as you think they should have, or as the Word of God says.

Maybe it's your children — you did your best. You did what you thought was right, but they didn't turn out the way they should have. You are experiencing an unbearable grief.

Maybe it's your mate, your employer, or_____ — you fill in the blank.

Or maybe you're bitter because you're poor, uneducated, sick, physically handicapped, or deformed.

Maybe it's because someone you love was taken from you or is suffering greatly. Maybe it's because you prayed, and God didn't answer.

You're bitter. There's no peace in your heart, and the devil is having a heyday. What are you to do?

Hebrews 12:1–17 is printed out below. Read it carefully and mark every use of the following words and their synonyms: *discipline, peace, bitterness, "let us."* Treat *holiness, righteousness,* and *sanctification* as one word, and mark them all the same way.

➤ HEBREWS 12:1–17

1 Therefore, since we have so great a cloud of witnesses surrounding us, let us also lay aside every encumbrance, and the sin which so easily entangles us, and let us run with endurance the race that is set before us,

2 fixing our eyes on Jesus, the author and perfecter of faith, who for the joy set before Him endured the cross, despising the shame, and has sat down at the right hand of the throne of God.

³ For consider Him who has endured such hostility by sinners against Himself, so that you may not grow weary and lose heart.

⁴ You have not yet resisted to the point of shedding blood in your striving against sin;

⁵ and you have forgotten the exhortation which is addressed to you as sons, "MY SON, DO NOT REGARD LIGHTLY THE DISCIPLINE OF THE LORD, NOR FAINT WHEN YOU ARE REPROVED BY HIM;

⁶ FOR THOSE WHOM THE LORD LOVES HE DISCIPLINES, AND HE SCOURGES EVERY SON WHOM HE RECEIVES."

⁷ It is for discipline that you endure; God deals with you as with sons; for what son is there whom *his* father does not discipline?

⁸ But if you are without discipline, of which all have become partakers, then you are illegitimate children and not sons.

⁹ Furthermore, we had earthly fathers to discipline us, and we respected them; shall we not much rather be subject to the Father of spirits, and live?

¹⁰ For they disciplined us for a short time as seemed best to them, but He disciplines *us* for *our* good, that we may share His holiness.

¹¹ All discipline for the moment seems not to be joyful, but sorrowful; yet to those who have been trained by it, afterwards it yields the peaceful fruit of righteousness.

¹² Therefore, strengthen the hands that are weak and the knees that are feeble,

¹³ and make straight paths for your feet, so that *the limb* which is lame may not be put out of joint, but rather be healed.

¹⁴ Pursue peace with all men, and the sanctification without which no one will see the Lord.

15 See to it that no one comes short of the grace of God; that no root of bitterness springing up causes trouble, and by it many be defiled;

16 that *there be* no immoral or godless person like Esau, who sold his own birthright for a *single* meal.

17 For you know that even afterwards, when he desired to inherit the blessing, he was rejected, for he found no place for repentance, though he sought for it with tears.

As we have seen in Colossians and Ephesians, those who belong to Jesus Christ are to put away all bitterness. You've also seen you are to be kind-hearted, compassionate, and forgiving toward others as God has been toward you in Christ Jesus. If you don't respond in this way, you'll be bitter.

What can you learn from Hebrews 12 that will help you deal with — or even prevent — bitterness? Write it out.

You'll have no peace to stand in, Beloved, if you don't submit to God. Meekness is the cure for bitterness. Meekness is accepting everything without murmuring or complaining because you realize that it was permitted by God and that it will serve an eternal purpose.

Remember, God is sovereign; He rules over all. Nothing can happen to you without God's permission. And if God permits it, even though in and of itself it is not good, God promises that it will work together for your good and that He'll use it to make you into the image of His Son.

You can put away your anger, forsake your bitterness, and put peace on your feet. This is part of the good news of the gospel of peace. Your Kinsman Redeemer will buy back the trauma, the pain, the disappointments and use them all to make you more like Jesus. This promise echoes throughout the chambers of His Word. Hush...listen...and do what He says. "And the God of peace will soon crush Satan under your feet" (Romans 16:20).

Write your prayer of affirmation in your notebook.

CHAPTER TEN

LORD, SATAN'S ATTACKING MY MIND! MY SHIELD! MY HELMET!

DAY ONE

T he hunter held his rifle as if it were the hand of his child rather than a weapon that could bring down a charging rhino or a lion in midair.

He was enjoying himself. Enraptured by the sights and sounds of the jungle, he wasn't bothered in the least that he hadn't ferreted out anything. Brilliant flashes of color winged by. Monkeys scurried up and down branches in hot pursuit of one another and then stopped to chatter. He wondered if they were accusing each other of cheating in their game of tag.

Suddenly, screeching filled the air. Adrenaline surged through the hunter's body. Without thinking, he lifted the rifle up under his chin and tightened his finger on the trigger. His eyes searched for the source of this chilling noise. In an instant he found his answer.

Relieved he put the strap of his rifle back over his shoulder. It was just a bird. His heart slowed. He grinned, almost sheepishly. He'd panicked over nothing. He moved closer. Why the racket?

The bird, who was darting back and forth to one particular tree seemed angry. Squinting to shut out the glare of the sun, he caught the movement of little ones in a nest. She must be the mother, but why the commotion? She must see something he couldn't, but what? Then he noticed the rustle of the leaves. A huge snake whose color blended with the color of the bark was making its way up the tree.

The hunter was captivated; he never thought to take his rifle and come to her rescue. Then as suddenly as the screeching began, silence pierced the air. The mother bird was gone.

He was puzzled. Where did she go?

The snake eased onto the long jutting branch housing the nest. At once the mother bird returned — a leaf in her beak. With uncanny precision she placed the leaf over her babies and flew to a nearby branch to take up her vigil.

The hunter's eyes never left the snake. It had reached its destination. As it arched its deadly head, its tongue flicked the air. The hunter winced. For a quick second he closed his eyes. As he hesitatingly looked back, to his surprise the nest covered by the leaf was still intact. The snake had frozen in midair. It was as if it had seen something it hadn't noticed before. Slowly the snake turned and slithered back down the tree.

The hunter was puzzled. What happened? Why had the snake forsaken the hunt after patiently making its way up the tree to its prey? How could a leaf calm a mother bird and ward off a snake?

These were the hunter's questions as he related the incident to the Africans gathered around the campfire. White teeth glistened in sharp contrast to dark skin, as they laughed and explained the ways of the jungle. The leaf the mother bird had laid over the nest to shield her young was poisonous to the snake.

What a wonderful picture for us! Our heavenly Father who put the instinct into the heart of the mother bird to protect her young and who provided the means to shield them from the serpent's fangs would not leave His own without a shield of faith, a helmet of salvation. The shield of faith is your heavenly Father's provision for the fiery darts of the serpent of old. A shield and a helmet — these will be our subject of study this week.

It stands to reason that at this point in his instructions regarding the armor, Paul would switch from the participle "having put on" to the participle "take up." It stands to reason that before a soldier would ever take up his shield, helmet, or sword he would have put on all the other pieces of his armor. The belt, breastplate, and shoes were essential clothing, but the shield and helmet were the soldier's primary defense against the enemy's attacks. The breastplate alone couldn't shield a soldier from the enemy's fiery darts, but the shield of faith was able to extinguish all of them.

Fiery darts were frightening missiles — arrows dipped in pitch and then set ablaze. When that fiery dart came blazing through the air, a soldier could drop his shield and run, leaving his backside unprotected, or he could stand fast with his shield in place. The shield, called a scutum, was made of iron, and shaped like a door. Its size alone provided good coverage. But it was also covered with layers of leather which were soaked in water just before the battle began. Water puts out fire!

Another incredible picture! Faith comes from believing the Word, and the Bible often likens the Word of God to water. The shield, soaked in water, was a shield of faith that quenched all the fiery darts of the enemy! Without faith, you can't please God (Hebrews 11:6). You'll go up in smoke! When you put on your belt, you're acknowledging truth — Jesus Christ and the Word of God. You're embracing it for what it is.

However, girding yourself with truth is not enough. You need a shield of faith to counteract the enemy's offense. When you use specific truths from God's Word to counteract the devil's lies and accusations, you're taking up the shield of faith! It is a defensive action! When the enemy attacks, the shield extinguishes the lie or accusation with an appropriate truth or promise that you've chosen to believe. Apparently there's not a single lie or accusation we can't extinguish. God says we will be able to extinguish all the flaming missiles of the evil one! It's awesome, isn't it! If we get burned, it's because we didn't construct a shield that was big enough or because we didn't soak it with enough water. Shields can dry out, so you must be in the Word day by day.

What are some of the flaming missiles the enemy has directed at you? Write them down. Next to each one record a promise or teaching that you can use to extinguish it. If you don't have "a leaf," leave it blank. If you are studying with a class, maybe someone can help you. Rest assured, God will not leave you unprotected. He'll send someone with the scripture you need!

DAY TWO

If the enemy couldn't demolish his foe with a fiery dart, he could always try to deliver a death blow to his head. A head wound would be a mortal wound. Thus, the helmet.

The soldier's helmet was usually made of bronze. Equipped with cheek pieces to protect the face, the helmet covered the whole head. Because of its weight, the helmet was lined with felt or sponge. Only an axe or hammer could pierce a good helmet.

With his head covered and his body shielded, the soldier had his personal defense in place. But what about yours and mine? How does all this translate to us? Let's look at it, and then we'll spend the rest of the week seeing what we are to do with the fiery darts of the enemy and the thoughts which would seek to crush our heads.

We've just discussed the enemy's fiery darts and our shield of defense. But because review is important for retention, let me say it again: A fiery dart would be anything the enemy would send your way in order to cause you not to believe or not to obey. When you hold up the shield of faith, you counteract these with the Word of God.

The belt is truth; the breastplate is righteousness; the shoes are peace; the shield is faith. The helmet is the assurance of salvation, the confidence that salvation brings. The helmet is symbolic of the fact that you belong to the Lord Jesus Christ and are a member of His forever family. When you put on the helmet, you demonstrate that you know and embrace your position in Christ. Thus, Paul begins his warfare epistle to the Ephesians with a eulogy to God for what we are and what we have in Christ.

When you put on your helmet of salvation, you acknowledge that the enemy cannot crush you, touch you, or do anything to you without your heavenly Father's permission. If the enemy does "seem" to gain the upper hand in thwarting you or does "seem" to have the victory, remember that Jesus Christ will always lead you in ultimate triumph. Be very aware that none of these things or events will separate you from the love of God.

The helmet of salvation covers the three aspects or tenses of salvation: I have been saved, I am being saved, and I shall be saved.

The first is justification — you have been saved from sin's penalty. That's the past tense — something which happened in your past, and because it did, you'll never be condemned.

The second is sanctification — the present tense of salvation. You are being saved from sin's power moment by moment as you live under His control and allow the indwelling Holy Spirit to lead you into all righteousness. Here you have a choice to walk by the Spirit or to walk by the flesh. If you quench the Holy Spirit by not letting Him carry out His will, or if you grieve Him by singular acts of sin, God will discipline you. But He will not cast you off forever. Your fellowship is broken but not your relationship. If you confess your sins by naming them for what they are, then God is faithful and just to forgive your sins and to cleanse you from all unrighteousness, and the fellowship is restored (1 John 1:9).

The third is glorification, and it is future. You will be saved from sin's presence and given a new body. Someday you'll die and be at home with your heavenly Father and the family of God. You'll sin no more. Isn't that something to look forward to?

No matter the battle, stand with your helmet on, confident because of your identity with Christ. The devil's blows will bounce off your head. You're on the winning side! The enemy will be defeated, and you will judge angels.

However, until your glorification, remember you're bone of His bone, flesh of His flesh — one with the Father, Son, and Holy Spirit. If you are absent from the body, there's only one place you can be and that's with the Lord. So don't fear what man or Satan would try to do to you. Simply walk according to the mind of Jesus Christ which became yours at salvation (1 Corinthians 2:16). God has not given you the spirit of fear, but power, love, and a sound mind — the mind of Christ (2 Timothy 1:7). As a result of salvation, you belong to Christ, and Christ belongs to God (1 Corinthians 3:23). God has said "'I WILL NEVER DESERT YOU, NOR WILL I EVER FORSAKE YOU,' so that we confidently say, 'THE LORD IS MY HELPER, I WILL NOT BE AFRAID. WHAT SHALL MAN DO TO ME?'" (Hebrews 13:5–6).

When it seems that the enemy has won the battle of the day, we sometimes forget that the war's not over — and the victor has already been named.

1. Look up the following verses, and note how it might appear that the enemy has won over the child of God.

a. Job 1:12–19; 2:7

b. 2 Corinthians 12:7–9 ("He has said" in verse 9 is in the perfect tense in the Greek, which means that when God said no, He meant no. Paul was not to ask again.)

c. 1 Thessalonians 2:18

d. Revelation 2:10

2. Now look up the following verses and record what you learn about the defeat of Satan and all his host.

a. Revelation 12:9–12

b. Revelation 16:12–16

c. Revelation 19:11–20:3

d. Revelation 20:7–10

The kingdoms of this world will become the kingdoms of our Christ, and He will rule forever and ever. Hallelujah!

DAY THREE

Have you ever had depression settle in like a bleak cold, rainy morning? The sun was bright the day before, but for some inexplicable reason today was gloomy, almost oppressive. You felt incredibly alone — except for questions, doubts, and accusations which harassed you.

I understand, and so do others.

Being alone was hard on James Fraser, a missionary to the Lisu tribe in inland China. Let me share an account from his biography, *Mountain Rain*. I can't recommend this book highly enough. There is so much to learn from Fraser's life about spiritual warfare.

The Lisu people were warm and hospitable, but for the most part they were not interested in James' Savior. He began to realize that he had appealed for prayer partners none too soon. He was sure though that the Lisu would soon be turning to Christ in large numbers, but it just hadn't happened. Then...

A strange and sinister shadow fell over James's spiritual life. He was perplexed, and found himself in deepening gloom. At first he put it down to his isolation: a sense of loneliness engulfed him from time to time, but gradually he became aware of an influence more far-reaching and soul-destroying than physical discomforts.

He was assailed by deep and treacherous doubts. Yea, hath God said? The question came to him again and again, as clearly as it came at the dawn of time. "Your prayers are not being answered, are they? No one wants to hear your message. The few who first believed have gone back, haven't they? You see, it doesn't work. You should never have stayed in this area on such a fool's errand. You've been in China five years and there's not much to show for it, is there? You thought you were called to be a missionary. It was pure imagination. You'd better leave it all, go back and admit it was a big mistake."

Day after day and night after night he wrestled with doubt and suicidal despair. Not once, but several times he stared over the dark ravine into the abyss. Why not end it all? The powers of darkness had him isolated; if they could get him now they could put an end to the work.

One day James received a copy of a magazine called *The Overcomer.* There he gained insight into his struggle with the enemy and how to get victory.

I read it over and over.... it showed me that deliverance from the power of the evil one comes through definite resistance on the ground of the Cross. I am an engineer and I want to see things work. I had found that much of the spiritual teaching one hears does not seem to work. My apprehension of other aspects of truth had broken down. The passive side of leaving everything to the Lord Jesus as our life, while blessedly true, was not all that was needed just then. Definite resistance on the ground of the Cross was what brought me light. For I found that it worked. I felt like a man perishing of thirst, to whom some beautiful, clear cold water had begun to flow.

People will tell you, after a helpful meeting perhaps, that such and such a truth is the secret of victory. No: we need different truths at different times. "Look to the Lord," some will say. "Resist the devil," is also Scripture. And I found it worked! That cloud of depression dispersed. I found that I could have victory in the spiritual realm whenever I wanted it. The Lord Himself resisted the devil vocally; "Get thee behind me, Satan!" I, in humble dependence on Him, did the same. I talked to Satan at that time, using the promises of Scripture as weapons. And they worked. Right then, the terrible oppression began to pass away. One had to learn, gradually, how to use the new-found weapon of resistance. I had so much to learn! It seemed as if God was saying, "You are crying to me to do a big work among the Lisu; I am wanting to do a big work in you."[1]

Can you relate? Have you experienced times when doubts assailed you, when you wondered what your life was worth anyway? Have you doubted whether you've ever heard God? Or even if you're saved?

Is your self-image a minus ten? Do you hate who and what you are or what's been done to you? Do you think you're too fat, even though people say you're too thin? Have you decided not to eat, to exercise excessively, or to help the process of getting thin by even taking laxatives? Does being in control of your body give you a sense of power? Are you afraid to give God control for fear He'll make you fat?

Have you felt like a failure as a mate, a parent, a son or daughter, a lover, a child of God? Has someone you loved failed or hurt you? Are you having a hard time forgetting it? Have you wanted to run away from it all?

Are you tempted to throw up your hands and say, "What's the use?" Have you thought of finding solace or oblivion in what you know is wrong for a child of God? Have you been tempted to just go ahead and satisfy the flesh because nothing is really going to change anyway? Or have you felt like you had a right to indulge yourself, your appetites, in some sort of self-destructing vengeance?

Are all sorts of thoughts clamoring for attention? Does vengeance keep pushing its way through the crowd, wanting to share its plan for getting even?

Have you thought of simply ending it all? Have you gone so far as thinking of a way to do it?

Listen! Can't you hear the trumpet? It's war! Those are not falling stars! They're the flaming missiles of the evil one.

Get off your bed. Get dressed. Where's your belt, your breastplate? Pick up your shield. Put on your helmet. Stand — oops, don't forget your shoes!

Get your transmitter. Call your Commanding Officer. Ask Him to bring to your remembrance His commandments and precepts. Cry out His promises. Bring your thoughts captive. Do not run away. Do what you're supposed to do — stand.

The Captain of the Host is at your side with His sword in His hand. "Consecrate yourselves, for...the LORD will do wonders among you" (Joshua 3:5). He was there for Joshua, for Jehoshaphat! He's there for you — the same, yesterday, today, and forever (Hebrews 13:8)!

Second Chronicles 20:1–23 is printed out below. Read through it, and ask the Father to speak to your heart, to show you through Jehoshaphat's example how to meet the enemy. Remember "whatever was written in earlier times was written for our instruction, that through perseverance and the encouragement of the Scriptures we might have hope" (Romans 15:4).

➤ 2 CHRONICLES 20:1–23

1 Now it came about after this that the sons of Moab and the sons of Ammon, together with some of the Meunites, came to make war against Jehoshaphat.

2 Then some came and reported to Jehoshaphat, saying, "A great multitude is coming against you from beyond the sea, out of Aram and behold, they are in Hazazon-tamar (that is Engedi)."

3 And Jehoshaphat was afraid and turned his attention to seek the LORD; and proclaimed a fast throughout all Judah.

4 So Judah gathered together to seek help from the LORD; they even came from all the cities of Judah to seek the LORD.

5 Then Jehoshaphat stood in the assembly of Judah and Jerusalem, in the house of the LORD before the new court,

6 and he said, "O LORD, the God of our fathers, art Thou not God in the heavens? And art Thou not ruler over all the kingdoms of the nations? Power and might are in Thy hand so that no one can stand against Thee.

7 "Didst Thou not, O our God, drive out the inhabitants of this land

before Thy people Israel, and give it to the descendants of Abraham Thy friend forever?

8 "And they lived in it, and have built Thee a sanctuary there for Thy name, saying,

9 'Should evil come upon us, the sword, *or* judgment, or pestilence, or famine, we will stand before this house and before Thee (for Thy name is in this house) and cry to Thee in our distress, and Thou wilt hear and deliver us.'

10 "And now behold, the sons of Ammon and Moab and Mount Seir, whom Thou didst not let Israel invade when they came out of the land of Egypt (they turned aside from them and did not destroy them),

11 behold *how* they are rewarding us, by coming to drive us out from Thy possession which Thou hast given us as an inheritance.

12 "O our God, wilt Thou not judge them? For we are powerless before this great multitude who are coming against us; nor do we know what to do, but our eyes are on Thee."

13 And all Judah was standing before the LORD, with their infants, their wives, and their children.

14 Then in the midst of the assembly the Spirit of the LORD came upon Jahaziel the son of Zechariah, the son of Benaiah, the son of Jeiel, the son of Mattaniah, the Levite of the sons of Asaph;

15 and he said, "Listen, all Judah and the inhabitants of Jerusalem and King Jehoshaphat: thus says the LORD to you, 'Do not fear or be dismayed because of this great multitude, for the battle is not yours but God's.

16 'Tomorrow go down against them. Behold, they will come up by the ascent of Ziz, and you will find them at the end of the valley in front of the wilderness of Jeruel.

17 'You *need* not fight in this *battle;* station yourselves, stand and see the salvation of the LORD on your behalf, O Judah and Jerusalem.' Do not fear or be dismayed; tomorrow go out to face them, for the LORD is with you."

18 And Jehoshaphat bowed his head with *his* face to the ground, and all Judah and the inhabitants of Jerusalem fell down before the LORD, worshiping the LORD.

19 And the Levites, from the sons of the Kohathites and of the sons of the Korahites, stood up to praise the LORD God of Israel, with a very loud voice.

20 And they rose early in the morning and went out to the wilderness of Tekoa; and when they went out, Jehoshaphat stood and said, "Listen to me, O Judah and inhabitants of Jerusalem, put your trust in the LORD your God, and you will be established. Put your trust in His prophets and succeed."

21 And when he had consulted with the people, he appointed those who sang to the LORD and those who praised *Him* in holy attire, as they went out before the army and said, "Give thanks to the LORD, for His lovingkindness is everlasting."

22 And when they began singing and praising, the LORD set ambushes against the sons of Ammon, Moab, and Mount Seir, who had come against Judah; so they were routed.

23 For the sons of Ammon and Moab rose up against the inhabitants of Mount Seir destroying *them* completely, and when they had finished with the inhabitants of Seir, they helped to destroy one another.

Note below the specific things Jehoshaphat did and the order in which he did them.

What did you learn that you can apply to your own life, especially in warfare?

D A Y   F O U R

The woman was brazen. "I'm going to have your husband."

From everything Sue knew, the woman was right. Sue was tempted to give up, to let her have him. After all these years, he still hadn't come to know the Lord. Was there any hope he'd give this woman up and come back home?

Her only son had walked away. Now she might lose her husband. It seemed too much to bear. Sue began to withdraw. She even wrote me to ask if she should continue to lead Precept when her life was in such disarray. Wouldn't the fact that she had a rebellious child and an adulterous husband bring shame on Precept Ministries if anyone found out?

One morning as Sue poured over the Scriptures, the Spirit seemed to put neon lights around Nahum 2:1: "The one who scatters has come up against you. Man the fortress, watch the road; strengthen your back, summon all *your* strength."

Suddenly it was clear — she was in a fierce spiritual battle. She had to launch an attack against the enemy of her soul.

Second Chronicles 20, which you studied yesterday, became Sue's battle plan from God. She poured over it daily, along with many other scriptures. As she waited upon the Lord, He led her step by step.

Waiting is important. Our problem is that we want the war to be over in a day. If it's not, we wave the white flag or we turn to the flesh. We follow our own reasoning, or we run to other counselors, not waiting for the Lord to lead us to counselors of His choice. Or we go for counseling without getting into the Word of God for ourselves. We rely on another human being to figure out what we should do. If someone else tells us what to do, we think we don't have to take the responsibility for our own actions. If it doesn't work, we can blame our counselor. Basically we want a short war.

Many a marriage, child, or relationship can be lost because we don't want to go to war. Take heed, my friend. Wars are rarely won in days or months.

Let me share some more of what Sue wrote in her journal. As you read, keep your Bible open to 2 Chronicles 20. Also, watch how Sue uses the shield of faith against every fiery dart!

In the first two verses of 2 Chronicles 20 I saw how a great multitude came against me. Adultery, lust of the eyes, lust of the flesh, pride of life, marital separation. "For the lips of an adulteress drip honey, and smoother than oil is her speech;...and he will be held with the cords of his sin. He will die for lack of instruction, and in the greatness of his folly he will go astray...for many are the victims she has cast down, and numerous are all her slain. Her house is the way to Sheol, descending to the chambers of death" (Proverbs 5:3, 22–23; 7:26–27). "'For I hate divorce,' says the LORD, the God of Israel" (Malachi 2:16).

I faced the enemy without, and the enemy within (verse 3). Like Jehoshaphat, fear came in a fierce wave pounding every part of my being. "Thy face, O LORD, I shall seek" (Psalm 27:8).

Verses 3–4: I called a solemn assembly of the righteous who prayed fervently. "Is not this the fast that I have chosen: to loose the bonds of wickedness, to undo the bands of the yoke, to let the oppressed go free, and that you break every (enslaving) yoke?" (Isaiah 58:6, Amplified Bible). "Not to us, O LORD, not to us, but to Thy name give glory because of Thy lovingkindness, because of Thy truth" (Psalm 115:1).

Verses 6–12: Only when my prayers were God centered (verse 12) did I leave my prayer closet with His peace. Fear subsides in the presence of Almighty God. "Do not fear, for I am with you; do not anxiously look about you, for I am your God. I will strengthen you; surely I will help you; surely I will uphold you with My righteous right hand" (Isaiah 41:10).

Counsel from two people wiser than me kept me on track when I would have used the wrong weapons. What a temptation it was to retaliate against my husband and this woman — especially verbally. In order not to use my voice for destruction but for creating, I kept this scripture ever on my tongue, "Set a guard, O LORD, over my mouth; keep watch over the door of my lips" (Psalm 141:3). "For the weapons of our warfare are not of the flesh, but divinely powerful for the destruction of fortresses" (2 Corinthians 10:4). Even though I received wise counsel, every word I said and every step I took came from the Holy Spirit directly to me.

On April 10, 1989, I wrote, "Lord, you want me to go in on them — in the house he gave her money to buy and money to maintain? Confront them together in their love nest? 'But the Lord is with me as a mighty and terrible one; therefore my persecutors will stumble, and they will not overcome me. They will be utterly put to shame, for they will not deal wisely or prosper (in their schemes); their eternal dishonor will never be forgotten'" (Jeremiah 20:11, Amplified Bible).

I did confront them, and I could hear in my mind the swish of the sword of the Lord as He was in command of that conversation. This was the first crack in the fortress. After this I thought I was through, but the Lord wouldn't let me sleep that night. "But Lord I don't want to show him unconditional love." (I can hardly even say the word.) "Haven't I had enough humiliation? What about my pride?" Then came James 4:6, "GOD IS OPPOSED TO THE PROUD, BUT GIVES GRACE TO THE HUMBLE."

"But Lord, I still don't understand this battle plan. Why continue in this unconditional love? What is the purpose?" His answer came from Proverbs 9. "The other woman calls him to death, but you call him to life. She is the foolish woman, noisy, simple, and open to all forms of evil; she willfully and recklessly knows nothing whatever of eternal value. She sits at the door of her house calling to those who pass by but he does not know the dead are there. You as a contrast are wisdom who goes into the streets calling him to come eat of the bread and drink of the spiritual wine that is in your house. She represents death but you represent life." Or "do you think lightly of the riches of His kindness and forbearance and patience, not knowing that the kindness of God leads you to repentance?" (Romans 2:4).

In April and May, it seemed as if things were on the mend, but from July through August things were not so good. There was no progress in our relationship just regression and deterioration. Then another turning point came as my husband began to call and come to see me almost every day. Then, October 27, I found them spending the night together.

Tuesday, after much prayer, I requested that he come to the house in the evening because I needed to talk to him. "Lord, I am so very weary of all this. I have nothing left to give and am tired. Just do something, I don't care but just act and bring this to some kind of a conclusion." I uttered this in frustration and weariness.

Then the scripture came, "It is time for the Lord to act, *for* they have broken Thy law" (Psalm 119:126). "The king's heart is *like* channels of water in the hand of the LORD; He turns it wherever He wishes" (Proverbs 21:1).

Then came 2 Chronicles 20:22, "When they began singing"…so I walked down my front sidewalk and across the porch singing and praising the Lord for a long time. God told me I wouldn't have to fight. The battle was His. So I let Him have it and watched as He destroyed the enemy.

My husband came up the sidewalk and onto our porch. I told him that she had won, that I would give up, that I was through trying.

He said that wasn't true. We weren't finished.

I told him to make a decision — either he wanted me or her. It didn't really matter to me anymore but to stop playing these silly games and make a choice. It could not be both ways.

He said he didn't want her but he did want me and with that he told me what he was willing to do about it.

Second Chronicles 20:22–23 came true before my very eyes! That was Tuesday. On Saturday "she" appeared at my front door step to inform me, "I just came to tell you that you can have him back because I don't want him any longer," and she turned to leave.

I did not answer her but took note of where she was standing on my porch and how she'd walked on the sidewalk — the very same places where I had stood and sung and praised the Lord just a few days before. I thought, "You don't stand a chance; you are standing on holy ground!"

My husband told me that she called him twice that day (Saturday) and was waiting at his apartment for him. He made her leave immediately. Each time he told her he never wanted to see her again and to leave us alone. It was all over. Her visit to me was within twenty minutes of her face-to-face confrontation with my husband. "No weapon that is formed against you shall prosper" (Isaiah 54:17). "But in the end she is bitter as wormwood" (Proverbs 5:4).

The spoils of war are being collected. Roses in the middle of the week, attentiveness, conversation, vacation, a new sensitivity. I will continue to praise and thank Him (verse 26).

One week later, like the father of the prodigal son, I killed the fatted calf and put a ring on his finger, and we celebrated. He wants to wear his wedding band now. There is a greater celebration coming when my husband believes in Jesus Christ as his personal Lord and Savior. I believe God will finish what He has started.

What have I learned in all this? Too much to put to pen now, except for this one thing: How I hurt my Lord with my unfaithfulness when I have one foot on the worldly path and one foot on the spiritual path, yet

He remains ever faithful. He did not and will never leave me or forsake me. Praise and glory to Him!

Sue sent her battle plan from 2 Chronicles 20:

Enemy without (v. 2).

Enemy within (v. 3).

Involve others (v. 4).

Acknowledge Him (v. 6).

Remember His promises and greatness (vs. 7–8).

God-focused prayer (v. 12).

Solution revealed through another (v. 14).

Battle plan: Go early; go singing; no fear; no fighting; no dismay;
    stand; see.

Response to battle plan (v. 18).

The battle: Not yours; is God's; enemy destroyed each other (vss. 15, 23;
    Psalm 141:10).

Gather spoils (v. 25).

Bless the Lord (v. 26).

DAY FIVE

I've said it before, but it bears repeating: Satan's primary objective is to get us into sin. His target is your mind, or as the New Testament refers to it, your heart. (The Jews believed that you thought with your heart.)

Sin doesn't originate in your actions; it begins in your mind. If you don't learn to control your thoughts, you'll find yourself ensnared by the devil. The following letter illustrates this so well:

As I listened to your program this week, it was as if you were talking about me. I had been married for many years, had teenage boys, but was so unhappy at home. I felt empty. My husband had always been a good provider, but he wouldn't show those little expressions of love that

I needed. He never remembered birthdays, anniversaries, Mother's Day (he said I wasn't his mother), or Valentine's Day. He rarely said, "I love you," unless I asked him.

Then, I met this woman. I was drawn to her. It started off as my wanting to help her, then I wanted to be with her all of the time. I would make excuses to go see her. I suspected that she had at one time been a lesbian. My mind started thinking what it would be like to be with her. We never had an affair, but I nearly lost my home and family because I got to where I didn't care.

I was tired of being taken advantage of at home. It seemed like all they wanted was a maid and cook. So I rebelled against it all.

I never told my husband; as a matter of fact, I denied it. I could not imagine me, a Christian of some twenty-five years, even considering it. I cried a lot. I stayed in constant prayer. I couldn't sleep; I lost a lot of weight. I just couldn't imagine what was happening to me.

It still scares me to death to think that I could let Satan come in and do such a thing. I had to realize that I wasn't above anything. (I thought I was.)

I thought a Christian wouldn't even be thinking such things. I thought I nearly hated my husband (a trick of Satan's). Now I realize I do love him and how terribly stupid I was. If husbands could only realize how we women crave our husband's attention. I'm not saying it was my husband's fault. I know I am responsible for my own actions, but I wouldn't have had that need if things had been right at home.

Please tell women not to ever start thinking about being with anybody whether male or female. I have (or I am) learning that when Satan brings these ideas to my mind to give them to the Lord right then and not dwell on them. I have depended on several verses to help me: 1 Corinthians 10:13; Philippians 3:13; 4:8.

O my friend, do you hear her admonition? What do you think about? What thoughts are you entertaining that you shouldn't?

Look up the following verses, and note what you learn about the heart (mind). Then you'll understand why it's Satan's primary target.

1. Proverbs 4:23

2. Proverbs 23:7 (Watch the context, but note that the man says one thing, but there's something else in his heart.)

3. Matthew 15:18–19

4. 2 Corinthians 10:3–6 (You'll also want to note the context of this passage.)

5. 2 Corinthians 11:3

6. Philippians 4:8

7. Write a brief summary of what you have learned about the mind.

What happens when ungodly thoughts go unchecked? A thought can become an action. If it is repeated enough, it becomes a habit. Eventually it can become a base of oppression for the enemy — what I'll call a stronghold.

Satan wants to ensnare Christians because when God's children are caught in sin, God has to discipline us. A child of God who's involved in sin is not ready to be used of God. Can you see then why Satan moves as he does?

Listen to 2 Timothy 2:20–22:

Now in a large house there are not only gold and silver vessels, but also vessels of wood and of earthenware, and some to honor and some to dishonor. Therefore, if a man cleanses himself from these *things,* he will be a vessel for honor, sanctified, useful to the Master, prepared for every good work. Now flee from youthful lusts, and pursue righteousness, faith, love *and* peace, with those who call on the Lord from a pure heart.

Read that again carefully. Note the *if.* What's a person to do in order to be useful to the Master, prepared for every good work? Write it out.

In your present state, my friend, are you useful to the Master? Why?

Second Timothy 2:24–26 goes on to say how the bondservant of the Lord is to respond to those caught in the devil's snare. Read it and note what happens to the one ensnared by Satan.

> And the Lord's bond-servant must not be quarrelsome, but be kind to all, able to teach, patient when wronged, with gentleness correcting those who are in opposition, if perhaps God may grant them repentance leading to the knowledge of the truth, and they may come to their senses *and escape* from the snare of the devil, having been held captive by him to do his will.

What happens to those ensnared by the devil?

Satan not only targets your thoughts, he also targets your dreams. Let me share one more illustration that shows how the enemy can use dreams to influence us, and then we'll call it a day.

> I became involved with my associate pastor in 1970. It all started by my dreaming about him. Then I started attending one of his morning Bible studies. I began to notice his attention toward me was not what it should have been, but I must admit it was what I wanted. It had all become so real in my dreams that when the affair became a reality it was even more wonderful.

Let me pause a minute to tell you why I was attracted to this man. He was all I wanted my husband to be spiritually, and I was drawn to him because I saw (I thought) Jesus Christ in him.

The moment I gave him the first sign I was interested (my big mistake) we were off and running for about six months. It was so ugly and at the same time so wonderful.

As I look back over this mess, I realized how Satan never let us get caught. We met in all kinds of places day and night. We talked about how wrong it was. Every time we parted, we were never going to call or see each other again. But that desire was there and would not go away until the pastor found out about it when the secretary happened to pick up the phone and listen to our conversation.

The pastor called us in separately and we told our story. He was asked to leave the church. He told the church without mentioning my name.

I went home that night and told my husband. We wept together and he forgave me. I know God has forgiven me, but, oh my, it has been a long time in coming that I can forgive myself.

I never thought God could or would use me ever again. You see I had only been saved four years when this happened. I couldn't believe something like this could happen, because this was my lifestyle before I was saved and I just knew I loved God too much to do this to Him now! So you see I let my guard down, feeling safe and secure, and Satan stepped right in and said, "Who do you think you are?" Oh my, how he can and will deceive us if we are not in the Word and on our knees daily.

Well, it has been twenty years. I live two thousand miles from that church, and I am teaching Sunday school in a Spirit-filled church. Hardly a day goes by after all this time that I am not reminded of what Jesus forgave me, and that He loves me in spite of it. Praise His Holy Name.

There's something I don't want you to miss. The dear woman kept the helmet of her salvation on! Although she sinned, she did not allow the enemy to convince her that God wouldn't have anything to do with her anymore, or that He would cast her off forever. She survived Satan's accusations because she covered her head with her helmet. Remember that, Beloved, and do the same.

However, if sin is the habit of your life and you realize that you're the same as you've always been, that you're not a new creature in Christ Jesus, then in all probability you're not saved. Examine yourself to see if you're in the faith (2 Corinthians 13:5). The Lord doesn't have you examine yourself in order to condemn you, rather He does it so you won't be deceived and consequently perish. If it's the devil causing you to doubt your salvation, he'll try to convince you that God won't ever save you because of who you are or because of what you've done. Satan condemns; God gives hope. That's how you can tell the difference.

DAY SIX

Satan not only puts thoughts in your mind, many times disguising them as your own, but sometimes they seem to be voices. Listen...

At the age of twenty-six I wanted the Lord in my life. I had gotten on some drugs, and almost killed myself. I was due for back surgery. I never would tell my doctor that I had taken drugs. I was so worried that something would happen to me in surgery. One night it was like out of the blue. I was sitting at the table, and the fear of death came over me so bad that I went into our guest bedroom, laid on the bed, and called on Jesus to please save me. Until then I had never asked Jesus into my life.

But I've also started having terrible thoughts against God. (I mean nasty, vulgar thoughts.) Thoughts I would never want to say to anyone.

For the longest time I would not talk to anyone about my problems. It was terrible...inside was a voice telling me not to tell anyone, so I walked around thinking "there's no hope." I thought about killing myself. But I knew better. But I felt like with these thoughts I didn't deserve to live.

I have called on Him to save me. But, Kay, what about these thoughts that run through my mind? Can you please help me? I need some kind of understanding, for I don't want to have such thoughts. Is it just Satan trying to drive me crazy and keep me worried all the time?

Can I be saved with these thoughts? Please, Kay, write me soon!

Bless her heart! The enemy's trying to deliver a death blow to this young woman's head as he bashes in her helmet of salvation. She's also having a hard time with her shield of faith. She's just a babe in Christ. She needs to soak her shield in the water of the Word. Yet we have to believe that God has permitted all of this and that it is not more than she can bear. This is God's promise in 1 Corinthians 10:13. It's yours, too — write it out and then spend the weekend memorizing it so you can whip it out when you think you're facing more than you can bear.

Now, although the question may not be necessary, I'll ask it anyway, "Where are these voices coming from?" Obviously they are not from God. But how do I know that? Because, Beloved, the thoughts are not in accordance with God's character or His Word. Are these thoughts in accordance with the lies of the enemy? Yes, they are. Of course the devil would like her to think that these are her thoughts — or God's. Just as long she doesn't see them as from him!

You might be thinking these thoughts come from an ungodly past. Not necessarily. Yesterday I was talking to a dear and spiritually mature friend who's been discipled by the most godly woman she has ever known. The woman who discipled her is very old, but very alert. She lives in constant communion with the Lord and has walked with Him in great intimacy for decades. Right now she's writing about the last days! Recently she told my friend that she was being tormented by "voices." She said that if she told others she felt that they would say it was simply senility finally creeping in. She knows it's the enemy, and so does my friend.

What are these voices? They are fiery darts from the enemy. Satan is real, my friend. He's a spirit with a personality. And although he is not omnipresent or omniscient, he has a host of evil entities working with him — evil spirits, demons with varying ranks and responsibilities. Ephesians 1:21; 3:10; and 6:12 show us this. We're in a warfare! We must learn to ask the Lord, "Is it warfare?" And if He answers yes, we need to cry, "Teach me to stand!"

As this age comes to a close, the war is going to escalate. Satan's end is determined. As you've seen, the Book of Revelation records it. Revelation also tells us Satan will not surrender. He'll give it all he has. He'll fight to the death.

And what will be Satan's first and primary battleground? Your mind.

Let's look at 2 Corinthians 10:3–5 again. Read it carefully.

For though we walk in the flesh, we do not war according to the flesh, for the weapons of our warfare are not of the flesh, but divinely powerful for the destruction of fortresses. We are destroying speculations and every lofty thing raised up against the knowledge of God, and we are taking every thought captive to the obedience of Christ.

Let me help you understand the context in which these verses were written. No church Paul ministered to had more problems than the church at Corinth. Plus, there were people there who did not like Paul. Physically, Paul was not what Greeks admired. Further, his speech lacked eloquence. They were enamored with eloquence and the art of rhetoric. Thus, many preferred the silver-tongued Apollos to Paul. On top of all this they also felt Paul was two-faced — one way when he was with them, another way in his letters. They really weren't sure Paul was a genuine apostle. It was rough ministering to this church he'd fathered in the gospel! Can you relate? I can. Leadership is never easy. The devil will see to that!

The Corinthians looked at things as they were outwardly (10:7). Their thoughts were speculations, empty speculations. Because they embraced them, these thoughts became strongholds of wrong thinking. As a result, they couldn't believe or wouldn't be convinced they were wrong.

That's the context — now the principles for warfare.

First, we must recognize that when others misunderstand us, it may be spiritual warfare. Spiritual battles are not fought with flesh and blood weapons. "A successful campaign can be waged in the spiritual realm only as worldly weapons are abandoned and total reliance is placed on the spiritual weaponry, which is divinely potent for demolishing apparently impregnable fortresses where evil is entrenched and from which the gospel is attacked."[2]

Second, we need to see that people can be held in bondage by wrong thoughts, worldly philosophies, worldly wisdom, wrong doctrine, and all sorts of lies from the father of lies. These are fortresses of wrong thinking which need to be torn down, destroyed. Any speculation (imagination) or thinking that is contrary to God, to His Word, and to our position in Christ and what God says about us is to be destroyed. We are not to allow these thoughts to continue. If we do, Satan will be the victor. Any thought which would lead us to disobedience or unbelief is not from God, and it, too, must be dealt with. We have the weapons to bring down those strongholds.

The key is Paul's example: "We are taking every thought captive to the obedience of Christ." In the Greek construction he uses a present active participle, indicating that this is "a continual struggle and warfare."[3]

Aichmalōtizō means "to lead away captive" or "to subjugate, to bring under control." This, then, is what we must do with every thought: Subjugate it to Christ! And we must do it continually.

Now with that said, I want to take the principles we have studied and share with you how I believe strongholds of wrong thinking are erected in our own minds.

The enemy will send a fiery dart (thought) to our mind: a lie, a thought of rejection, a wrong doctrine, a deprecating thought, a suggestion to do evil, whatever.

When the thought comes, we should bring it captive to Jesus Christ:

1. Evaluate the thought. Frisk it at the door of your mind. Philippians 4:8 it! "Finally, brethren, whatever is true, whatever is honorable, whatever is right, whatever is pure, whatever is lovely, whatever is of good repute, if

there is any excellence and if anything worthy of praise, let your mind dwell on these things."

2. Reject this thought if it doesn't meet the qualifications (2 Corinthians 10:5) and replace it (Philippians 4:8; Isaiah 26:3).

If the thought does not meet the qualifications of Philippians 4:8, we must not consider or entertain it. We must take it captive! If we don't, it can become a stronghold of wrong thinking, a fortress which will hold us prisoner. We will become the captive, instead of the captor.

The acceptance of a wrong thought can then lead to

An action
　　Which creates an appetite
　　　　Which becomes a weakness
　　　　　　Which becomes a habit
　　　　　　　　Which brings oppression from the enemy.

Think about it. Next week we'll talk about what to do if you find yourself, or a loved one, held hostage by the enemy.

Tomorrow, since Ephesians deals with family relationships, I want us to see specifically how the enemy is targeting the family.

D A Y   S E V E N

Satan has targeted the family unit for destruction. His success is phenomenal.

Why the family? Look at Ephesians 3:15 and write it out.

There is some debate over exactly what the phrase "in heaven and on earth" means in respect to families. However, we know one thing for sure — whatever family in heaven and on earth is being referred to, there is only one Father, our Father God. He is the Father of fathers, the supreme example of fatherhood. From Him every family in heaven and on earth derives its name. Therefore, every family is to be modeled after His example of love and righteousness. The first mention of the family in the Book of Ephesians is in chapter 3. But the standard for the family is presented in the practical segment of Ephesians, the segment where we're told how to walk in the light of our wealth.

Take a minute and read Ephesians 5:22–6:4. What relationships are mentioned? Note these below.

Satan has targeted the family because the relationship between the husband and wife and between the parents and children are to be earthly examples of our heavenly Father and His family. If people want to know what it's like to belong to God, they should be able to look at Christians' relationships and homes and get a taste of heaven.

The devil's principalities and powers rule over nations. The family is the backbone of any nation. Families produce the nation's leaders. Study Hitler's family, and you'll see how he got his start. The saga of the Mafia is portrayed in "Godfather," demonstrating again the significant impact of the family as we see how the devil used these Sicilians to spread crime, murder, gambling, drugs, alcohol, and prostitution throughout our country on a wholesale level — a country founded on biblical values and a fear of God.

One of the greatest threats to Satan's progress will be a committed Christian husband and wife who are determined to raise godly children for the furtherance of the kingdom of God. Families such as these will be on Satan's bombing run. Because the more committed Christian families there are in a nation, the greater will be their collective influence upon that nation.

The second family unit Satan targets is a family where both parents are present but only one is a committed Christian. Why? First Corinthians 7:14

tells us "the unbelieving husband is sanctified through his wife, and the unbelieving wife is sanctified through her believing husband; for otherwise your children are unclean, but now they are holy."

One Christian parent in a family has a sanctifying effect on that family unit. They serve as salt to stop the spread of corruption and to make the others thirst for Christ. They are also light. They dispel darkness and manifest to the family the light of Christ by their visible good works. This is why God doesn't want the believer to leave the unbeliever — and why Satan counsels so many to get a divorce.

Now, what is the tempter's strategy for breaking up the family unit? He knows the weakness of our flesh — remember we once walked in the lusts of our flesh when we were sons of disobedience. He's going to do everything he can to entice us to sin. One of his most wicked devices is pornography — it's destroying marital relationships because it leads to sexual perversion. This is why it is imperative, first that we fulfill our sexual roles in marriage, and second that we remember that if we look upon others to lust after them in our heart, it is adultery — and God judges adultery.

Look up Hebrews 13:4 and write it out.

Now turn to 1 Corinthians 7:3–5 in your Bible. You can mark your red pitchfork again. Read the verses, then write out below how we make our mates vulnerable to Satan.

250 LORD, IS IT WARFARE? TEACH ME TO STAND

Satan will also do everything he can to keep us from fulfilling our family responsibilities to our children. Children follow in their parents' footsteps. They also often reap the harvest of their parents' sins. Satan will do all he can to keep parents from loving and nurturing their children. His desire is to turn the hearts of the fathers from their children, and the children from their fathers. Alienation is his game.

O beloved, guard your family, guard your marriage. Walk as Paul teaches you to walk in Ephesians 5:15–6:4.

What will be your prayer of affirmation this week, Beloved? Also, record any new insights on Satan on your list.

LORD, HOW DO I TAKE THE OFFENSE AGAINST SATAN?

A ssailed by evil thoughts? Tormented by a besetting sin? Hindered in your service for God? Sick but don't know why? Loved ones blind to salvation? You're not alone. And it could be warfare. When James Fraser, missionary to China, was assailed by evil thoughts, he wrote:

> These thoughts were present with me even when I was preaching. I went out of the city to a hidden gully on the hillside, one of my prayer-haunts, and there voiced my determined resistance to Satan in the matter. I claimed deliverance on the ground of my Redeemer's victory on the Cross. I even shouted my resistance to Satan and all his thoughts. The obsession collapsed then and there, like a pack of cards, to return no more.
>
> In times of conflict I still find deliverance through repeating Scriptures out loud, appropriate Scripture, brought to my mind through the Holy Spirit. It is like crashing through opposition. "Resist the devil and he will flee from you."[1]

One of my "sons" in the Lord, Steve Rowan, missionary to Lima, Peru, wrote in one of his prayer letters:

In Peru there are five New Testament translations that are in the final stages of revision, but Satan is trying his best to thwart their completion. Each of the translation teams has experienced serious health problems that have stopped progress.

In the spring of 1990, when I was teaching in Hong Kong, I picked up OMS International's publication "On Borrowed Time," a little front-and-back handout for "Monitoring Hong Kong Life in Its Countdown to 1997." I read:

Spiritual war rages in the area. Pastor Tony Kwan in Macau reports that several members of his church have been attacked physically at night by a 'presence' and only the Name of Jesus has brought relief. He says, "This is not TV or a movie, this is *real*! Pray that we will be strong in the Lord to overcome."

Joseph Carroll from the Evangelical Institute of Greenville, South Carolina, wrote:

I am convinced that one of the reasons why the Lord led us to commence the Institute was…many of our graduates who are now on foreign fields have testified that they could never have maintained their spiritual equilibrium had they not mastered the basic principles enunciated in our course on spiritual warfare. More than ever this course is needful as the enemy is now accelerating his activity as evidenced in the New Age movement and the rapid formulating of organizations which are leading to the day of the antichrist.

Graham Smith, an Australian pastor, sat in our breakfast room and told us of a fellow minister who rescued three girls from a witches' coven. Afterwards all sorts of harassment ensued. At the church furniture would move all of a sudden. You couldn't see anyone moving it. He had several near accidents in which people from the coven tried to force him off the road. Then quite suddenly his young son became very sick. They discovered a tumor in a critical position on his spine. After X-rays and examination by several doctors, his son was taken to the Royal Children's Hospital in Brisbane. There the need for surgery was confirmed. As the minister continued to seek the Lord, he deduced that this was a satanic attack. He gathered others for prayer to resist the enemy. When the surgeon opened up the little boy, the tumor was gone. He simply sewed him back up. The boy is fine.

I received this short but sweet letter from a young mother who was led to the Lord by one of our staff and has taken seven of our Precept courses.

Regular and spiritual warfare prayers, a daily quiet time, a daily Precept study, let alone a heart surrendered to the Lord and His will, were not enough to deliver me from defeat. I was led by the Lord to seek Judy for counseling. She prayed with me, and the Lord was so gracious to deliver me of my strongholds. The fruit has been so tremendous that my husband has noticed.

I love the Lord with all my heart. He is the "joy of my desire" as sung on a praise and worship tape.

The Holy Spirit keeps bearing witness that I have been set free, free spiritually to be part of the army that the Lord Himself is raising up despite Satan's schemes to interfere.

The director of my daily radio program, "How Can I Live?" received this letter:

For over thirty years I have been "addicted" to soap operas. I had tried everything I knew to stop watching — prayer, claiming Scripture, etc. But they had such a grip on me. Then after reading about Kay's release from the grip immoral dreams had on her by demanding that the spirit leave her, I was able to do the same thing. Praise the Lord, I feel as if a heavy weight has been taken off my shoulders and I can continue to grow spiritually. It's almost like being born again.

Yes, beloved student, it is warfare, but don't be afraid of the lion's roar.
The Lord is on your side! You needn't stand dressed in your belt, breastplate,
and shoes with your knees knocking, shield shaking, and your helmet sway-
ing on your head. You have a sharp, two-edged sword and a "walkie-talkie."
We'll learn about these in this final, critical week.

As we finish this study on warfare, let me remind you once again that
questions and differences of opinions on the subject of warfare are to be
expected because the body of Jesus Christ has varying viewpoints on the
topics. If you're doing this study in a group setting, you've probably already
realized this fact. Christians are divided on a lot of things, and all of us sin-
cerely believe we're right, especially if we've done a lot of inductive study on
our own and believe we've handled the subject with integrity.

So what are we to do? We should continue to study the subject with an
open heart, telling the Lord we want to be led into truth and kept from error.
At the same time, we must realize that even then we may not be in total
agreement. Oneness in doctrine will happen when we get to heaven because
then we won't see through a glass darkly. We'll know and understand truth
in all its purity because we will sit at His feet.

Until then, we are to strive to keep the unity of the Spirit in the bond of
peace. The seven essentials for the unity of Spirit are listed in Ephesians
4:4–6. Read Ephesians 4:1–6, and list how we are to walk in a manner worthy of our Lord, and then list the seven essentials.

THE SEVEN ESSENTIALS

HOW TO WALK WORTHY   OF UNITY

HOW TO WALK WORTHY

THE SEVEN ESSENTIALS
OF UNITY

Make these seven essentials the basis of your fellowship, and keep the unity of the Spirit until you come to the unity of the faith. Remember what you have learned about the shoes of peace, and walk accordingly — lest Satan deceive you.

After you read through the rest of the instructions that follow, read Ephesians 6:10–18 on your knees.

As you read, put on each piece of the armor by faith in prayer. Remember the significance of each piece, and tell God you want to live accordingly. For example, when you come to the belt of truth, tell God that you believe His Word is truth and that you want His truth to hold everything in your life in its proper place.

As you pray, the Lord will lead you. Your words don't have to be fancy or eloquent, nor your prayer long. Simply talk it through with your Father. This exercise is what I call praying back scripture to God. When you pray this way, you know you have the petitions you've desired because you have fulfilled John 15:7.

Also pray back aloud to God the principles you have learned in this passage. For instance, when you come to "stand firm," you know that to stand firm means to hold your position. Think through the truths of Ephesians 1. Thank God that He chose you in Christ Jesus before the world was ever created. Thank Him for adopting you into His family, for being your Father, etc.

Tomorrow we'll look at the sword of the Spirit.

Paul doesn't leave us in the dark about the meaning of the sword of the Spirit. He says it is "the Word of God."

"But," you may ask, "if the sword of the Spirit is the Word of God, how does it differ from the belt of truth and the shield of faith?"

First, it is both a defensive weapon and an offensive weapon. You don't put the sword on! You take it up.

Second, it does not refer to the entire Bible, from Genesis to Revelation. The English transliteration of the Greek word used in Ephesians 6:17 for *word* is *rhēma,* not *logos.*

Both words are used to describe the Word of God. *Logos* "denotes 'the expression of thought' — not the mere name of an object...and 'the Personal Word,' a title of the Son of God." *Rhēma* "denotes 'that which is spoken, what is uttered in speech or writing.'... The significance of *rhēma* (as distinct from *logos)* is exemplified in the injunction to take 'the sword of the Spirit, which is the word of God.'... Here the reference is not to the whole Bible as such, but to the individual scripture which the Spirit brings to our remembrance for use in time of need, a prerequisite being the regular storing of the mind with Scripture."[2]

The word used for *sword* in this passage is *machaira* and "signifies the short, straight sword used by the Roman soldier."[3] It was used for hand-to-hand combat and required skill.

The sword was put in the scabbard or sheath which hung from the belt of truth. Neat picture, isn't it? The sword symbolized a specific verse or segment of truth needed in a particular conflict with the enemy. We see Jesus use Scripture in this way when Satan tempted Him (Luke 4:1–13).

Can you see how critical it is that we're skilled in the Word of God? If we hear or experience something and don't bring it to the plumb line of the Word to determine if it is accurate, then we can get off balance. Don't go off into battle unskilled in the use of your sword.

1. Look up the following verses and write out what you learn about the Son's triumph over the devil. You've looked up some of these earlier, but I

want you to see them grouped together. It will help you understand why you have the authority you do. (The meaning of *power* or *domain* in the Greek is "authority.")

    a. Colossians 1:13

    b. Colossians 2:15

    c. John 12:31

    d. Hebrews 2:14

    e. 1 John 3:8

    2. Now how could you use these particular verses as your sword in warfare?

When God became man and began His public ministry, it seemed that hell broke loose. The demons recognized Him and often created a scene, falling at His feet or crying out, "Ha! What do we have to do with You, Jesus of Nazareth? Have You come to destroy us? I know who You are — the Holy One of God!" (Luke 4:34). Why this sudden outburst? What was happening?

3. Matthew 12:22–32, 43–45 is printed out for you. It will help you see how to use your sword. Read it carefully and mark every reference to Satan and his demons. When you finish, I'll ask you some questions.

➤ MATTHEW 12:22-32

22 Then there was brought to Him a demon-possessed man *who was* blind and dumb, and He healed him, so that the dumb man spoke and saw.

23 And all the multitudes were amazed, and *began* to say, "This *man* cannot be the Son of David, can he?"

24 But when the Pharisees heard it, they said, "This man casts out demons only by Beelzebul the ruler of the demons."

25 And knowing their thoughts He said to them, "Any kingdom divided against itself is laid waste; and any city or house divided against itself shall not stand.

26 "And if Satan casts out Satan, he is divided against himself; how then shall his kingdom stand?

27 "And if I by Beelzebul cast out demons, by whom do your sons cast them out? Consequently they shall be your judges.

28 "But if I cast out demons by the Spirit of God, then the kingdom of God has come upon you.

29 "Or how can anyone enter the strong man's house and carry off his property, unless he first binds the strong *man?* And then he will plunder his house.

30 "He who is not with Me is against Me; and he who does not gather with Me scatters.

31 "Therefore I say to you, any sin and blasphemy shall be forgiven men, but blasphemy against the Spirit shall not be forgiven.

32 "And whoever shall speak a word against the Son of Man, it shall be forgiven him; but whoever shall speak against the Holy Spirit, it shall not be forgiven him, either in this age, or in the *age* to come."

➤ MATTHEW 12:43–45

43 "Now when the unclean spirit goes out of a man, it passes through waterless places, seeking rest, and does not find *it*.

44 "Then it says, 'I will return to my house from which I came'; and when it comes, it finds it unoccupied, swept, and put in order.

45 "Then it goes, and takes along with it seven other spirits more wicked than itself, and they go in and live there; and the last state of that man becomes worse than the first. That is the way it will also be with this evil generation."

a. What did the crowd accuse Jesus of doing?

b. How was Jesus casting out demons? How did Jesus say He did it?

c. What did the casting out of demons show?

d. In what way do you think it showed it?

Luke is the chronological yardstick for the other gospels. The account that you just studied in Matthew is also recorded in Luke 11:14–26. (See what preceded this event.)

After being tempted by the devil, Jesus returned to Galilee in the power of the Spirit. While there, He went to his hometown of Nazareth. On the Sabbath, He entered the synagogue, took the scroll, and read from Isaiah 61.

4. Read Luke 4:18–21, and list the things which were being fulfilled before their eyes.

5. Do you see any relationship between the Isaiah passage Jesus read that day and what Jesus was doing in the passages we just studied in Luke 11 and Matthew 12? What?

As you read through the Gospels, you'll see sixteen accounts of Jesus and His disciples encountering demons. However, we know in Jesus' three-and-a-half years of public ministry there were other encounters with demons because other passages tell us Jesus went throughout all Galilee preaching and casting out demons (Mark 1:34–39; Matthew 4:23–25). We also know that His confrontations with the kingdom of darkness occurred right up to the end of His public ministry (Luke 13:32).

Why all these clashes with demons? Because confronting the enemy and setting captives free was an integral part of our Lord's mission. The demons recognized Jesus and trembled because they knew their fate.

The kingdom of God had come. With it came the authority of heaven — authority that had to be obeyed. Jesus cast out demons by the Spirit of God. He bound the strong man and plundered his house, reclaiming souls for the kingdom, proclaiming release to the captives and setting free the downtrodden.

And when His hour came, He paid the price for our redemption, conquered death, and ascended to the Father. However, before He went to sit at the right hand of God, He commissioned you to "occupy" until He returns.

Satan is strong, but he is not strong enough to resist God! Don't tremble or be alarmed. God has given you His Spirit, the same One who through Jesus cast out demons. He has given you His Sword, the Word of God. And He has given you a direct line to His throne room through prayer. You needn't always live on the defensive — you can take the offensive!

DAY   THREE

The Sword of the Spirit and prayer are the Christian's two offensive weapons in warfare.

Years ago as I was teaching Ephesians 6 on the Christian's armor, God showed me how to describe prayer in respect to modern day weaponry — the walkie-talkie. Prayer is our means of staying in communication with God, so as "we walkie, we should talkie!" Warfare prayer is the means of knowing how to advance on the enemy for the release of captives. It's not only a defensive but an offensive attack led by our Commander-in-Chief.

I've seen enough war movies to know that communication with the command post is imperative. The movie *A Bridge Too Far* was a reenactment of Operation Market Garden, a plan devised by General Montgomery to seize seven key bridges. These bridges would then be used as supply lines so the British could outflank the West Wall and drive into Germany.

Operation Market Garden was the biggest operation since D-Day. Yet behind the scenes there raged a battle of rivaling egos — Patton's and Montgomery's. Both needed supplies in their arenas of war, but Monty persuaded President Eisenhower that Operation Market Garden was the way to go. In Monty's eagerness to get on with his plan, basic principles of war were ignored. Thousands were lost in that operation, primarily because they ignored the principle of communication. The radios were old and did not work properly. But those who were responsible for sending the radios to the battle zone were confident that if they weren't strong enough to cover the specified range, it wouldn't matter in the end.

But it did! The movie chronicles their poor judgment in gory Technicolor. Our men watched American planes drop supplies behind enemy lines. Due to faulty radio equipment the necessary ground cover could not be ordered. Men were slaughtered. One division was cut off from another with no way of knowing what to do. Communication was impossible. The rivers ran red. Market Garden failed.

And you will fail too, Beloved, if you ignore your offensive weapons: the Word and prayer. What would happen to the kingdom of darkness if believers ever learned to wield their swords skillfully in hand-to-hand combat as they cried to their Supreme Commander-in-Chief to call out more forces? Let's find out.

As we studied the first two chapters of Ephesians, it was clear that positionally we are seated in heavenly places with our Lord Jesus Christ — far above all rule and authority and power and dominion and every name that is named. There is none above us but our heavenly Father.

1. Read Paul's prayer in Ephesians 3:14–21, and fill in the chart that follows:

WHAT PAUL PRAYS WE'LL KNOW	WHAT GOD IS ABLE TO DO FOR US

WHAT PAUL PRAYS
WE'LL KNOW

WHAT GOD IS ABLE
TO DO FOR US

Power is essential in warfare. And if you want victory, you'll need power greater than your enemy's. From what you've seen, it should be obvious that you have sufficient power. It's not simply because God is on your side, but because He has given you power. In case you need a little more evidence, look up the following verses and record what you learn.

1. Acts 1:8 (The English transliteration of the Greek word for *power* is *dunamis,* which means "power, ability," physical or moral "power in action."[4])

2. 1 John 4:4

Power is one thing. Authority is another. Together they are unconquerable, especially if there is no authority or power that can override your authority and power. And who can override God's authority and power? No one!

During His three-and-a-half years of public ministry, there was never an incident when Jesus gave a command and the devil or his demons did not obey. As the Son of Man, Jesus had God's absolute authority and absolute power at His disposal. It was this authority and power He used, not His own. You can do the same!

Look up the following verses and note what you learn from each about Jesus' authority and how He did or didn't exercise it.

1. Matthew 4:10

2. Luke 4:31–37

3. Mark 9:17–29

4. Luke 13:10–17

5. Luke 22:31 (If you are using a KJV Bible, in the original Greek language the word translated *desired* means "obtained by asking or demanding permission.")

6. John 19:10–11

Tomorrow, we'll look at the Christian's authority.

DAY FOUR

Beloved, I want you to understand that because of the work of your Kinsman Redeemer you have the power and the authority to overcome the evil one.

Let me quote what the *Expositor's Bible Commentary* has to say about overcoming the evil one based on 1 John 2:13b.

The description of the community as "young men" who "are strong" and "have overcome" adds a new dimension. Believers are to see themselves as not only in conflict with the enemy but as having perceived the victory in Christ's name and by his power. The victory obviously was gained through Christ's death, and now his followers have the task under his leadership of establishing his reign over the world and the devil. This victory, seen as already realized, does not promise that believers shall be removed from the heat and peril of the battlefield. But it does assure them that if they are faithful they will overcome the "evil one." As

Christ has been victorious over the evil one, so they too may commit themselves to the conflict without fear... After again referring to the "fathers," John, "concludes by addressing the young men as those in whom 'the word of God lives.' They were indeed 'strong' as the children of faith, but the author reminds them that their strength ultimately depends on one fact alone — the Word of God abiding or living in them.[5]

At salvation God's power and authority over the evil one is given to every believer. However, God's power is not seen as mightily in some believers as in others either because some don't know the power and authority that is theirs or they don't appropriate it. If you use the offensive weapons of the word and prayer, you appropriate your power and authority.

In Luke 9:1–2 we read, "And He called the twelve together, and gave them power and authority over all the demons, and to heal diseases. And He sent them out to proclaim the kingdom of God, and to perform healing."

There it is — power and authority given to the twelve. Are you nodding your head and saying, "That's right. Jesus gave it to the twelve but that's not us!"

Read Luke 10:1–20 and answer the following questions:

1. How many did Jesus send out?

2. What were they sent to do? Don't get caught up in details; just give the broad picture.

3. When they came back, what were they excited about?

4. What had Jesus seen?

5. What authority did Jesus give them?

6. What are they to rejoice in?

When Jesus commissioned the seventy, there is no record that He told them they would have the power and authority to cast out demons. Maybe this insight explains why they were so excited when it happened. Apparently they found themselves confronted by the enemy and simply did what they had seen Jesus do when he dealt with demons. It worked! They were filled with joy.

When they returned, Jesus confirmed that He was watching Satan fall from heaven like lightning. That's an interesting statement, isn't it? They dealt with demons, and Jesus saw Satan falling from heaven.

In commenting on this, F. F. Bruce says, "The kingdom has come, 'the success of the disciples is regarded as a symbol and earnest of the complete overthrow of Satan.'"[6] "When the disciples exorcise demons, the forces of evil are shaken, symbolizing the defeat of Satan himself."[7]

Why does Jesus tell them not to rejoice that the demons are subject to them but to rejoice that their names are written in heaven? Could it be because He wants them to understand that their authority over the evil one and all his demons is the birthright of every child of God? I think so. In fact, I think that's why He didn't tell them they had this authority when He sent them out. Rather, He let them experience it on their own and then explained why they had it. "'Do not rejoice' does not exclude the disciples' taking joy in spiritual victories."[8]

Are you going to say, "But, Kay, that was the seventy who had been following Jesus — they had authority, but do we?" Let's look at Matthew 16:15–20.

➤ MATTHEW 16:15-20

15 He said to them, "But who do you say that I am?"

16 And Simon Peter answered and said, "Thou art the Christ, the Son of the living God."

17 And Jesus answered and said to him, "Blessed are you, Simon Barjona, because flesh and blood did not reveal *this* to you, but My Father who is in heaven.

18 "And I also say to you that you are Peter, and upon this rock I will build My church; and the gates of Hades shall not overpower it.

19 "I will give you the keys of the kingdom of heaven; and whatever you shall bind on earth shall be bound in heaven, and whatever you shall loose on earth shall be loosed in heaven."

20 Then He warned the disciples that they should tell no one that He was the Christ.

Here was a promise that the gates of hell would not overpower the church. "The 'gates of Hades' have been taken to represent the strength of Satan and his cohorts (since 'gates' can refer to 'fortifications').... The church, because Jesus is building it, cannot be defeated by the hosts of darkness."[9]

We are the church (Ephesians 1–2). The church is not a building but a body — a body comprised of all those who have believed on and received the Lord Jesus Christ. The gates of hell can't overpower you! You need not fear the enemy — just fear God. When I say that you should fear God, remember that I mean a reverential trust in and an awesome respect of Him. If you truly fear God, you will not allow yourself to fear the enemy. There is no need to. Remember where you're seated!

Keys were a symbol of authority. Peter wasn't the only one who had the keys to the kingdom, not the only believer with authority. You too can bind and loose. The *International Bible Commentary* says "the keys of the kingdom of heaven are to be understood in the light of Isaiah 22:22; and the authority to bind and loose is not of admission and exclusion, but deciding what is and what is not the Lord's will. This latter promise in 18:18 extended not merely to the other disciples, but by inference to all spiritual Christians."[10]

The verbal construction of binding and loosing implies that you have the authority to bind on earth *whatever has already been bound in heaven,* and you have the authority to loose on earth *what has already been loosed in heaven.* In other words, you have the authority to execute the Father's will on earth.

Because Jesus has come to earth "heaven's rule has thereby broken in. Thus Jesus' disciples, in accordance with His gospel of the kingdom, take up the ministry of the keys and bind and loose on earth what has with the coming of the kingdom been bound and loosed in heaven."[11]

Some believe that using the "keys of the kingdom" has to do only with introducing people into the kingdom or telling them that if they don't receive Jesus Christ they will perish in hell. While it's true they will perish, I personally do not believe this explanation gives the full meaning of the phrase. If it did, then *whoever* would seem more logical, since it would be people who would be included or excluded from the kingdom. The term *whatever* seems to be more inclusive. Now, hang on, while I explain my thinking.

Jesus, as our Kinsman Redeemer, has won back for us what we lost in Adam. We now belong to the kingdom of heaven. We have received the power and authority to act as God's vice-regents on earth. However, this truth doesn't mean a believer can go into the "wholesale" business of binding and loosing — *indiscriminately* binding *all* world leaders, binding *all* sorts of infirmities, and binding the devil and his demons so that they cannot blind the minds of all the unsaved people in the world. Such action is ludicrous. Jesus didn't do that.

Remember, our authority is a bestowed authority and cannot be used contrary to or independently of the One who gave it to us. If we try, we'll fail. But if God tells us to act in a particular situation, then we'd better — and with confidence since we are doing the will of the Father. Thus, we begin to understand the role of faith which moves mountains. Faith always finds its strength not in the one believing but in the object of faith. Faith that moves mountains means that when God lets me know His will, I am to pray or act accordingly. God will accomplish whatever He directed me to act on. We see the principle in 1 John 5:14: "if we ask anything according to His will, He will do it."

Now, let's look at John 14:10–14. Philip has just asked Jesus to show them the Father, to which Jesus replies:

➤ JOHN 14:10–14

10 "Do you not believe that I am in the Father, and the Father is in Me? The words that I say to you I do not speak on My own initiative, but the Father abiding in Me does His works.

11 "Believe Me that I am in the Father, and the Father in Me; otherwise believe on account of the works themselves.

12 "Truly, truly, I say to you, he who believes in Me, the works that I do shall he do also; and greater works than these shall he do; because I go to the Father.

13 "And whatever you ask in My name, that will I do, that the Father may be glorified in the Son.

14 "If you ask Me anything in My name, I will do *it.*

15 "If you love Me, you will keep My commandments."

Jesus never acted independently of God. He always did what the Father told Him to do and always said what the Father told Him to say. God wants the same from us. Jesus walked by the Spirit, and by the Spirit of God He cast out demons. The same Holy Spirit is in us! When we walk under His control, not quenching or grieving Him, we will do the works that Jesus did. Why? We have the same Spirit, the same authority, and the same power. As a matter of fact, Jesus said that we would do greater works than His because He was going to the Father.

We're here to carry on our Lord's work. In order to do that, the Father has given us His authority and His power. Our problem is that we don't know it, or we know it and don't appropriate it, or we don't believe it's for today and, therefore, we live accordingly. Our faith is small. It moves sand castles, not mountains.

Read the Book of Acts; there is your example. Oh, I know that some would tell you we can't live that way today, but I would have to ask when or where God tells us differently? Beloved, don't just live in the Epistles; consider the whole counsel of the Word. If the Old Testament was for our learning, our example, what about the Gospels and Acts as well as the Epistles and Revelation?

Just before Jesus ascended, He said, "All authority has been given to Me in heaven and on earth. Go therefore and make disciples of all the nations, baptizing them in the name of the Father and the Son and the Holy Spirit, teaching them to observe all that I commanded you; and lo, I am with you always, even to the end of the age" (Matthew 28:18–20).

The One who has all authority told you to go. He sent the twelve, the seventy, and now it's you! His promise is the same: He'll be with you always, all the days, "even to the end of the age."

Take up your sword and go — the gates of hell will not overpower you.

DAY FIVE

The day the Lord set me free from the torment of immoral thoughts, attractions, and dreams, I recognized I was in a spiritual warfare and needed to exercise the authority which was mine. I used the sword of the Spirit and prayed.

Although I wasn't aware of it, I basically followed the pattern of James 4:7–8: "Submit therefore to God. Resist the devil and he will flee from you. Draw near to God and He will draw near to you. Cleanse your hands, you sinners; and purify your hearts, you double-minded."

To submit to the Lord is to align yourself under His authority. *Submit* is an aorist passive imperative verb in the Greek language. It's a command. Therefore, we're to obey. Second, it's in the passive voice. Therefore the subject receives the action of the verb; God is there ready to exercise His authority, but we are commanded to receive it.

On the other hand, in the Greek, *resist* is an aorist active imperative. Once again it is a command, but the active voice indicates that the subject performs the action rather than receives the action, as in the passive voice. The aorist imperative calls for urgent action. Because "he will flee" is in the future tense, it indicates that when you take your stand against the devil, *then* he will flee from you. In other words, resisting is not passive; it's active. We must resist!

I didn't know all these technicalities when I walked into the bathroom at the Evangelical Institute's conference center and locked the door. All I knew was that the oppression from my immoral dream was very heavy, and I needed help. I thought I finally saw what the problem was.

"Lord, all I can assume is that this is demonic, and I'm asking you in the name of your Son, the Lord Jesus Christ, and by His blood to set me free." Then I proceeded to tell God again how sorry I was for my past and that I wanted none of it. I named lustful thoughts and immorality for what they were. Then I asked God to set me free from any way in which the enemy had gained ground in my life. I asked Him to forgive me for any contacts I had ever had with anything from the occult. I remembered that someone had once tried to hypnotize me and that we tried to raise a coffee pot off the table through levitation. I told God that I didn't want anything ever to do with Satan because my body was His temple. I told him that I wanted every nook and cranny of my being to be filled with Him.

Then I commanded the spirit of immorality to leave me alone. I quoted aloud every verse I knew about my position in Christ over the enemy.

Among those verses was Revelation 12:11 where we read that they overcame the enemy by the blood of the Lamb, the word of their testimony, and by not loving their lives unto death. I claimed the blood of the Lord Jesus Christ which cleansed me from all sin and gave me forgiveness of sin. I reminded the devil and all his demons that because I had been saved (my testimony), greater was Jesus who was in me than Satan who's in the world. I rehearsed the fact that I was seated in the heavenlies above his power. Then I told Satan that I would die before I would give in to him — loving my life not unto death.

I thanked God once again and reminded Him I wanted His Spirit to fill every bit of me. I remembered the verse about the evil spirit going out, wandering around, then coming back and finding the house empty and taking in seven more spirits with him. Neither the devil nor his cohorts were going to have a place with me.

That day God set me free! There have been times when I have been on the edge of an immoral dream, but as soon as I awaken, I simply tell the enemy and his host that I want none of it. I command him to be gone, just as Jesus did.

I've shared this experience many times, and it has helped many who were plagued with things they couldn't shake — no matter how hard they tried, no matter how near they drew to God. When they have heard what God did for me, they have followed the pattern of James 4 and resisted the devil and have had victory.

I could tell a lot of war stories, but I'll use a very brief one. A woman who came to Bible study and later joined our staff was plagued with disabling nausea for years. Her only relief came when she could lie down and sleep. As the nausea began to occur more frequently, it crippled her. She went to doctors, to clinics, yet received no diagnosis or cure. She decided it must be nerves, but she asked God to show her. Then she heard my testimony about my dreams. As she was driving home from church one Sunday, the Lord confirmed to her that her problem was with the enemy. So she did what I had done, and from that day on she has had no trouble. At times when the sensation would start to come back, she would remind the enemy

that he had no place in her and that he had to depart. It's been years now —
and as she said, "The Lord has done it."

O Beloved, how we need to remember that our Lord is the deliverer, not
us. It's His authority and His power in us. Our role is simply to exercise it
under His leadership.

Some people object to using the terms *binding* and *loosing* in relationship
to Satan because they are so misused. However, we must realize that they are
used in relationship to the enemy. Of course Jesus talked about binding the
strong man when the Pharisees accused him of casting out demons by
Beelzebul. Then in Luke 13:10–16 we have the account of a daughter of
Abraham who, for eighteen years, had a "sickness caused by a spirit." When
Jesus freed her from her sickness, He said to the synagogue officials who
objected because He did it on the Sabbath: "And this woman, a daughter of
Abraham as she is, whom Satan *has bound* for eighteen long years, should
she not have been *released* from this bond on the Sabbath day?" The words
bound and *released* are from the same Greek words as *bind* (*bound*) and
loose(*d*) in Matthew 16:19.

Not long ago some friends shared the following story with us.

When John and I first met, he had a condition called spondelitus — a
rheumatoid arthritis of the spine. He had suffered with it for four years
at that point. The doctors had done everything they could — but nothing seemed to help. He could not run at all, and walked with a limp.
He had sought prayer from his pastor as well as different pastors and
teachers that came through the church. He had been anointed with oil,
and had them also lay hands on him — nothing happened. The pain
continued to persist. The doctors told him that within two to three
years this condition would move up his spine and leave his back totally
rigid — he would not be able to bend it at all. We dated for a year and
got engaged. I knew the pain he was suffering and that the future could
be clouded with this illness, but I loved him and I believed God would
take care of us.

One Sunday afternoon we were at John's parents' home for dinner.

We were getting ready to leave for evening church when he realized that the pain in his spine was just too great — he couldn't even stand. I felt so bad for him I asked if I could pray. He agreed — I think mainly to humor me because he felt so defeated because nothing had happened when others had prayed.

As I began to pray, all I can tell you is that a sense of authority began to arise in me which I had never experienced before or since that day. God showed me clearly that John was being afflicted physically by a demon. The name of it came clearly into my mind. Its name was Gemini (a sign of the zodiac). Also interestingly enough Gemini contains stars that represent twins sitting together. John is a twin. God told me to cast it out, and not to be afraid. I began to do that, calling it by name. As I did, John fell backward onto the bed he was sitting on, writhing in pain.

He told me later that as I spoke the name Gemini, it was as if a knife had been plunged in his back. He began screaming in pain, but I remained calm and very unemotional through it all. I was sure John's parents would come running into the room immediately because of all the noise, but they never heard a thing; even the dog never budged. God apparently shut their ears.

As I continued to pray, the pain subsided and turned into a dull ache — and finally a few days later, just a bruised feeling was left. That lasted a few more days, and then left. John has been free from it ever since. This happened twenty years ago.

Now, my friend, what should you do when you meet the enemy head on? Cry, "Lord, it's warfare! You have taught me to stand, and I will do what you have taught me to do." Put on the armor and stand firm in the Lord and in the strength of His might. Submit to God, resist the devil, and he will flee from you. Then draw near to Him. Listen to Thomas White's wise words of exhortation.

Many people mistakenly think that dealing with the evil one requires some deep level of knowledge and a super-spirituality and that it involves a long, laborious struggle. Jesus identified Satan as the "father of lies," the master of deceit. As such, it is the truth of the Word of God that dispels and expels the lies. While many of the devil's devices may appear complex, breaking them is scripturally simple. *Faith* in the supremacy and sufficiency of Jesus' name (Matthew 11:22–24; Matthew 18:18–20), *confidence* in the power of his atoning blood (Revelation 12:11), *courage* to claim and use our authority in resisting evil (Luke 10:19), and total *trust* in the imminent power of the Holy Spirit (Acts 10:38) will break oppression. Dealing with evil requires tools the ordinary Christian has at hand. The Lord will move according to his purpose if conditions for victory are being met. Dealing with the deceiver requires a "go for it" kind of spiritual guts that engages the gears of faith.

Trust the Lord to help you get over hesitation and fear. You will probably feel weak and unprepared. You will sometimes be miserably slow to respond correctly. It always amazes me how we know the right way to respond, but fail to do it. You will make mistakes. Don't give up — God will help you. He was there for Moses, Gideon, David, Jeremiah, and others as they stood against evil. He'll be there for you too. To call on his name in a crisis somehow sets in mysterious motion the manifestation of his presence. When you pray and resolve to stand, the Lord of Hosts will show himself strong. Remember, you have the authority to resist evil.

*Pray...reaffirm through praise...*repent of any known sin...ask in prayer for God's wisdom (James 1:5, 6) and a sharpening of discernment (1 John 2:20, 27). Invite the Holy Spirit to take full control of the circumstance you are facing.

Realize your position in Christ. Think of your true identity as enthroned with the Savior (Ephesians 2:6).

Rely on the supremacy and sufficiency of Jesus' name (Philippians 2:9–11), on the power of his atoning blood (Colossians 1:13–20; Revelation 12:11).

Remove the ground of oppression. Moral compromise, deception, and exploitation of vulnerabilities are the chief avenues used to influence people.

Many pastors, missionaries, counselors, and lay persons have suddenly come face-to-face with a clear case of demonic manifestation. Often they have no formal training in the how-to's of deliverance. But the greatest preparation is pre-occupation with the person of Jesus, and an unshakable faith in his triumph over evil. This fearless faith quickly makes up for any lack of training.[12]

Be occupied with Jesus, His Word, and prayer, and not with the devil. Then your offensive weapons will be in perfect working order.

If it's warfare, you have been taught to stand. Therefore when the enemy:

> attacks the veracity of God's Word, put on *the belt of truth;*
> would lead you into sin, or remind you of sins you've already confessed, put on the *breastplate of righteousness;*
> would bring disharmony or enmity between you and others, put on the *shoes of peace;*
> would cause you to doubt or fear, take up your *shield of faith;*
> would cause you to doubt your salvation or try to move you from confidence in your position in Christ, take the *helmet of salvation.*

Take the victory with the *sword of the Spirit...*getting your orders from headquarters in *prayer.*

DAY SIX

"We will devote ourselves to prayer, and to the ministry of the word" (Acts 6:4). I wonder what would have happened to Christianity if the men who made this statement had been caught up in the affairs of a growing church and its multiple needs and hadn't made prayer a priority. Maybe Christianity wouldn't have reached as far as quickly and as effectively.

I wonder if the "dark ages" of church history could be directly related to the lack of people who saw prayer as more than a way to have their personal, spiritual, emotional, or material needs met.

I wonder where many nations would be if a few saints had not beseeched God tirelessly for revival. How deep would the degradation in their nation be if God had not moved in answer to prayer?

I wonder where we would be as a nation if the shepherds of the sheep had not neglected prayer. If grabbing hold of the horns of the altar in intercession had been their priority rather than numbers and programs. Or if Christian ministries had sought God rather than Madison Avenue for direction.

I wonder how many more we could see set free from sin, from the power of the enemy, if we understood the offensive dimension of prayer.

I wonder how many more nations we could reach, evangelize, and disciple if Wednesday night prayer meetings were just that — prayer meetings where our focus would be on intercession for the nations of the world rather than personal needs.

I wonder where our government officials and our nation would be morally if we had diligently obeyed our Lord's injunction to pray for kings and rulers and all in authority so that we might live peaceable and godly lives.

Yes, God is sovereign. He rules. But mystery of mysteries, prayer affects the work of God in the lives of men and nations. I don't understand — I don't have to. I am simply to obey. And, as I write this, I tell you that I have not prayed as I should have. If I could change only one thing in my past — and that's all I would be allowed to change — I would choose to have prayed more.

I cling to Romans 8:28–30, but I know I should have been more diligent in prayer for family, friends, ministry, our government, our nation, our world. What about you, Beloved?

With God it's never too late until He takes you home. But since we're both still here, let's see what we can learn and then put into practice.

We will not cover the whole subject of prayer; we'll only look at the warfare aspect of prayer. Because I believe prayer is part of our armor, to neglect it in a book on spiritual warfare would be to miss a vital part of our armor.

Ephesians 6:18–20 says: "With all prayer and petition pray at all times in the Spirit, and with this in view, be on the alert with all perseverance and petition for all the saints, and *pray* on my behalf, that utterance may be given to me in the opening of my mouth, to make known with boldness the mystery of the gospel, for which I am an ambassador in chains; that in *proclaiming* it I may speak boldly, as I ought to speak."

I think a careful study of these verses shows you two aspects of prayer as it relates to warfare. Even as part of the armor is defensive and the other offensive, so it seems to be with prayer.

The defensive aspect is stated first as Paul instructs us to pray at all times in the Spirit, being *on the alert* with all perseverance and petition for all the saints.

"Being on the alert" is in the present tense in the Greek, which speaks of a habitual action, indicating a great sensitivity to the Holy Spirit. The word means "to stay awake, to lie sleepless, to pass a sleepless night, to suffer from insomnia, to be watchful, to be vigilant."[13] The definition reminds me of two of my intimate friends, Evelyn and Mia. Many night hours are spent in intercession as the Lord awakens them for prayer. Convicting, isn't it?

Let's look at *perseverance*. The word speaks of constancy. "The verb was used in the papyri in the sense of holding out or waiting, e.g., waiting until one's trial came before the court or diligently remaining at one's work."[14] As I read this verse, I can't help but think of Luke 11, which is Jesus' response to the disciples when they ask Him to teach them to pray. First, He gives them a pattern for prayer in what we call The Lord's Prayer.[15] Then, in verses 5–13, He gives them some principles for prayer that will keep us from discouragement and weariness. So read Luke 11:5–13, and record what you learn. Keep in mind that the verbs *asking, seeking,* and *knocking* are all in the present tense in the Greek, which indicates habitual or continuous action.

► LUKE 11:5–13

5 And He said to them, "Suppose one of you shall have a friend, and shall go to him at midnight, and say to him, 'Friend, lend me three loaves;

6 for a friend of mine has come to me from a journey, and I have nothing to set before him';

7 and from inside he shall answer and say, 'Do not bother me; the door has already been shut and my children and I are in bed; I cannot get up and give you *anything.*'

8 "I tell you, even though he will not get up and give him *anything* because he is his friend, yet because of his persistence he will get up and give him as much as he needs.

9 "And I say to you, ask, and it shall be given to you; seek, and you shall find; knock, and it shall be opened to you.

10 "For everyone who asks, receives; and he who seeks, finds; and to him who knocks, it shall be opened.

11 "Now suppose one of you fathers is asked by his son for a fish; he will not give him a snake instead of a fish, will he?

12 "Or *if* he is asked for an egg, he will not give him a scorpion, will he?

13 "If you then, being evil, know how to give good gifts to your children, how much more shall *your* heavenly Father give the Holy Spirit to those who ask Him?"

Our Lord gives us an example of defensive warfare praying in Luke 22:31–32. Look it up and write it out.

Now look at Luke 22:40–46. Record what you learn about prayer from this passage.

➤ LUKE 22:40–46

40 And when He arrived at the place, He said to them, "Pray that you may not enter into temptation."

41 And He withdrew from them about a stone's throw, and He knelt down and *began* to pray,

42 saying, "Father, if Thou art willing, remove this cup from Me; yet not My will, but Thine be done."

43 Now an angel from heaven appeared to Him, strengthening Him.

44 And being in agony He was praying very fervently; and His sweat became like drops of blood, falling down upon the ground.

45 And when He rose from prayer, He came to the disciples and found them sleeping from sorrow,

46 and said to them, "Why are you sleeping? Rise and pray that you may not enter into temptation."

How does such defensive prayer work? Paul tells us our prayer is to be "in the Spirit," which, as I understand it, would be to pray under the leadership and direction of the Holy Spirit. Thus, as you have your quiet time, ask God to make you sensitive to all that you ought to pray for. What a difference this kind of praying could make in the way we raise our children!

Paul gives us a good example of defensive prayer in Ephesians 1 and 3 as he prays we will know and understand some important truths — truths the enemy would love to keep us blinded to. Remember the enemy will do everything he can to snatch God's Word from our hearts because His truth sets us free! Keep that in mind as you pray, Beloved.

Because there's so much I want to share with you, I felt frustrated about it all until I received Evelyn Christenson's book last week. I thought, *Lord, what beautiful timing. My dear sister must have been listening to the Lord as she autographed* Battling the Prince of Darkness *and dropped it in the mail.* This book on warfare prayer is written by a woman who has had far more experience than I have. Get it and study it. You'll learn much. Victor Books is the publisher, and a Leader's Guide is available to go with the book. Obviously I haven't had time to read it all, but I can't wait to sit at Evelyn's feet and learn from her.

Finally, I want us to take a look at Ephesians 6:19–20. I think we can get a glimpse of the offensive aspect of warfare praying as Paul requests prayer on his behalf that utterance may be given him to make known with boldness the mystery of the gospel.

We often forget that the world lies in the power of the evil one and that men remain his captives because the god of this world has blinded their eyes (2 Corinthians 4:4). The parable of the sower in Mark 4 teaches us that sometimes when the Word of God is sown, the evil one comes and snatches it away. How are they going to be saved? Yes, God is sovereign. Remember Ephesians 1:4 says that God chose us before the foundation of the world. Yet, mystery of mysteries, prayer plays a critical role in bringing people to Christ.

Look at this excerpt from James Fraser's biography, *Mountain Rain:*

James learned more and more that prayer was the only weapon that could drive back the forces of darkness. He had preached; he had taught; he had discussed; but there was little fruit. He wrote to His prayer-partners: "About twelve men at Tantsah have professed their intention of being Christians. Of these, few or none come regularly to the services, nor do I know of any who have definitely renounced demonolatry, i.e. of those who are responsible members of their families. The 'strong man' has not yet been bound, if I may put it so. The majority of the people are too afraid of their demons to turn to God as yet. Still, God is leading me onward and I am quite hopeful. I do not intend to be in too much of a hurry, and yet I will cry to God for a blessed work of grace among the Lisu as long as He lends me breath."

Great were the strides in his understanding of prayer during these days. His own exercises in prayer gave him experience in the things of God, a knowledge of God; a friendship with God. His study of prayer in the Bible gave him a grasp of the whole vital subject in relation to the work of God. The Holy Spirit was opening up to him a whole new dimension of power through which he could become a prince with Him and prevail.

"If two of you," he wrote, "shall agree…" I feel even when praying alone that there are two concerned in the prayer, God and myself.… I do not think that a petition which misses the mind of God will ever be answered (1 John 5:14). *Personally I feel the need of trusting Him to lead me in prayer as well as in other matters. I find it well to preface prayer not only by meditation but by the definite request that I may be directed into the channels of prayer to which the Holy Spirit is beckoning me.* I also find it helpful to make a short list, like notes prepared for a sermon, before every season of prayer. The mind needs to be guided as well as the spirit attuned. I can thus get my thoughts in order, and having prepared my prayer can put the notes on the table or chair before me, kneel down and get down to business"[16] (italics mine).

O Beloved, may we be motivated or convicted (whichever is necessary) to get down to business using the weapon of prayer to rescue the perishing from the jaws of the devourer.

DAY SEVEN

Arthur Mathews was a valiant warrior for our Lord. Isobel Kuhn wrote his story in *Green Leaves in Drought Time,* and ever since reading about him, I have greatly admired him. A few years ago I learned that his book of thirty-one daily studies on spiritual warfare is required reading for all OMF missionaries. It's an inexpensive investment of great value. Listen to what Mathews says about offensive prayer:

> There are two aspects of prayer that we need to take a closer look at. One is illustrated for us in Philippians 1:19, where Paul says this: "For I (the missionary at the front line) know that this (situation that I am in) shall turn to my salvation through your prayer and the supply of the Spirit of Jesus Christ." Paul is the main spearhead of missionary attack for His Lord. But even though he has achieved his objective in reaching an almost lifetime goal, he is bound and held in a Roman prison. In this situation he is bursting with praise as he realizes that the prayers of his friends at Philippi are channeling the supply of the Spirit of his conquering Lord into his situation. It is this fact of supporting prayer that is turning apparent loss into stepping-stones for the furtherance of the gospel. The Church at Philippi is part and parcel of the main offensive. It is their responsibility to see that the necessary supplies get through to their brave soldier at the front. Faithfully they devote themselves to their mission, so that Paul is able to record victories even though he is chained and unable to go out preaching.
>
> But there is another aspect of prayer that has a completely different approach and function, and yet is a vital, though often neglected, part of the main offensive of God's missionary program. This aspect is put before us in the words of the Lord Jesus, "How can one enter into a strong man's house, and spoil his goods?" (Matthew 12:29, KJV). Victory can be hastened and casualties lessened by infiltrating into the enemy's vulnerable control zone, where plans for attack are conceived and from which the orders are issued. This area is not marked on our atlases as a geographic point, but that does not make it any less real. To the believer the heavenlies are more real than the temporal things of earth. Satan's control zone is vulnerable, because he is a defeated foe. Christ crushed his head for him at Calvary, and that victory means that every believer who holds his position in Christ by faith is co-sharer in the triumph of

that mighty act. The devil must yield ground before the believer who resists him with the delegated authority of the "stronger than the strong."

Jesus says, "Whatsoever ye shall bind on earth shall be bound in heaven" (Matthew 18:18). The temerity of this aspect of prayer warfare appalls many and, because the results are not easily measured, is often put to one side. But it is a way of victory....

In my own experience long-range penetration in prayer has been a watershed, and I now realize that my earlier appreciation of prayer values was only half developed. *But there are cautions that need to be sounded. The enemy is a real person, and he is spirit; therefore at no time dare we move against him or any of his wicked spirits with weapons that are not spiritual, and then only under the leading of the Spirit of God. In the warfare it is not for us to pick and choose at will where we think we should attack. We must be first submissive to God. That is the order of priority James gives us, "Submit yourselves to God. Resist the devil, and he will flee from you"* (James 4:7).

Recently a burden was placed on my heart for two specific areas in Southeast Asia. The enemy was staging strong opposition to the progress of the gospel, and it was borne in on me that God was waiting for someone to resist the devil. The burden persisted; so asserting my position with Christ in the heavenlies on the basis of God's Word and strengthened with His might, I took unto me the whole armor of God in order to stand against the wiles of the devil and to withstand his opposition to the gospel. Some time passed and then the news from the missionaries in both those places began to change. The resisting powers in both cases were weakened, making possible victories for the Lord. I would never mention this, but so many are shy of this kind of warfare and need a definite example to guide them; so for that reason alone I have included this personal testimony.

On the last day before General Wingate's expedition crossed the Chindwin and entered enemy-held territory, he issued his battle order of the day. It included this sentence: "Finally, knowing the vanity of man's effort and the confusion of his purpose, let us pray that God may accept our services and direct our endeavors, so that when we have done all, we may see the fruit of our labors and be satisfied"[17] (italics mine).

I read what Arthur Mathews says, and it brings to mind an account Neil Anderson, author of *Victory Over the Darkness* and *The Bondage Breaker*, tells. Missionaries from Argentina shared how they had struggled for years in trying to penetrate that land with the gospel, yet they had only fifty or sixty people in their churches. However, in recent years they have experienced tremendous growth where now those same churches have memberships in the hundreds and thousands. What made the difference? For years they had thought their enemy was the corrupt political power of Argentina, and they never looked beyond this human power to the prince of the power of the air. They mistakenly thought their warfare was against flesh and blood.

As they evangelized, it was as if they went to Satan's prison and urged the prisoners to come out, but the guards were on duty and the gates secured. *Then after seeking the Lord in prayer,* God showed them that those who were held prisoners could not walk out of the prison unless someone opened its gate and took care of the guard and his watchtower so the prisoners could come out.

With this insight, their strategy changed. They sent teams of prayer warriors into cities and villages several weeks in advance of the evangelistic teams. The prayer teams would bind the enemy who was blinding the hearts and minds of these people. Then when the evangelistic teams followed, for the first time there was incredible response to the gospel and growth to the church.

Oh, the power of watching and praying with all prayer and supplication *in the Spirit.*

Such prayer is not only needed on mission fields but in our own homes. Many parents are experiencing traumatic and disconcerting trials with their children these days and are so frustrated because there seems to be no solution in sight. They don't know what's happening, but it's disrupting their family life and many times threatens to destroy all they've prayed for.

I wonder how much of it is warfare? Our children live in an environment increasingly permeated by the powers of darkness. As I stated earlier, a trip through a toy store and a good look at the most popular toys will be witness enough. Take a look at the screens that mesmerize people for hours. All those things and more are enforced and sealed on moldable minds in full color. Add these influences to the things which are being promoted and taught in public schools, and it's obvious someone is out to destroy not only their values but their relationship with their families.

I suggest you get "Child Abuse in the Classroom" edited by Phyllis Schafly. It contains excerpts from the Official Transcript of Proceedings before the Department of Education. "The testimonies prove how federally funded curricula in the public schools have encouraged children to commit suicide, to believe that killing, lying, cheating, and stealing are sometimes okay, to engage in premarital sex, to have an abortion, to experiment with illegal drugs, to study anti-religious and occult practices contrary to their own religion, and to reject their parent's authority and value system."[18]

Evil is blatant. Satan is gaining fast. Oh, Christian soldier, pray defensively for your children, grandchildren, and the children of this nation. Satan desires to have them. Pray they don't enter into temptation but that they are delivered from the evil one.

And be open to the fact that you may have to pray offensively. If your child or grandchild starts to exhibit unusual or unmanageable behavior, go to the Lord in prayer and ask Him to show you how to pray for your child. It may be that He will lead you into offensive warfare praying where you take the authority which is yours and resist the devil.

Our cry has been "Lord, Is It Warfare? Teach Me To Stand!" What you have learned, you have not learned just for yourself. This is a call to arms. Be His valiant warrior.

As for God, His way is blameless;
The word of the LORD is tried;
He is a shield to all who take refuge in Him.
For who is God, but the LORD?
And who is a rock, except our God,

The God who girds me with strength,
And makes my way blameless?
He makes my feet like hinds' *feet*,
And sets me upon my high places.
He trains my hands for battle,
So that my arms can bend a bow of bronze.
Thou hast also given me the shield of Thy salvation,
And Thy right hand upholds me;
And Thy gentleness makes me great.
Thou dost enlarge my steps under me,
And my feet have not slipped.

I pursued my enemies and overtook them,
And I did not turn back until they were consumed.
I shattered them, so that they were not able to rise;
They fell under my feet.
For Thou has girded me with strength for battle.
(Psalm 18:30–39a)

Go forth, Beloved. Live in such a way as to manifest the manifold wisdom of God to the principalities and powers in the heavenly places so that once again our Lord may see Satan falling from heaven like lightning!

EPHESIANS

1 Paul, an apostle of Christ Jesus by the will of God, to the saints who are at Ephesus, and *who are* faithful in Christ Jesus:

2 Grace to you and peace from God our Father and the Lord Jesus Christ.

3 Blessed *be* the God and Father of our Lord Jesus Christ, who has blessed us with every spiritual blessing in the heavenly *places* in Christ,

4 just as He chose us in Him before the foundation of the world, that we should be holy and blameless before Him. In love

5 He predestined us to adoption as sons through Jesus Christ to Himself, according to the kind intention of His will,

6 to the praise of the glory of His grace, which He freely bestowed on us in the Beloved.

7 In Him we have redemption through His blood, the forgiveness of our trespasses, according to the riches of His grace,

8 which He lavished upon us. In all wisdom and insight

9 He made known to us the mystery of His will, according to His kind intention which He purposed in Him

10 with a view to an administration suitable to the fulness of the times, *that is,* the summing up of all things in Christ, things in the heavens and things upon the earth. In Him

11 also we have obtained an inheritance, having been predestined according to His purpose who works all things after the counsel of His will,

12 to the end that we who were the first to hope in Christ should be to the praise of His glory.

13 In Him, you also, after listening to the message of truth, the gospel of your salvation — having also believed, you were sealed in Him with the Holy Spirit of promise,

14 who is given as a pledge of our inheritance, with a view to the redemption of *God's own* possession, to the praise of His glory.

15 For this reason I too, having heard of the faith in the Lord Jesus which *exists* among you, and your love for all the saints,

16 do not cease giving thanks for you, while making mention *of you* in my prayers;

17 that the God of our Lord Jesus Christ, the Father of glory, may give to you a spirit of wisdom and of revelation in the knowledge of Him.

18 *I pray that* the eyes of your heart may be enlightened, so that you may know what is the hope of His calling, what are the riches of the glory of His inheritance in the saints,

19 and what is the surpassing greatness of His power toward us who believe. *These are* in accordance with the working of the strength of His might

20 which He brought about in Christ, when He raised Him from the dead, and seated Him at His right hand in the heavenly *places,*

21 far above all rule and authority and power and dominion, and every name that is named, not only in this age, but also in the one to come.

22 And He put all things in subjection under His feet, and gave Him as head over all things to the church,

23 which is His body, the fulness of Him who fills all in all.

CHAPTER 2

1 And you were dead in your trespasses and sins,

2 in which you formerly walked according to the course of this world, according to the prince of the power of the air, of the spirit that is now working in the sons of disobedience.

3 Among them we too all formerly lived in the lusts of our flesh, indulging the desires of the flesh and of the mind, and were by nature children of wrath, even as the rest.

4 But God, being rich in mercy, because of His great love with which He loved us,

5 even when we were dead in our transgressions, made us alive together with Christ (by grace you have been saved),

6 and raised us up with Him, and seated us with Him in the heavenly *places,* in Christ Jesus,

7 in order that in the ages to come He might show the surpassing riches of His grace in kindness toward us in Christ Jesus.

8 For by grace you have been saved through faith; and that not of yourselves, *it is* the gift of God;

9 not as a result of works, that no one should boast.

10 For we are His workmanship, created in Christ Jesus for good works, which God prepared beforehand, that we should walk in them.

11 Therefore remember, that formerly you, the Gentiles in the flesh, who are called "Uncircumcision" by the so-called "Circumcision," *which is* performed in the flesh by human hands —

12 *remember* that you were at that time separate from Christ, excluded from the commonwealth of Israel, and strangers to the covenants of promise, having no hope and without God in the world.

13 But now in Christ Jesus you who formerly were far off have been brought near by the blood of Christ.

14 For He Himself is our peace, who made both *groups into* one, and broke down the barrier of the dividing wall,

15 by abolishing in His flesh the enmity, *which is* the Law of commandments *contained* in ordinances, that in Himself He might make the two into one new man, *thus* establishing peace,

16 and might reconcile them both in one body to God through the cross, by it having put to death the enmity.

17 AND HE CAME AND PREACHED PEACE TO YOU WHO WERE FAR AWAY, AND PEACE TO THOSE WHO WERE NEAR;

18 for through Him we both have our access in one Spirit to the Father.

19 So then you are no longer strangers and aliens, but you are fellow citizens with the saints, and are of God's household,

20 having been built upon the foundation of the apostles and prophets, Christ Jesus Himself being the corner *stone,*

21 in whom the whole building, being fitted together is growing into a holy temple in the Lord;

22 in whom you also are being built together into a dwelling of God in the Spirit.

CHAPTER 3

1 For this reason I, Paul, the prisoner of Christ Jesus for the sake of you Gentiles —

2 if indeed you have heard of the stewardship of God's grace which was given to me for you;

3 that by revelation there was made known to me the mystery, as I wrote before in brief.

4 And by referring to this, when you read you can understand my insight into the mystery of Christ,

5 which in other generations was not made known to the sons of men, as it has now been revealed to His holy apostles and prophets in the Spirit;

6 *to be specific,* that the Gentiles are fellow heirs and fellow members of the body, and fellow partakers of the promise in Christ Jesus through the gospel,

7 of which I was made a minister, according to the gift of God's grace which was given to me according to the working of His power.

8 To me, the very least of all saints, this grace was given, to preach to the Gentiles the unfathomable riches of Christ,

9 and to bring to light what is the administration of the mystery which for ages has been hidden in God, who created all things;

10 in order that the manifold wisdom of God might now be made known through the church to the rulers and the authorities in the heavenly *places.*

11 *This was* in accordance with the eternal purpose which He carried out in Christ Jesus our Lord,

12 in whom we have boldness and confident access through faith in Him.

13 Therefore I ask you not to lose heart at my tribulations on your behalf, for they are your glory.

14 For this reason, I bow my knees before the Father,

15 from whom every family in heaven and on earth derives its name,

16 that He would grant you, according to the riches of His glory, to be strengthened with power through His Spirit in the inner man;

17 so that Christ may dwell in your hearts through faith; *and* that you, being rooted and grounded in love,

18 may be able to comprehend with all the saints what is the breadth and length and height and depth,

19 and to know the love of Christ which surpasses knowledge, that you may be filled up to all the fulness of God.

20 Now to Him who is able to do exceeding abundantly beyond all that we ask or think, according to the power that works within us,

21 to Him *be* the glory in the church and in Christ Jesus to all generations forever and ever. Amen.

CHAPTER 4

1 I, therefore, the prisoner of the Lord, entreat you to walk in a manner worthy of the calling with which you have been called,

2 with all humility and gentleness, with patience, showing forbearance to one another in love,

3 being diligent to preserve the unity of the Spirit in the bond of peace.

4 *There is* one body and one Spirit, just as also you were called in one hope of your calling;

5 one Lord, one faith, one baptism,

6 one God and Father of all who is over all and through all and in all.

7 But to each one of us grace was given according to the measure of Christ's gift.

8 Therefore it says,

"WHEN HE ASCENDED ON HIGH,
HE LED CAPTIVE A HOST OF CAPTIVES,
AND HE GAVE GIFTS TO MEN."

9 (Now this *expression,* "He ascended," what does it mean except that He also had descended into the lower parts of the earth?

10 He who descended is Himself also He who ascended far above all the heavens, that He might fill all things.)

11 And He gave some *as* apostles, and some *as* prophets, and some *as* evangelists, and some *as* pastors and teachers,

12 for the equipping of the saints for the work of service, to the building up of the body of Christ;

13 until we all attain to the unity of the faith, and of the knowledge of the Son of God, to a mature man, to the measure of the stature which belongs to the fulness of Christ.

14 As a result, we are no longer to be children, tossed here and there by waves, and carried about by every wind of doctrine, by the trickery of men, by craftiness in deceitful scheming;

15 but speaking the truth in love, we are to grow up in all *aspects* into Him, who is the head, *even* Christ,

16 from whom the whole body, being fitted and held together by that which every joint supplies, according to the proper working of each individual part, causes the growth of the body for the building up of itself in love.

17 This I say therefore, and affirm together with the Lord, that you walk no longer just as the Gentiles also walk, in the futility of their mind,

18 being darkened in their understanding, excluded from the life of God, because of the ignorance that is in them, because of the hardness of their heart;

19 and they, having become callous, have given themselves over to sensuality, for the practice of every kind of impurity with greediness.

20 But you did not learn Christ in this way,

21 if indeed you have heard Him and have been taught in Him, just as truth is in Jesus,

22 that, in reference to your former manner of life, you lay aside the old self, which is being corrupted in accordance with the lusts of deceit,

23 and that you be renewed in the spirit of your mind,

24 and put on the new self, which in *the likeness of* God has been created in righteousness and holiness of the truth.

25 Therefore, laying aside falsehood, SPEAK TRUTH, EACH ONE *of you,* WITH HIS NEIGHBOR, for we are members of one another.

26 BE ANGRY, AND *yet* DO NOT SIN; do not let the sun go down on your anger,

27 and do not give the devil an opportunity.

28 Let him who steals steal no longer; but rather let him labor, performing with his own hands what is good, in order that he may have *something* to share with him who has need.

29 Let no unwholesome word proceed from your mouth, but only such *a word* as is good for edification according to the need *of the moment,* that it may give grace to those who hear.

30 And do not grieve the Holy Spirit of God, by whom you were sealed for the day of redemption.

31 Let all bitterness and wrath and anger and clamor and slander be put away from you, along with all malice.

32 And be kind to one another, tender-hearted, forgiving each other, just as God in Christ also has forgiven you.

CHAPTER 5

1 Therefore be imitators of God, as beloved children;

2 and walk in love, just as Christ also loved you, and gave Himself up for us, an offering and a sacrifice to God as a fragrant aroma.

3 But do not let immorality or any impurity or greed even be named among you, as is proper among saints;

4 and *there must be no* filthiness and silly talk, or coarse jesting, which are not fitting, but rather giving of thanks.

5 For this you know with certainty, that no immoral or impure person or covetous man, who is an idolater, has an inheritance in the kingdom of Christ and God.

⁶ Let no one deceive you with empty words, for because of these things the wrath of God comes upon the sons of disobedience.

⁷ Therefore do not be partakers with them;

⁸ for you were formerly darkness, but now you are light in the Lord; walk as children of light

⁹ (for the fruit of the light *consists* in all goodness and righteousness and truth),

¹⁰ trying to learn what is pleasing to the Lord.

¹¹ And do not participate in the unfruitful deeds of darkness, but instead even expose them;

¹² for it is disgraceful even to speak of the things which are done by them in secret.

¹³ But all things become visible when they are exposed by the light, for everything that becomes visible is light.

¹⁴ For this reason it says,

"Awake, sleeper,

And arise from the dead,

And Christ will shine on you."

¹⁵ Therefore be careful how you walk, not as unwise men, but as wise,

¹⁶ making the most of your time, because the days are evil.

¹⁷ So then do not be foolish, but understand what the will of the Lord is.

¹⁸ And do not get drunk with wine, for that is dissipation, but be filled with the Spirit,

¹⁹ speaking to one another in psalms and hymns and spiritual songs, singing and making melody with your heart to the Lord;

²⁰ always giving thanks for all things in the name of our Lord Jesus Christ to God, even the Father;

²¹ and be subject to one another in the fear of Christ.

²² Wives, *be subject* to your own husbands, as to the Lord.

²³ For the husband is the head of the wife, as Christ also is the head of the church, He Himself *being* the Savior of the body.

²⁴ But as the church is subject to Christ, so also the wives *ought to be* to their husbands in everything.

25 Husbands, love your wives, just as Christ also loved the church and gave Himself up for her;

26 that He might sanctify her, having cleansed her by the washing of water with the word,

27 that He might present to Himself the church in all her glory, having no spot or wrinkle or any such thing; but that she should be holy and blameless.

28 So husbands ought also to love their own wives as their own bodies. He who loves his own wife loves himself;

29 for no one ever hated his own flesh, but nourishes and cherishes it, just as Christ also *does* the church,

30 because we are members of His body.

31 FOR THIS CAUSE A MAN SHALL LEAVE HIS FATHER AND MOTHER, AND SHALL CLEAVE TO HIS WIFE; AND THE TWO SHALL BECOME ONE FLESH.

32 This mystery is great; but I am speaking with reference to Christ and the church.

33 Nevertheless let each individual among you also love his own wife even as himself; and *let* the wife *see to it* that she respect her husband.

CHAPTER 6

1 Children, obey your parents in the Lord, for this is right.

2 HONOR YOUR FATHER AND MOTHER (which is the first commandment with a promise),

3 THAT IT MAY BE WELL WITH YOU, AND THAT YOU MAY LIVE LONG ON THE EARTH.

4 And, fathers, do not provoke your children to anger; but bring them up in the discipline and instruction of the Lord.

5 Slaves, be obedient to those who are your masters according to the flesh, with fear and trembling, in the sincerity of your heart, as to Christ;

6 not by way of eyeservice, as men-pleasers, but as slaves of Christ, doing the will of God from the heart.

⁷ With good will render service, as to the Lord, and not to men,

⁸ knowing that whatever good thing each one does, this he will receive back from the Lord, whether slave or free.

⁹ And, masters, do the same things to them, and give up threatening, knowing that both their Master and yours is in heaven, and there is no partiality with Him.

¹⁰ Finally, be strong in the Lord, and in the strength of His might.

¹¹ Put on the full armor of God, that you may be able to stand firm against the schemes of the devil.

¹² For our struggle is not against flesh and blood, but against the rulers, against the powers, against the world forces of this darkness, against the spiritual *forces* of wickedness in the heavenly *places*.

¹³ Therefore, take up the full armor of God, that you may be able to resist in the evil day, and having done everything, to stand firm.

¹⁴ Stand firm therefore, HAVING GIRDED YOUR LOINS WITH TRUTH, and HAVING PUT ON THE BREASTPLATE OF RIGHTEOUSNESS,

¹⁵ and having shod YOUR FEET WITH THE PREPARATION OF THE GOSPEL OF PEACE;

¹⁶ in addition to all, taking up the shield of faith with which you will be able to extinguish all the flaming missiles of the evil *one*.

¹⁷ And take THE HELMET OF SALVATION, and the sword of the Spirit, which is the word of God.

¹⁸ With all prayer and petition pray at all times in the Spirit, and with this in view, be on the alert with all perseverance and petition for all the saints,

¹⁹ and *pray* on my behalf, that utterance may be given to me in the opening of my mouth, to make known with boldness the mystery of the gospel,

²⁰ for which I am an ambassador in chains; that in *proclaiming* it I may speak boldly, as I ought to speak.

²¹ But that you also may know about my circumstances, how I am doing, Tychicus, the beloved brother and faithful minister in the Lord, will make everything known to you.

22 And I have sent him to you for this very purpose, so that you may know about us, and that he may comfort your hearts.

23 Peace be to the brethren, and love with faith, from God the Father and the Lord Jesus Christ.

24 Grace be with all those who love our Lord Jesus Christ with *a love* incorruptible.

GROUP DISCUSSION QUESTIONS

If you want to use *Lord, Is It Warfare? Teach Me to Stand* as a group study, we suggest the following:

1. Prayerfully commit the study to the Lord, seeking His direction in every step. Choose someone to lead the study who will diligently prepare to lead the discussion time.

2. Begin your first class by listening to the audio or video taped *introductory* lesson to the study. Each student should do the homework for Week One before the next class. Then you would meet, have your discussion, and listen to the lecture tape for Week One, etc.

3. Encourage each student to purchase a book and do the study at home week by week. Each week will require an average of one to two hours of study, depending on the topic.

4. When you meet as a group, begin with a forty- to sixty-minute class discussion. (Audio tapes are available to assist the person leading the discussion.) Then listen to the sixty-minute audio or video teaching tape which supplements each week's lesson. The teaching tape should always follow the class discussion, not precede it.

5. Write or call to receive information on how to order the teaching tapes and discussion leader tapes which supplement the following questions.

PRECEPT MINISTRIES
P. O. BOX 182218
CHATTANOOGA, TN 37422–7218
(423) 892-6814

The following questions can be used to stimulate discussion.

CHAPTER ONE

If you are a child of God, what can you know about warfare? Whom is the warfare with? Why can you be certain that it will come? What must you know in order to stand and not be deceived?

1. The Book of Ephesians focuses on the Christian's warfare like no other book. What are some of the significant historical facts about the city of Ephesus in Paul's day that help in understanding this book?

   a. What was the religious environment like? Whom did they worship? What kind of a goddess was she? Where did they believe she came from?

   b. In 1 Corinthians 10:19–21, what power does Paul say an idol has?

   c. What was the temple like? What were some of the activities that went on in the temple? Why was the temple so important to the commerce of the day?

   d. What were some of the other evil practices that were common in Ephesus?

2. The events in Acts 19 took place in Ephesus. How do these events further explain the historical and religious background of Ephesus?

   a. How long did Paul stay in Ephesus? How and to whom did he proclaim the gospel?

   b. How was the power of God specifically manifested? What did you learn about evil spirits and the Jewish exorcists? What were these exorcists attempting to do?

   c. How did many in Ephesus respond to the preaching of the gospel? What did those who believed do with their magic books? How does this event reveal the work of the enemy in Ephesus? What does it show about the power of God?

   d. What was the conflict that the gospel brought? Who was involved? Why?

3. When the children of Israel entered the land, what were God's warnings concerning these same evil practices that were taking place in Ephesus (Deuteronomy 18:9–14 and Leviticus 19:26–28)?

    a. What did God specifically tell them not to do? Why? What did He tell them to do?

    b. How do you see these kinds of things in our Western culture today? Have you ever been involved in any of these? If you have, what do you need to do?

4. According to the Book of Ephesians, what is true of you if you are in Him? What has happened to you?

    a. What has God blessed you with? What do you have through His blood? What have you obtained in Him? With whom have you been sealed?

    b. Where is Christ now seated? Specifically, what is He seated above? Why is this significant in spiritual warfare?

    c. Who were you? What were you like? What did God do?

    d. As a believer, where are you now seated? Where does this place you? Why is this significant in the light of warfare? What is your position?

    e. What did Jesus do for both Jew and Gentile?

5. In Ephesians 4–6, what specific instructions does Paul give concerning your walk?

6. The Christian's struggle is explained in Ephesians 6:10–20. According to these verses the struggle is with whom?

    a. What does the Greek word translated *struggle* or *wrestle* mean? What does that tell you?

    b. What does the Greek word for *schemes* mean?

    c. What specific instructions are given in these verses?

    d. Describe the Christian's armor that is to be put on for this struggle. What are the weapons?

7. Do you understand your position in Christ? Are you walking as you ought?

    a. What will have to change in your life as a result of this study?

    b. Will you determine that the Word of God will have priority in your life so that you can know how to stand firm against the enemy?

CHAPTER TWO

Last week you saw that if you are a child of God, you can know you will have to battle the enemy.

You were reminded of your position in Christ, which places you with Him above all rule and authority, and of your responsibility to walk in a manner worthy of your calling.

You also learned that in warfare you are to be strong in the Lord and in the strength of His might, that you are to stand firm in the armor of God against the schemes of the devil.

How did the devil get to be the devil? Was he created, or has he always existed? Where did demons come from? Did God create evil?

1. What did God create (John 1:1–3; Nehemiah 9:5–6; and Colossians 1:15–16)? Did God create anything evil?

   a. In Psalm 103:19–22, what did you learn about God's throne, God's power, and the angels?

   b. What did you learn about the angels in Hebrews 1:7–9, 13–14? What do they do?

2. Where did Satan come from?

   a. According to Ezekiel 28:11–15, what are some of the names that he was called? Where was he? How did he get there? What was he like? How do you know he was not a man?

   b. What happened to him according to Ezekiel 28:16–19? Why is there controversy over this passage?

   c. How did Satan become the adversary of God and man in Isaiah 14:3–15? What was Satan called? What did his name mean? What were his five "I wills"? What place did he want? What happened to him?

   d. What was the sin that Satan committed? What happened as a result? How does 1 Timothy 3:6 support the belief that Isaiah 14:12–14 is referring to the devil? How does this passage compare with Ezekiel 28:11–19?

   e. According to Psalm 75:6–7, where does exaltation come from? How does Daniel 2:20–21 explain who reigns?

f. Do you have any "I wills" in your life? According to James 4:13–17, if you say "I will," what are you doing? What should your attitude be according to Philippians 2:5–11?

3. Where did demons come from? Key: What was Satan called in Isaiah 14?

a. According to Job 38:4–7, who are the morning stars? How does that term parallel the term "sons of God"?

b. What did you learn in Job 1:6 and 2:1 about the "sons of God"? What did you learn from these verses about Satan? How do they parallel Ezekiel 28 and Isaiah 14?

c. What did you learn about the stars in Revelation 1:20 and 9:1–2? Who are the stars?

d. What happened to a third of the stars according to Revelation 12:3–4 and 12:7–9?

e. Is there redemption for Satan or the angels who defected with him? What has been prepared for them?

f. According to Job 38:7, when God created the heavens and earth, where were the angels?

4. What did you learn about the serpent and his tactics in Genesis 3? How was he described?

a. Was the serpent Satan? How does Revelation 12:9 describe Satan? How does this parallel Genesis 3?

b. Whom did he attack or whom did Satan cause to doubt God? How did he question God's Word? How did he deny God's Word? How did he exchange God's Word for a lie?

c. What did Satan say that eating the fruit of the tree of the knowledge of good and evil would do for Eve? How did this parallel the sin that resulted in his own fall?

d. What did you learn about Satan's future? What did God promise on that day? What has been true since that day?

e. Because Adam lost his right to rule the earth, what did Satan become according to Ephesians 2:1–3?

5. According to Paul's prayer in Ephesians 1:15–23, what three truths

concerning your position and power do you need to be absolutely certain about? Where is Jesus Christ seated? What is in subjection to Him? Whom does that include? What does that mean for you if you are in Him?

6. Have you seen self as the root of sin? Is your life turned to your way or God's way? Do you realize that if you are running your own life, then you are trying to be like the Most High?

7. What are five "I wills" that you can use to counteract Satan's "I wills"?

CHAPTER THREE

Last week you looked at the origin of Satan, his sin, his fall, and the angels he took with him. You learned that Satan was created blameless by God. But you saw too that because of his desire to make himself like the Most High, God cast him from the holy mountain, along with the angels who rebelled with him.

You also saw that Satan's desire is to control man. You studied the fall of man in the Garden of Eden and examined Satan's tactics. You saw that Satan, in essence, lured Adam and Eve into the same sin that caused his fall: pride.

You were reminded that immediately after man's fall, God cursed the serpent and promised a Redeemer. The Redeemer has paid the price of death for your sin, has been raised by God, and seated at His right hand far above all rule and authority. All powers are in subjection to Him, and you are seated with Him in heavenly places.

Who is in charge anyway? Is the devil in charge, or is God in charge? What is the devil like? What does he do? What are his limits, and what is his relationship to God?

1. Who is the enemy? What is the meaning of the Greek word for *devil* and the Hebrew word for *Satan,* and what do these reveal about the enemy?

    a. What has the devil done from the beginning (1 John 3:8)? What did Jesus call the devil (John 8:44)?

    b. Does Satan work alone? Who works with him (Ephesians 6:12)?

2. What does Satan do? Specifically, what do these scriptures reveal about his work?

    a. What control does he have over those dead in trespasses and sins (Ephesians 2:2)? How does this explain his work?

    b. How does he disguise himself (2 Corinthians 11:14–15)? What does this indicate about the way he works?

    c. What has he done to the minds of the unbelieving? Why (2 Corinthians 4:4)?

    d. What does the enemy do to the one who hears and does not understand (Matthew 13:19)?

    e. What influence did the enemy have on Ananias in Acts 5:3? Any parallel with John 8:44?

    f. What truths did you learn about the enemy's work when Jesus told Peter that Satan desired to sift him like wheat (Luke 22:31)?

    g. In 1 Thessalonians 2:18 Paul said he had wanted to come to them but did not make it. Why? What had Satan done? What is the warning here? What can Satan do?

    h. Why did Paul send to find out about their faith in 1 Thessalonians 3:5? What was his fear about Satan?

    i. What did you learn about the enemy's work in the parable of the wheat and the tares (Matthew 13:24–30, 38–39)?

    j. What might those mentioned in 2 Timothy 2:25–26 escape from? How do you see the work of the enemy here?

    k. What does 1 Timothy 3:7 show of the enemy's tactics?

    l. What did Satan do to the daughter of Abraham (Luke 13:16)? What does this indicate about Satan's work?

    m. How was Jesus' healing ministry described in Acts 10:38? What does this verse show about Satan?

3. What are Satan's limits? What is his relationship to God?

    a. What is God sovereign over? Who is included in the army of heaven (Daniel 4:34–35)?

    b. In 1 Corinthians 10:13 God says that He will not allow you to be tempted beyond that which you are able to bear. What does this show about God's sovereign rule over Satan's power?

c. What did you learn about Satan's limits in Luke 22:31 when Jesus told Peter that Satan desired permission to sift him like wheat?

4. How does the Book of Job illustrate Satan's character, his work, his limits, and his relationship to God?

a. What does the fact that Satan presented himself before God show you about Satan's access to God?

b. What does Satan's roaming the earth indicate about his awareness of man?

c. What did God bring to Satan's attention? What did God say about Job? What does this tell you about Job?

d. Why did Satan say that Job had served God? How did he know that God had placed a hedge about Job? What does this show that God can do?

e. Could Satan deal with Job as he wanted? Why not? What did he have to do? How did Satan attack Job? What do these attacks show about Satan's power?

f. How did Job respond to each of Satan's attacks? What does this show about the kind of man Satan targets? What happened in the end?

g. How can you reconcile this account of Satan's attack on Job with God's words "I have wounded and it is I who heal...causing well-being and creating calamity" (Deuteronomy 32:39 and Isaiah 45:6–7)? Who was in control?

h. Did Job lose his integrity? What did Job say that he had not denied (Job 6:10)?

i. How did Job's trial end? When did God restore Job's fortunes? What were Job's final words (Job 42:5–6)?

5. According to 1 Peter 5:6–11, what were those who received this letter undergoing?

a. What is Peter's warning? How is the devil described? What does he do?

b. What does Peter say that you are to do? What is God going to do?

6. What will many fall away from in the last days? Why (1 Timothy 4:1)?

    a. What kind of time is coming upon this earth (Revelation 12:7, 12)?

    b. What did you learn about the lawless one who is coming at the end times? What will he be like (2 Thessalonians 2:9)?

7. Will you be on the alert? Will you stand firm?

CHAPTER FOUR

Last week you looked at Satan's character and his work. You learned that he is your adversary and your accuser and that he has been a murderer and a liar from the beginning. You saw that he blinds the eyes of the unbelieving, that he thwarts, tempts, sifts, afflicts physically, and oppresses.

You saw that, although he is powerful, his authority and power are limited by God. You also saw clearly illustrated from the life of Job that Satan has access to God and that he targets the upright.

You saw that you are to be on the alert and to resist him, firm in the faith.

Who are the living dead? What is their state, how did they get there, and what are they like? How is it possible to be set free, and what comes with this freedom?

1. What is the state of a lost person, according to Ephesians 2:1–3? How are they walking? Whose rule are they under? What are they indulging? What are they by nature?

2. How did man end up in this state of sin described in Ephesians 2? Was this God's purpose for man?

    a. How did God create man? What responsibility was man given? Where did God place man? What provision did God make for man (Genesis 1:27–28; Genesis 2:7–9)?

    b. What were God's clear instructions to Adam when He placed him in the garden? What did God say that the consequences would be for disobedience (Genesis 2:16–17)?

    c. What were Satan's tactics? What were the serpent's first four recorded words in Genesis 3:1? What was Eve's response in Genesis 3:3?

d. How did Satan deny God's Word? When Satan said, "You surely shall not die," what was he doing? How did he make a subtle accusation against God? What was the ultimate temptation (Genesis 3:4–5)?

e. What was Eve's response? Adam's? How is Eve's response explained in 1 Timothy 2:14? Why was Adam not deceived? What does this tell you about his sin?

f. What was the judgment pronounced on the serpent in Genesis 3:14–15? What was the promise?

g. What was the result of Adam's sin, according to Romans 5:12? What happened to the whole world as a result of his sin? From that point on, the whole world has been in whose power (1 John 5:19)?

h. What did Satan become (Ephesians 2:1–3)? What responsibility had originally been given to man (Genesis 1:27–28)?

3. How does Paul describe those dead in sin in Romans? What is man like, or what can man be like apart from God?

a. The wrath of God is revealed against what? Whom is His wrath against? Why? What about God is evident to men? Where is it evident (Romans 1:18–20)?

b. When men reject the knowledge of God, what happens? What exchanges are made? What does God do? What course of life begins? Where does it end (Romans 1:21–32)?

c. What did you learn about those without God in Romans 3:10–18? What are they like?

d. What were you like when Christ died for you (Romans 5:6–8, 10)?

e. What is Paul's warning concerning the last days in 2 Timothy 3:1–8? What will men be like? Does this sound like man is going to get better and better?

4. How is it possible for you to be freed from Satan's domain, to have a life of righteousness and peace? How did God accomplish this?

a. Explain how you were saved, according to Ephesians 2:8–9.

b. What has God done for you, according to Ephesians 2:4–7? Why? Where were you, according to Ephesians 2:11–13?

c. What is His purpose in saving you (Ephesians 2:10)?

5. What belongs to you if you are in Him, according to Ephesians 1?

a. What has God provided in Him that takes care of your sins? In Him you have what?

b. Whom has God sealed you with in Him?

c. Where has He seated Him? What does that provide for you?

6. What is your security in Him, according to John 10:27–30?

7. Have you been doubting God's Word, God's character, His love, His goodness? Have you thought you might be better off if you ran your own life? Or have you come to Him, crying out to Him to save you, giving Him rulership over your life?

CHAPTER FIVE

Last week you looked at the state of the lost. You saw that they are walking in sin, living under the rule of Satan, and indulging the flesh and the mind. You learned that God created man in His image to rule the earth; but as a result of Adam's disobedience, Satan gained the rulership of the world. Sin and death entered the world by one man, and from that point all others were born in sin. You saw that the lost can be freed from Satan's domain and have a life of righteousness and peace by God's grace through faith in Jesus Christ.

What is the difference between life under Satan and life under God?

1. What is life like under Satan?

a. What is the state of the lost person? Whose control is he under? How did he get there? Where is he in relationship to Christ (Ephesians 2)?

b. What did you learn in Revelation 20:11–22:21 concerning the future of the lost? At which judgment do the lost have to stand? How are they judged (Revelation 20:11–13)? What happens to them (Revelation 20:14–15)? Specifically, who will be cast into the lake of fire? How are they described (Revelation 21:8)?

2. What is life like under God?

    a. What is the grace of God? What does His grace include?

    b. What were you like when God loved you (Ephesians 2:4–5)? What did God do for you because of His grace (Ephesians 1:5–9; 2:4–7)? Why?

    c. What is the relationship of God's grace to salvation? How were you saved? How is faith explained? How were you not saved? What is the place of works (Ephesians 2:8–10)?

    d. How does Romans 8:31–32 explain what grace is?

    e. What is God's mercy? What is the relationship between God's mercy and salvation (Titus 3:5)? How did God cause you to be born again (1 Peter 1:3)? How did Paul describe his own salvation (1 Timothy 1:16)?

    f. Once you receive God's mercy, what are you called to do (Romans 12:1)? What will happen to those who give mercy (Matthew 5:7)? What will happen to those who refuse to show mercy (James 2:13)?

    g. What is the peace of God? What brings peace (Romans 5:1)? What prevents a person from having this peace?

3. If you do not have the peace of God in your heart because you cannot accept the fact that Jesus has taken your guilt, what might the problem be? What insight do the following scriptures give?

    a. What did you learn about unbelief from this illustration concerning the children of Israel? Why did some of the children of Israel not enter the land (Hebrews 3:18–19)? What is synonymous with unbelief?

    b. What do you need to remember according to Romans 14:23?

    c. How must sin be viewed according to Psalm 51? If you have confessed your sin, what can you know that you have from God (John 1:9)? What would failure to accept God's cleansing represent?

    d. What does God say has happened to you through the offering of the body of Jesus Christ (Hebrews 10:10)? What takes care of an evil conscience (guilt)? What is the confidence you can now have (Hebrews 10:14–22)?

    e. What does God do with your sins (Hebrews 10:17; Micah 7:19; Isaiah 38:17; 43:25)?

4. If the lack of peace is an attack from the enemy, what do you need to remember?

    a. Where are you seated (Ephesians 2:6)? What does it mean to be seated with Christ in the heavenly places (Ephesians 1:20–23)? What kind of position do you have?

    b. How is it possible to be living here on earth and to be seated with Christ at the same time?

5. If the enemy's tactic is to isolate you and cut you off from fellowship with others, what do you need to remember? If you have been saved, what has happened to you?

    a. What is your relationship to God? What has He done for you (Ephesians 2:11–22)?

    b. Will He ever leave you (Hebrews 13:5–6)? Will God forget (Isaiah 49:14–16)?

6. If the enemy does not leave when you stand, what are you to do?

7. In Ephesians 1:18–19, Paul prays for three things that you need to know in holding your position. What are they?

    a. What is the hope of His calling (1 John 3:2–3)? What will the future of the redeemed be like, according to Revelation 20:11–22:21? What will God do in this new heaven and new earth (Revelation 21:3–4)?

    b. What are the riches of the glory of His inheritance in the saints? Based on Ephesians 1–2, what is His inheritance in the saints?

    c. What is the surpassing greatness of His power toward you who believe? What kind of power is it (Ephesians 2:6; 3:7, 16, 20)?

8. Will you stand against the enemy's attack, confident because of what God has done for you, looking in hope to the future?

CHAPTER SIX

Last week you looked briefly at those who are under Satan. You saw that those under Satan are dead in sin, are living under the control of Satan, and are without God and without hope in the world. You saw that one day they will stand at the Great White Throne judgment, that they will be judged according to their deeds, and that ultimately they will be cast into the lake of fire.

You also looked at those who are under God. You saw that they are saved by His grace and His mercy and that the result of justification is peace with God and the removal of guilt over sins.

You evaluated the fact that although the result of salvation is peace with God, this peace often eludes believers. You saw that when peace eludes, the problem is usually one of two things: either unbelief or an attack from the enemy.

You saw that if the problem is unbelief, then the solution is to accept by faith God's forgiveness. If the problem is an attack from the enemy, the solution is to stand firm against him. You saw that being seated with Christ in heavenly places is your position of power over the enemy.

You also saw that the future hope of the believer is that one day he will dwell with God in the new heaven and the new earth.

Was God caught off guard by Satan's temptation and man's sin in the Garden of Eden? What was God's plan for redemption? How is this plan seen in the law of the kinsman redeemer? How did Jesus fulfill the law of kinsman redeemer?

1. Was God caught off guard by Satan's temptation and man's sin in the Garden of Eden? How does Paul explain this in Ephesians 1:9–10 and Ephesians 3:8–10? What does the word *administration* mean? What was God's plan?

    a. When was God's plan of redemption first revealed to the devil? What happened to mankind as a result of Adam's sin? What did God tell Satan would happen?

    b. How was Abraham a part of God's plan? Who came forth from the nation that God made of Abraham?

    c. Why did Jesus have to be born of a virgin and of God? How did that qualify Him as the Redeemer? Why did Satan have to tempt Jesus?

d. What did the crucifixion and the resurrection offer?

e. After Jesus' ascension, whom did He send? What did those indwelt by the Holy Spirit become?

f. According to Ephesians 3:8–10, after being freed from sin's slavery and Satan's dominion, what then would the church reveal to the angelic and demonic hosts? In the end, what will Jesus deliver up to God?

2. What Old Testament teaching contained God's plan of redemption? What did the kinsman redeemer have the right to do?

a. What are the three Old Testament words for redeem? What do these three words have in common?

b. How was the law of the kinsman redeemer explained in Leviticus 25:47–55? What qualifications of the kinsman redeemer are seen in this passage? Why would a person need redeeming? Who had the right of redemption? What obviously did the redeemer have to have? Could a man redeem himself? How? What determined the cost of redemption?

c. How was the law of the kinsman redeemer explained in Deuteronomy 25:5–10? What was the responsibility of a brother if his brother died and left a widow? Why? What was a kinsman to do if he did not want to marry the widow? What qualification does this show that a kinsman redeemer had to have?

d. How does the Book of Ruth illustrate the law of the kinsman redeemer? Why did Ruth need a redeemer? When Boaz offered the nearest kinsman the opportunity to redeem the property and Ruth, why did he refuse? What must the kinsman redeemer be willing to jeopardize (Ruth 4:6)? What qualification does this show that a kinsman redeemer must have?

3. How did Jesus fulfill the qualifications and responsibilities of the law of the kinsman redeemer to become your Kinsman Redeemer?

a. What is the first qualification of the kinsman redeemer? What relationship did the kinsman redeemer have to be (Leviticus 25:47–49)? What did Jesus have to partake of in order to become your Kinsman Redeemer? Why (Hebrews 2:14–16)? How was this accomplished (Matthew 1:18; Luke 1:35)?

b. What was the second qualification for the kinsman redeemer? What did the kinsman redeemer have to have the ability to do (Leviticus 25:4749)? What are the Greek words for *redeem*?

c. What would be the price to redeem from the slave market of sin (1 Peter 1:18–19; Ephesians 1:7–8)? Why blood (Leviticus 17:11)? Why not the blood of animals (Hebrews 10:4–10)? What does Jesus' blood free you from (Colossians 1:13–14)?

d. How does John 8:34–36 relate to the teaching on the kinsman redeemer? What does committing sin do to the sinner? According to this passage, what does Jesus do?

e. What was the third qualification of the kinsman redeemer? What must be the kinsman redeemer's desire (Deuteronomy 25:5–10)? How did Jesus fulfill that qualification? How is His desire to redeem you explained in Hebrews 10:4–10?

f. What was the fourth qualification of the kinsman redeemer (Ruth 4:6)? How did Jesus fulfill this qualification? What was Jesus' cry to the Father in the Garden of Gethsemane (Luke 22:42, 44; Matthew 26:36–44)? How was Jesus' suffering in the garden explained in Hebrews 5:7–9? What did Jesus lay aside (Philippians 2:6–7)?

g. What is the significance of the story of Boaz in relationship to Jesus, your Kinsman Redeemer?

4. Have you thanked and worshiped Jesus for His willingness to redeem you?

CHAPTER SEVEN

Last week you looked at the fact that God was not caught off guard by Adam's sin in the garden but that God had a plan for man's redemption. You saw that the Old Testament teaching of the kinsman redeemer gives a picture of the redemption that you have in Jesus Christ. You saw that in order to redeem another, the kinsman redeemer had to be a blood relative and further that he had to have the ability to redeem, the desire to redeem, and a willingness to jeopardize his own inheritance. You saw how Jesus fulfilled each of these qualifications in order to become your Kinsman Redeemer. You looked at the story of Ruth and Boaz as an illustration of the law of the kinsman redeemer. You also saw how this story relates to Jesus, your Kinsman Redeemer.

What will you do when you are tempted by Satan?

1. What was the responsibility of the kinsman redeemer concerning the murder of a blood relative? What was he to do? Why?

    a. What law did God give concerning murder in Genesis 9:5–6? Why did God say that He gave this law? What commandment was given in Exodus 20:13? Does Exodus 20:13 contradict Genesis 9:5–6? Why?

    b. What happens to the man who murders another? Why (Deuteronomy 19:10–13)?

    c. Who was the avenger of blood? How does the meaning of the Hebrew word for *avenger of blood* explain who the avenger of blood is?

    d. According to Numbers 35:16–34, if the murder was deliberate, what was the blood avenger to do to the murderer? What if the killing was unintentional? What was the manslayer's protection from the blood avenger?

    e. What evidence was necessary in order to convict the murderer? Could there be a ransom for murder? Why? What does murder do to the land?

2. How does this responsibility of the kinsman redeemer as the blood avenger relate to Jesus Christ, your Kinsman Redeemer? Why do you need a blood avenger?

    a. Who did Jesus say that Satan is in John 8:44? Why? What did Satan do to God's creation in the Garden of Eden? Whose blood had to be avenged? How would this avenging begin to take place? How is this explained in the prophecy given in Genesis 3:15? When did this crushing of the serpent's head take place?

b. What did Jesus say was going to happen to Satan (John 12:23–33)? When Jesus talked about being lifted up and all men being drawn to Him, what was He talking about?

c. When will your blood avenger put Satan to death and fulfill Numbers 35:17, 19?

3. Is it your responsibility to take revenge?

a. What does God say about taking revenge on another (Romans 12:17–21)? If you have been wounded, how are you to respond? Why? What is God's assurance in regard to your enemies?

b. Does this mean that the lawless go unpunished? Whom was the law made for (1 Timothy 1:9–11)? What if the guilty go unpunished (Romans 2:8–10)?

4. What was the kinsman's responsibility concerning the land that had been lost by a relative? What was he to do (Leviticus 25:23–25)?

a. How does this responsibility relate to your Kinsman Redeemer? What land needs redeeming? When man sinned, what happened to the land that he had been given authority over?

b. What is Satan's position in the world? How did Jesus and Paul refer to him (John 14:30; 2 Corinthians 4:3–4)? Is this a permanent position?

c. What does Paul say about Jesus in Colossians 2:9–10? According to Colossians 2:11–15, what did Christ accomplish in His death, burial, and resurrection? How does this compare with John 12:23–33? How do these passages explain Satan's head being crushed?

d. How does Hebrews 2:14 further explain what Jesus did as your Kinsman Redeemer? What is the power of death? Why is it critical to know that your sins are forgiven?

e. In the Gospels, what did the demons do when they recognized Jesus as the Son of God (Mark 5:7–8)? What did Jesus let them know (Matthew 12:28)?

f. What did the demons know (Psalm 110:1)? What does it mean to be under someone's feet?

g. According to Revelation 5:1–6:1, what will it be like when your Kinsman Redeemer stands as the just avenger and begins His final cleansing? What did you learn about the book? What will the Lamb do? How does this book compare with the scroll in Jeremiah 32:6–15?

h. Ultimately, what will happen to the devil and his angels, along with death (Revelation 20:10, 14)?

5. Why is Jesus' temptation critical to man's redemption? How does His temptation relate to His ability to open the title deed to the earth?

a. When did the devil's first temptation of Jesus come (Matthew 4:1–11)?

b. In what ways did the devil tempt Jesus? How did Jesus respond each time? How did Satan respond to Jesus? How does Jesus' temptation parallel with Adam and Eve's?

c. If Jesus had yielded to any of these three temptations, would there have been temporal benefit?

d. If Jesus had yielded to any or all three, how would it have affected His relationship with God?

e. How did Jesus finally get rid of the devil?

6. What are you going to do when you face the temptation of the enemy? What will you do when you come face to face with demons?

a. What have you learned about your Kinsman Redeemer that shows who you are, what has been done for you, and how you can stand?

b. What are some of the principles from Jesus' temptation that can teach you to stand victoriously in warfare?

CHAPTER EIGHT

Last week you looked at the responsibility of the kinsman redeemer to be the judicial executioner of the murderer of a blood relative. You saw that Jesus fulfilled the responsibility as your blood avenger by crushing the head of Satan, your murderer, at Calvary. You also saw that at Calvary Jesus removed Satan's power and authority over you and will ultimately cast Satan into the lake of fire. You also looked at the responsibility of the kinsman redeemer to drive the squatters from the land that he had repossessed. You saw that Jesus fulfilled the responsibility to redeem the land by disarming the rulers and authorities at the cross. You saw that ultimately Jesus will be given the title deed of the earth and will cleanse the earth of all rulers and authorities by casting them into the lake of fire. Finally, you looked at Satan's temptation of Jesus. You learned principles from Satan's temptation and Jesus' response that you can use in order to stand victoriously in warfare.

For victory in warfare against the enemy, what must you know about your position? How are you to walk? What must you know about the enemy? What must you do?

1. In order to stand firm against the enemy, what are you to remember concerning your position in Christ?

   a. What has God done for you that explains your position in Christ (Ephesians 1:4, 7, 13; 4:30)?

   b. Where has God seated you (Ephesians 2:6)? According to Ephesians 2:19; 3:6, you have become part of what? How do these things explain your position?

   c. What is God's provision that allows you to hold your position (Ephesians 3:16)?

   d. Why are these truths significant to warfare?

2. How are you to walk if you are going to have victory over the enemy?

   a. In Ephesians 4:1–6:9, what specific instructions are given concerning your walk?

   b. Why is obedience to these instructions so crucial in warfare?

3. What are the three enemies of the believer? How did they become enemies? How do these enemies relate to one another?

   a. What is to be your relationship to the world (Romans 12:1–2)?

   b. What is to be your relationship to the flesh (Galatians 5:16)? How did you walk before you were saved (Ephesians 2:1–3)?

   c. What is to be your relationship to the devil (James 4:7)?

   d. What are Satan's three objectives? Why does he want to destroy

GROUP DISCUSSION QUESTIONS 321

your unity with God? Why does he want to entice you into sin? Why would he want to lead you into false teaching?

4. What are you to do in order to have victory over the enemy?
   a. What are the first two specific instructions concerning your warfare with the enemy that are given in Ephesians 6:10–11?
   b. What does it mean to be strong in the Lord and in the strength of His might?
   c. What is the meaning of the Greek word for *full armor*? When was each piece of the armor provided?
   d. What does the Greek term for *stand firm* mean? What are you to stand firm against?

5. According to Ephesians 6:12, your struggle is with whom?
   a. How long will this struggle with the enemy last? What kind of a struggle will it be? How does the word *wrestle* (KJV) indicate the kind of combat?
   b. What did Paul mean by the phrase *world forces of this darkness?* How was this Greek term used?
   c. What did God say about astrology and the consequences of participating in it (Deuteronomy 17:2–7)?
   d. If you have been involved in any form of astrology, what should you do (1 John 1:9)? What did some of the Ephesian believers do in Acts 19?
   e. Who are the "spiritual forces of wickedness"? What do they do?
   f. In your struggle with the enemy, what do you need to remember (1 John 4:4; Revelation 12:11)? When tempted, what did Jesus command the enemy to do? What are you to do?

6. What two instructions does Paul give in Ephesians 6:13–14? Why? What does the term *take up* mean? What must you have done in order to stand firm (Ephesians 6:14–18)?

7. What is the first piece of the armor that is mentioned?
   a. Why does Paul begin with the belt of truth? What did the belt do for a soldier? What is the parallel?
   b. What did you learn in John 17:17 regarding the Word?

    c. In recent years how has the enemy had a victory concerning the truth of the Word?

8. What do you believe about the Word of God?

    a. What did God say about how the Word was given and why it was given (2 Peter 1:19–21; 2 Timothy 3:16–17)?

    b. What did Jesus say about the Law in Matthew 5:17–18? In Luke 24:25–27, what did Jesus say about the prophets? What does Jesus' reference to Jonah in Matthew 12:40 and to the creation account in Matthew 19:4–6 indicate?

    c. What was Paul's concern about the gospel in 2 Corinthians 11:2–15? What did Paul warn about Satan's strategy?

    d. What did Peter tell you to do with your mind in 1 Peter 1:13? What was his warning about the devil in 1 Peter 5:9?

9. According to 1 Timothy 4:1–3, what can happen to people who do not keep on the belt of truth? What does it take to keep from being deceived (1 Timothy 4:6–8)?

    a. What is the result of being properly equipped? What if a believer is led astray? Who is behind such tactics? Why? What should you do (Ephesians 4:15)?

    b. How does the belt of truth relate to walking in truthfulness (Ephesians 4:25)? What happened to Ananias and Sapphira (Acts 5)? Why? What role did the enemy play?

10. What about your belt of truth? Will you discipline yourself to study the Word of God? Will you walk in truth?

CHAPTER NINE

Last week you saw that the Book of Ephesians shows you how to battle the enemy by establishing your position with Him and by instructing you in how to walk and how to stand. You looked at the three enemies of the believer and their relationship to one another. You also looked at Satan's three objectives: to destroy your unity, to entice you into sin, and to lead you into false teaching. You saw that you are to "be strong in the Lord" and that you are to "put on the full armor of God" and to "take up the full armor of God." You looked at the fact that you are in hand-to-hand combat with the rulers, the powers, the "world forces of this darkness" and "spiritual forces of wickedness" in the heavenly places. You also learned what it means to have your "loins girded with the belt of truth." You saw that if you are going to stand firm in battle with the enemy that you must stand in the truth of the Word of God and that you must walk in truthfulness.

What are the next two pieces of armor that the believer must put on in order to stand firm against the schemes of the devil?

1. To stand firm against the enemy, the believer must put on the breast-plate of righteousness. What is the breastplate of righteousness? What is involved in putting on the breastplate of righteousness?

> a. What did the Roman soldier's breastplate cover? What is the parallel?
>
> b. According to 2 Corinthians 5:21, how does the child of God receive the breastplate of righteousness? What happened to your sins? What power does Satan no longer have over you?
>
> c. What do you need to remember when you face condemnation from the devil concerning sins that you know have been forgiven (Romans 8:1–2)? Can you be separated from the love of God? Why (Romans 8:31–39)?

2. Is being declared righteous all that there is to the breastplate of righteousness?

> a. What does God say about immorality and its physical and spiritual consequences (Romans 1:22–27; 1 Corinthians 6:9–11)?
>
> b. How was adultery defined, and what was the penalty in Leviticus 20:10–20?
>
> c. What command was given to believers concerning immorality in 1 Corinthians 6:18? Why? In Ephesians 5:1–13, why did Paul say that impurity is not even to be named among them?
>
> d. What did you learn about immorality in the church and the responsibility of believers from the passage in 1 Corinthians 5:1–5? What was the sin? What was the punishment to be?

e. According to Ephesians 4:17–20, what command is given to believers concerning their walk? How do the Gentiles walk?

f. What did you learn about the "old self" versus the "new self" in Ephesians 4:22–24 and Colossians 3:9?

g. What does Paul mean by the "old self" or the "old man"? What has happened to the old man and why (Romans 6:5–6)?

h. What specific instructions are given in Ephesians 4:25–32 concerning what to do and what not to do?

i. According to Ephesians 4:27, what does sin give to Satan? What is the Greek word for *opportunity*? How can sin in a believer's life become an open door to the enemy?

3. Why is the breastplate necessary to stand firm in warfare? What must you do to put it on?

4. To stand firm, your feet must be shod with the preparation of the gospel of peace. What does it mean to shoe your feet with the preparation of the gospel of peace? What is the believer's responsibility?

a. Describe the Roman soldier's sandals and why he needed them. What is the parallel?

b. How does Romans 10:15 relate to the responsibilities to shoe your feet with the preparation of the gospel of peace? Is evangelism the only emphasis here?

c. Who is your peace (Ephesians 2:14)? According to Ephesians 2:14–17, how and why did Jesus bring peace between Jew and Gentile? How did Paul say you are to walk in Ephesians 4:1–3?

5. What are some of the things that can keep you from walking righteously, affect your peace with God and others, and open the door to the enemy in your life?

a. What did you learn about anger and bitterness in Ephesians 4:25–32? When does anger become sin according to Galatians 5:19–20? How does letting anger rule or harboring anger give ground to the enemy?

b. If you are bitter and there is no peace in your heart, what are you to do (Ephesians 4:32)? What does bitterness do according to Hebrews 12?

6. What is the best defense that a Christian can have against the devil?

    a. Instead of anger and bitterness, what is to be your response when wronged by others? How are you to relate to and forgive others (Ephesians 4:32; Colossians 3:12–15)?

    b. In 2 Corinthians 2:5–11 why did Paul say that they were to forgive the one who had been punished? How would Satan take advantage if they failed to forgive? What is the warning to you?

    c. Briefly explain the parable in Matthew 18. According to this parable, what happens to those who don't forgive?

    d. What is to be your attitude toward your enemies (Matthew 5:44–47)?

7. What changes will you have to make in order to walk in righteousness and to do all that you can to live at peace with all men?

CHAPTER TEN

Last week you looked at the fact that in order to stand firm in warfare, the believer must put on the breastplate of righteousness. You saw that putting on the breastplate of righteousness includes not only being declared righteous but also walking righteously. You learned that in order to stand firm, you must shoe your feet with the preparation of the gospel of peace. You saw that this shoeing of your feet with the preparation of the gospel of peace not only involves peace with God but also living in peace with man. Finally, you saw that anger, bitterness, and unforgiveness can keep you from walking righteously and having peace and can open the door for the enemy to gain a foothold in your life.

What are the next two pieces of armor that the believer must take up in order to stand firm against the enemy? What do you need to know concerning the enemy's objectives? What principles concerning warfare do you need to understand?

1. To stand firm against the enemy, the believer must take up the shield of faith. Why (Ephesians 6:16)?

   a. Describe the Roman soldier's shield. What were the fiery darts like
     that were aimed at the Roman soldier? What is the parallel?

   b. What is the purpose of the shield of faith? What is a fiery dart?

   c. Is there any fiery dart that cannot be extinguished?

   d. Why is the belt of truth not enough (Hebrews 11:6)?

   e. What does this tell you about your need to know the Word of
     God?

   f. What are some of the flaming missiles the enemy has directed at
     you? Can you think of any promises or teachings that extinguish
     these missiles?

2. The next piece of armor that the believer is to take up is the helmet of
salvation. What was the purpose of the Roman soldier's helmet? How was it
made?

   a. What is the helmet of salvation? What does it mean to take up the
     helmet of salvation?

   b. What three aspects of salvation does the helmet cover?

   c. Whose mind do you have (1 Corinthians 2:16)? What kind of a
     mind is it (2 Timothy 1:7)?

   d. What is your security? What will God never do (Hebrews
     13:5–6)?

3. Why do you need the shield of faith and the helmet of salvation?
What is Satan's primary objective? What is his primary target? Why?

   a. Why are you told to watch over your heart in Proverbs 4:23? What
     is the relationship between who you are and what you think
     (Proverbs 23:7)? What comes out of the heart (Matthew
     15:18–19)?

   b. What are you to think (Philippians 4:8)? What happens when a
     thought goes unchecked?

   c. What are you to do to be useful to the Master (2 Timothy
     2:20–22)?

   d. How are you to respond to those caught in the devil's snare? Why?
     What has happened to them (2 Timothy 2:24–26)?

4. What principles can be learned about warfare in 2 Corinthians 10:3–6? What is the context of these verses?

   a. What was the attitude of some of the people in Corinth toward Paul? How were they looking at things? What were their thoughts? What did these thoughts become?

   b. What did you learn from Paul's example? What did he say that he was doing with these thoughts? Based on these verses, how are spiritual battles fought?

   c. How are strongholds of wrong thinking erected in your mind? When the wrong thought comes, how is it to be evaluated (Philippians 4:8)? What is to be done with it (2 Corinthians 10:5)?

   d. Why are you not to allow a wrong thought to continue?

5. What did you learn from Jehoshaphat's example concerning how to meet the enemy (2 Chronicles 20:1–23)? What principles can be seen in these verses that can be applied in warfare?

   a. What were the circumstances that Jehoshaphat faced?

   b. What specific things did Jehoshaphat do, and in what order did he do them?

6. Why has Satan targeted the family for destruction (Ephesians 3:15)? What family relationships and instructions are mentioned in Ephesians 5:22–6:4?

   a. What is the enemy's strategy for breaking up the family unit (Hebrews 13:4; 1 Corinthians 7:3–5)?

   b. What is God's instruction to the family when only one of the parents is a Christian (1 Corinthians 7:14)? Why would this situation be a target of Satan?

7. When it seems that the enemy has won the battle, what do you need to remember?

   a. How does it appear that the enemy won in Job 1:12–19; 2:7? Did he?

   b. What did you learn concerning Paul's thorn in 2 Corinthians 12:7–9?

    c. What did Satan do in 1 Thessalonians 2:18 and in Revelation 2:10?

    d. What will happen to Satan and his angels (Revelation 12:9–12)? What battle will be fought (Revelation 16:12–16)?

    e. When the Lord returns, what will happen to Satan (Revelation 19:11–20:2)? What is his ultimate end (Revelation 20:7–10)?

8. What will you do with the fiery darts from the enemy? Will you take up the shield of faith? Will you put on the helmet of salvation?

CHAPTER ELEVEN

Last week you saw that in order to stand firm against the enemy, you are to take up the shield of faith, using specific truths from God's Word to counter-act the devil's lies and accusations. You also learned that to take up the helmet of salvation is to know with absolute certainty that you belong to Christ. You looked at the fact that Satan's target is your mind and his desire is to build strongholds in your mind. You saw that his target also is the family. You learned principles of warfare from Paul's and Jehoshaphat's lives. You also saw that although Satan sometimes appears to be the victor, his ultimate end will be the lake of fire.

What are the believer's two offensive weapons? How are these weapons to be used, and what is the believer's power and authority in using them?

1. In Ephesians 6:17 Paul says to take the sword of the Spirit. What is this sword? Describe the Roman soldier's sword.

    a. What is the significance of the Greek word used for *sword?* What does the sword symbolize? How does Jesus' response to the devil at His temptation illustrate this?

    b. How does the sword of the Spirit differ from the belt of truth? How does it differ from the shield of faith?

2. What did Jesus' triumph over the devil accomplish? Why and how do you have the authority that you do?

    a. What deliverance did God bring about for you through Jesus (Colossians 1:13)?

b. What did Jesus' partaking of flesh and blood do to the devil (Hebrews 2:14)?

c. What did Jesus do to the rulers and authorities (Colossians 2:15)?

d. How could you use these verses as your sword in warfare?

3. How was Jesus' power and authority over Satan demonstrated in His public ministry?

a. When Jesus healed the demon-possessed man in Matthew 12:22–32, what did the crowd accuse Him of doing? How did Jesus say that He cast out demons? What did Jesus say casting out the demons showed? How did it show it?

b. When Jesus read from Isaiah in the synagogue, what things did He say were being fulfilled (Luke 4:18–21)? How does this relate to Jesus' healing of the demon-possessed man in Matthew 12:22–32?

c. How did Jesus exercise His authority over unclean spirits (Luke 4:31–37)?

d. What does the fact that Satan had to have permission to sift Peter show about Jesus' authority (Luke 22:31)?

e. How do these passages help you to see how to use your sword?

4. What authority did Jesus give the twelve in Luke 9:1–2?

a. In Luke 10:1–20 how many did Jesus send out? What were they sent to do? What authority did Jesus give them?

b. When they came back, what were they excited about? What had Jesus seen? What were they to rejoice in?

c. Why did Jesus tell them not to rejoice that the demons are subject to them, but to rejoice that their names are written in heaven?

5. In Matthew 16:15–20, what was Jesus' promise to Peter about the church?

a. What do the "gates of hell" represent? What does it mean that the gates of hell shall not overpower it?

b. What is the church? What did Jesus mean when He talked about the keys of the kingdom of heaven and binding and loosing? What are the limits of the believer's authority and power?

6. What power and authority belong to the believer?

      a. When Jesus said, "Greater works than these shall you do," what did He mean (John 14:10–15)?

      b. In Matthew 28:18–20 when Jesus gave the command to go and make disciples, what was His promise?

      c. In Paul's prayer in Ephesians 3:14–21, what does he pray that you will know? What is God able to do for us?

      d. What did Jesus tell the apostles that they would receive (Acts 1:8)? How is your power explained in 1 John 4:4?

7. What is warfare prayer? What does Paul instruct concerning prayer in Ephesians 6:18–20? What two aspects of warfare prayer do these verses show (Ephesians 6:18–20)?

      a. What is the defensive aspect of prayer? What does "be on the alert" mean? What does the word *perseverance* mean?

      b. How does this command to "be on the alert with all perseverance" relate to Jesus' instructions to ask, seek, and knock in Luke 11:9–10?

      c. In Luke 22:31 when Satan desired to sift Peter, what did Jesus say that He had done?

      d. What is the offensive aspect of prayer that you see in Ephesians 6:19–20?

8. Practically, how are authority and power over the enemy to be exercised?

      a. What does it mean to submit to God, resist the devil, and draw near to God?

      b. What is involved in putting on the armor of God?

9. If there are areas of disagreement with others on this subject, what are you to do (Ephesians 4:1–6)?

      a. What are the seven essentials of unity?

      b. Will you walk this way? Will you stand firm against the enemy?

NOTES

CHAPTER ONE:
LORD, IS IT WARFARE?

1. From time to time we will look at the definition of a word in the Hebrew or Greek. Since the Old Testament was written originally in Hebrew and since the New Testament was written originally in Koine Greek, sometimes it is helpful to go back to the original language to see the meaning of a word. There are many study tools to help you if you would like to do this type of digging. One excellent book to help you understand how to do more in-depth study is *How to Study Your Bible* (Harvest House Publishers, l994).

2. W. E. Vine, Merrill P. Unger, and William White, Jr., *An Expository Dictionary of Biblical Words* (Nashville, Tenn.: Thomas Nelson Publishers, 1984), 1228.

3. Ibid.

4. J. D. Douglas and Merrill C. Tenney, *The New International Dictionary of the Bible* (Grand Rapids, Mich.: Zondervan Publishing House, 1987), 316.

5. *The Expositor's Bible Commentary,* vol. 9 (Grand Rapids, Mich.: Zondervan Publishing House, 1981), 492.

6. Ibid., 492–93.

7. Dr. Sadan Gokovali, *Ephesus* (Turkey), 29.

8. *The Revell Bible Dictionary* (Old Tappan, N.J.: Fleming H. Revell Company, 1990), 342.

9. *The Expositor's Bible Commentary,* vol. 9, 496.

10. Gokovali, *Ephesus,* 31.

11. Clinton E. Arnold, *Ephesians: Power and Magic* (New York, N.Y.: Cambridge University Press, 1989), 47. Quoted from James H. Charlesworth, ed., *The Old Testament, Prolegomena for the Study of Christian Origins,* SNTSMS 54 (Cambridge University Press, 1985).

12. Ruth Paxson, *The Wealth, Walk, and Warfare of the Christian* (Old Tappan, N.J.: Fleming H. Revell Company, n.d.), 21.

13. Fritz Rienecker and Cleon Rogers, *Linguistic Key to the Greek New Testament* (Grand Rapids, Mich.: Zondervan Publishing House, 1976, 1980), 541.

CHAPTER TWO:
LORD, WHY DID YOU CREATE THE DEVIL?

1. Rienecker and Rogers, *Linguistic Key,* 623.

CHAPTER THREE:
LORD, SATAN'S ROARING—NEED I FEAR?

1. Vine, Unger, and White, Jr., *An Expository Dictionary,* 166.

CHAPTER FOUR:
LORD, I DON'T WANT TO BUY SATAN'S LIE!

1. The word translated *sorceries* is *pharmekia,* which means the use of drugs for magical purposes.

CHAPTER FIVE:

LORD, THE ENEMY'S ACCUSING ME!

1. William Barclay, *The Letters to the Galatians and Ephesians* (Philadelphia, Penn.: The Westminster Press, 1958), 120.

2. Charles R. Erdman, *The Epistle of Paul to the Ephesians* (Philadelphia, Penn.: The Westminster Press), 53.

3. By the way, if you want to understand the grace of God in a greater depth, and you want to know how to live in that grace day in and day out, I believe my *Lord* study on grace, *Lord, I Need Grace to Make It,* just might be the answer. It also makes excellent material for Sunday school classes or home Bible studies. Like most books in the *Lord* series, there are video and/or audio teaching tapes to accompany each lesson, plus leader discussion tapes done by Betsy Bird. (You may order the book and tapes from Precept Ministries, P. O. Box 182218, Chattanooga, Tennessee 37422.)

4. Fanny Crosby, from a hymn entitled "Rescue the Perishing."

5. Vine, Unger, and White, Jr., *An Expository Dictionary,* 403.

6. Ibid., 440–41.

7. Arnold, *Ephesians: Power and Magic,* 20.

8. Ibid., 22.

9. Ibid., 74–75.

CHAPTER SIX:

LORD, I NEED A KINSMAN REDEEMER!

1. Sean Sellers, *Web of Darkness* (Tulsa, Okla.: Victory House, Inc., 1990), 25.

2. Chris Elkins, *Heavenly Deception* (Wheaton, Ill.: Tyndale House Publishers, Inc., 1980).

3. Kay Arthur, *How to Overcome Strongholds* (Chattanooga, Tenn.: Precept Ministries, 1987).

4. Vine, Unger, and White, Jr., *An Expository Dictionary,* 313.

5. Lawrence O. Richards, *Expository Dictionary of Bible Words* (Grand Rapids, Mich.: Zondervan Publishing House, 1985), 516.

6. Ibid., 517.

7. Ibid., 516.

8. Ibid.

9. Vine, Unger, and White, Jr., *An Expository Dictionary,* 515.

10. Marvin R. Vincent, *Word Studies in the New Testament,* vol. 4 (Grand Rapids, Mich.: Wm. B. Eerdmans Publishing Co., 1969), 435.

11. Lawrence O. Richards, *Expository Dictionary of Bible Words,* 518.

CHAPTER SEVEN:

LORD, KINSMAN REDEEMER, HOW CAN SATAN BE DEFEATED?

1. Just think of how many innocent people would still be alive in the United States of America if we carried out the sentence of capital punishment as God ordained, rather than releasing murderers from prison to murder again and again.

2. Laird Harris, Gleason L. Archer, Jr., and Bruce K. Waltke, eds., *Theological Wordbook of the Old Testament,* vol. 1 (Chicago, Ill.: Moody Press, 1980), 144.

CHAPTER EIGHT:
LORD, HOW DO I PUT ON THE ARMOR? BELT ON TRUTH?

1. Rienecker and Rogers, *Linguistic Key,* 541.
2. Ibid.
3. Stott, *The Message of Ephesians,* 264.
4. Matthew 4:8–9; John 12:31; 14:30; 16:11; 1 John 5:19. Cf. also Ephesians 2:2.
5. Stott, *The Message of Ephesians,* 265.
6. Ibid., citing Lloyd-Jones, *Warfare,* 292.
7. Rienecker and Rogers, *Linguistic Key,* 541.
8. Ibid.
9. Dave Breese, *Seven Men Who Rule the World from the Grave* (Chicago, Ill.: Moody Press, 1990), 20.

CHAPTER NINE:
LORD, TEACH ME ABOUT THE BREASTPLATE AND SHOES

1. Marshal Alan Phillips, "Bible Doesn't Say What We Thought It Did," *The Los Angeles Times,* date unavailable.
2. Warren Wiersbe, *The Strategy of Satan* (Wheaton, Ill.: Tyndale House Publishers, 1979), 105.
3. Ibid., 114–15.
4. Kenneth S. Wuest, *Wuest's Word Studies from the Greek New Testament* (Grand Rapids, Mich.: Wm. B. Eerdmans Publishing Company, 1953), 144.
5. John MacArthur, Jr., *The Believer's Armor* (Panorama, Calif.: Word of Grace Communications, 1981), 38.
6. Rienecker and Rogers, *Linguistic Key,* 542.
7. A. T. Robertson, *Word Pictures in the New Testament,* vol. 4, *The Epistles of Paul* (Nashville, Tenn.: Broadman Press, 1931), 551.
8. Ibid., 541.
9. Rienecker and Rogers, *Linguistic Key,* 534.
10. Ibid.

CHAPTER TEN:
LORD, SATAN'S ATTACKING MY MIND! MY SHIELD! MY HELMET!

1. Eileen Crossman, *Mountain Rain: A New Biography of James O. Fraser* (Singapore: Overseas Missionary Fellowship, 1987), 67–69.
2. *The Expositor's Bible Commentary,* ed. Frank E. Gaebelein, vol. 10, 380.
3. Rienecker and Rogers, *Linguistic Key,* 486.

CHAPTER ELEVEN:
LORD, HOW DO I TAKE THE OFFENSE AGAINST SATAN?

1. Crossman, *Mountain Rain,* 72.
2. Vine, Unger, and White, Jr., *An Expository Dictionary,* 683.
3. Rienecker and Rogers, *Linguistic Key,* 542.
4. Vine, Unger, and White, Jr., *An Expository Dictionary,* 2.

5. *The Expositor's Bible Commentary,* vol. 12, 320–21.

6. *The International Bible Commentary,* ed. F. F. Bruce (Grand Rapids, Mich.: Zondervan, 1986), 1204.

7. *The Expositor's Bible Commentary,* vol. 8, 939.

8. Ibid., 939.

9. Ibid., 370.

10. *International Bible Commentary,* 1138–39.

11. *The Expositor's Bible Commentary,* 374.

12. Thomas B. White, *The Believer's Guide to Spiritual Warfare* (Ann Arbor, Mich.: Servant Publications, 1990), 46–50.

13. Rienecker and Rogers, *Linguistic Key,* 542.

14. Ibid., 542–43.

15. I've written a four-week study book, *Lord Teach Me to Pray in 28 Days,* which gives principles of praying based on the pattern Jesus gave His disciples in The Lord's Prayer. The book is published by Harvest House Publishers, and audio and video tapes on this subject are also available through Precept Ministries.

16. Crossman, *Mountain Rain,* 84–85.

17. R. Arthur Mathews, *Born for Battle* (Singapore: Overseas Missionary Fellowship, 1978), 44–48.

18. Phyllis Schafly, *Child Abuse in the Classroom* (Alton, Ill.: Pere Marquette Press, 1984).

DISCOVER GOD'S TRUTHS
FOR YOURSELF

Every book in Kay Arthur's powerful *Lord* Bible study series is designed to help you study *inductively* — to examine God's Word in depth and discern His truths for yourself, rather than relying on interpretations by others.

You can learn more about this life-changing study method in the revolutionary *International Inductive Study Bible,* the only Bible on the market that teaches you how to examine each book of the Bible — chapter by chapter — completely on your own.

Look for the *International Inductive Study Bible* at your local Christian bookstore.

For information about Kay's teaching ministry and about other study materials, write or call:

Precept Ministries
P. O. Box 182218
Chattanooga, Tennessee 37422
Attention: Information Department
(423) 892-6814